Last Rambles Amongst the Indians of the Rocky Mountains and the Andes

A Native American History

By George Catlin

Published by Pantianos Classics

ISBN-13: 978-1-78987-345-0

First published in 1868

Contents

Preface v

Chapter One - The Rattlesnakes' Den 6

Chapter Two - Gold Hunting in the Crystal Mountains 26

Chapter Three - Descent of the Yucayali 40

Chapter Four - The Flathead Indians 72

Chapter Five - California 89

Chapter Six - Rio de Janeiro 99

Chapter Seven - Buenos Ayres 118

Chapter Eight - Tierra del Fuego 135

Chapter Nine - The Indians, Where From? 142

Chapter Ten - The Indians, Who Are They? 149

Chapter Eleven - The Indians, Where Are They Going? 156

Preface

It was said by a very great man that "Nothing can be more proper than that old people should write books for young folks, and that young folks should read them; for old people have the greatest amount of experience, and young people have the greatest amount of time to profit by it."

Considering myself now belonging to the first of this category, and with a good share of the experience referred to, I shall take infinite pleasure in presenting this second volume of "Life amongst the Indians" to the readers of my first volume, who now amount, as far as I am able to learn, to some thing approaching 60,000.

These will doubtless search with avidity, when this volume comes forth, the means of commencing where the other volume left off, and of following me through the rest of the wanderings of my errant and chequered life; and if it falls into others' hands, they should not cut its pages until they have called upon the publishers for the first volume, that they may appreciate the vast plains and rivers and forests, with their peoples and their animal creations, east of the Rocky Mountains and the Andes, before they undertake to follow me amongst rocks and snows, and through scenes that transpire on the cindered plains and pine-dressed mountains and shores of the Pacific Ocean.

Without the first volume, the reading of this will be like coming in at the play at the end of the second or third act; the plot will be misunderstood, as the great and warlike and picturesque tribes of the prairies, the Sioux, the Comanches, the Osages, the Pawnees, &c, and their noble sports in the chase, and the stories of the *"Kettle of Gold,"* and the *"Old Sawmill-Lick,"* with *"John Darrow,"* and *"Johnny O'Neil,"* &c, will all be lost; and much, therefore, that is to be said in this volume would be unappreciated.

This is all I need say in the Preface, for the reader, with these suggestions, will be able to follow me, and to appreciate what I shall have to say and to show in the following pages.

THE AUTHOR

The Rocky Mountains and the Andes

Chapter One - The Rattlesnakes' Den

Readers of my first volume will have preserved some impression of the shape and position of my father's plantation in the picturesque little valley of the Ocquago, on the bank of the Susquehanna river, hemmed in with huge mountains on either side, and in which was situated the "Old Sawmill Lick," and the scene of the "Kettle of Gold," which have been described in the first volume.

As has been said, though not the place of my nativity, it was the tapis on which my boyish days were spent, and rife with legends of Indian lore; its natural features, and its incidents stamped upon my youthful mind impressions which easily beguile me in this, as in my first volume, again to loiter a little about it before I start off with my young readers to the vast and boundless regions where the principal scenes of this little book are to be laid.

"John Darrow" is recollected, and faithful "Johnny O'Neil," and their singular and respective characters will be better stereotyped in the little episode which is here to follow.

Ocquago (Ohk-qua-gúh), the Indian name of a straight mountain, of six or eight miles in length, in the southern part of the State of New York, having the cool and limpid river Susquehanna gliding along at its western base, and a fertile valley of rich alluvion from one to two miles in breadth on the opposite shore, barricaded by the Randolph Mountains on the west.

In the middle of this little valley lay my father's plantation, and above and below it, during the days of my boyhood, some eight or ten farms of less dimensions, and also bordering on the river shore, were under cultivation; which, together with labourers, hunters, fishermen, &c, counted a population of something like two hundred persons.

This picturesque, but insignificant little valley, which at that time had acquired no place in history, having been settled but a few years, nevertheless had its traditions of an exciting interest, as the rendezvous of "Brant," the famous and terrible Mohawk chief, and his army during the frontier war, in which the *"Wyoming massacre"* took place, and the finale of which was the subsequent *déroute* of Brant and his Indian forces, through the valley of the Ocquago, and beyond the Randolph Mountains, to the sources of the Susquehana, by the Pennsylvania militia.

These events, and their attendant cruelties, both savage and civil, too recent at that time to be called traditions, accounted (as stated in the first volume) for the vivid and unfading impressions which I received, at an early age, of Indians, of "Indian massacres," &c. And the singular adventures here to follow will show how I received at the same age impressions not less exciting, nor less lasting, but of another kind, indicated in the heading of this chapter.

Though the Indians had disappeared, and nothing but their oral history, and their bones, and their implements ploughed up in our fields, remained of them, there was yet another enemy, even more numerous, more cruel, and more deadly, and threatening to be more unconquerable and inexterminable to deal with.

The banks and the meadows of the Susquehanna, in the beautiful valleys of Wyoming, Tioga, Chenango, Ocquago, and Otsego, were probably more infested than any other portions of the globe, with rattlesnakes of all colours, and various dimensions, that struck at the heels of all that was mortal, man or beast,' in the meadows or fields of grain, in which they crawled and wallowed during the summer season.

Of these localities, the little valley of the Ocquago seemed to be the most cruelly inflicted by this terrible scourge, and no doubt so, from its limited dimensions and peculiar position, receiving the concentration of these reptiles in the summer months, from the desolate mountains surrounding it.

During the hay-making and harvesting season these poisonous creatures were exceedingly dangerous to the lives of the labourers, and from my father's fields their frightful carcasses were daily brought in by my father's hired men, with their heads cut off by the scythe, or killed by the cudgel. And every summer, more or less lives of men, of women, or of children, as well as of horses, of dogs, and other animals were destroyed, in the otherwise peaceable and happy little valley, by these hidden and deadly enemies.

With the habits and peculiarities of an enemy so deadly and so universal (and consequently so "respectable") as this, in the mountains and valleys of America, it may be well for the reader to be made a little more familiar in this place, for they are an enemy more dangerous than Indians, and will probably demand a large space in the narrations of incidents to be given in the following pages, as well as those mentioned in the former volume.

As a natural history fact, and known to all the inhabitants of those parts where they abound, how curious that these reptiles, after spending the summer season in the grassy valleys, and on the banks of the rivers and lakes, at the first indication of frost in the fall of the year, *en masse,* and simultaneously, from instinct, commence a pilgrimage across rivers, Across lakes, and up the mountain sides, no matter what distance, to the "Rattlesnakes' Den," their winter's rendezvous, where not only hundreds, but thousands, assemble. And in their inapproachable cavern, in a torpid state, they await the coming of spring, and the beginning of summer, when they venture forth again, and descend into the valleys, for another summer's campaign.

How curious the fact also, that, in their summer's peregrinations, the male and female are always in company; and how wonderful that instinct that enables them to track each other, and never to lose that company, though, when met, two are never seen together, but are generally within hearing of each other's rattle, or not far distant, following on the trail! Most generally, if we irritate -the one, and make it sound its rattle, we hear in the distance the sound of the other's rattle, in answer; and if we kill the one* we meet, and leave its carcass overnight, we find the other by its side, or near it, the next morning.

And a Rattlesnake Trap! (who has ever heard of it?) first invented, no doubt, by Buel Rowley, one of my father's labouring men; the same who ploughed up the "kettle of gold," and the rusty tomahawk, which it will be recollected left its indelible mark on my left cheek-bone.

Well, the "Rattlesnake Trap," here it is:

A simple log of wood, some three or four feet in length, and the size of a man's leg, or larger, with a hollow through it, large enough for the reptile to crawl through, but not sufficiently spacious for it to turn about; its forward extremity being partially closed, to prevent the snake from passing out. Rowley, from a practical knowledge he had gained of the close manner in which this creature follows the trail of its mate, conceived the plan of conducting it into a hollow tube from which it could not escape, being unable to retreat in its straitened and confined position, and checked by the reversed position of its scales.

This ingenious machine was lodged in my father's woodhouse, [1] and when a rattlesnake was killed in any of his fields, the trap was transported to a position near the spot, when the carcass of the snake was gently dragged towards it through the grass, by a thong, and pulled through the hollow of the log. After which a tenpenny nail or two driven into the forward end was sufficient to prevent the living snake from passing through, and at the same time to allow the light to enter.

The carcass of the dead snake was then lifted from the ground and carried away; and on Rowley's shoulder the next morning the rattlesnake trap was almost invariably transported back to the woodhouse; the tail of the snake, with its rattles, hanging out, a harmless and amusing toy for the women and children to play with, for by touching them, or striking the log, they were instantly set in motion, and the expression and crescendo of their music controlled by the harmless rage that was boiling within.

Curiosity satisfied (and that curious propensity of the most of mankind "to finger danger when it is iron bound"), Rowley's pincers withdrew the nails in front of the cage, which was then passed between the bars of the fence, enclosing a field containing a number of hogs, and clipping the tail with its rattles as a trophy, the imprisoned reptile lost no time in launching itself out of its prison, and into the jaws of "the old sow," which stood ready, and whose fore feet were instantly upon it and held it, whilst she exhibited her swinish taste, by tearing it to pieces and devouring every morsel of it!

My father had learned (I don't know how) that the bite of a rattlesnake was not poisonous to the flesh of swine, and that those reptiles were invariably devoured by hogs that happened to come upon them; both of which singular facts I often saw confirmed in my father's fields of swine, when he had ordered these living serpents to be thrown amongst them.

Rowley's trap, for which he had no patent, was soon adopted in the other parts of the valley, and his enviable standing, as a public benefactor, was soon evident from the number of tails with rattles which were sent to him, and which he had demanded as a sort of Royalty for his invention.

And yet, a *greater trap* than this awaited those poisonous beasts, which were at that time almost threatening the existence of the otherwise happy little colony of the valley of the Ocquago a trap which, by way of comparison, might be called a *wholesale trap - a cataclysm - a catastrophe,* as will be seen, which rescued the valley from its dangers, and gained for its inventor, honours, though not immortal, yet of an enviable character, while they lasted. (We shall see anon).

The Rattlesnake in Rowley's Trap

"Darrow" (recollect the empire which his Nimrodic celebrity had gained over my youthful mind my consummate admiration of his deer-stalking and panther-hunting qualities), Darrow, not a long time after the scene at the "Old Sawmill Lick," and, I think, early in the spring of 1810, said to me one day whilst he and I were working in the field together, "George, I intend to play the devil with the rattlesnakes this spring - they've had it all in their own way long enough. You recollect poor Mary Judkins, George?"

"Yes, Mr. Darrow, I was close by her when she was bit last summer. I heard her scream when she was struck. There was a whole wagon-load of us, boys and girls, out on Bowman's ridge picking whortleberries; she was reaching her hand forward when the snake jumped from a rock before her, and about even with her face, and bit her right in the vein of her neck! She gave one scream, and fell backwards, close by me, and never got up. All the party gathered around her, and put her into the wagon, quite dead, and carried her home: and her neck and her arms were just the colour of the rattle snake itself, which we found under the rocks and killed."

"And that good soul, Heth, George, bitten on the floor of his own house!"

"Yes; that I didn't see, Mr. Darrow, but I heard of it."

"It's getting too bad, George. These devils are increasing at such a rate that it's almost as much as a man's life is worth to work in the fields amongst them. Now, George, I know where all these beasts come from; I know the very house they all live in; and you and I will make a smash among 'em, George, before many days come around."

Darrow then related to me what at that time was new to me, and which has been mentioned in a former page, that these reptiles all leave the valley at the first appearance of frosty nights in the fall of the year, and congregate in one immense cavern, where they spend the winter in a torpid state, and start off in pairs for the valleys as soon as the weather is warm enough in the spring of the year; and that for a week or two before the nights are warm enough for their travels, during the warmth of the sun in the middle of the spring days, they come out of their den, not only in hundreds, but by thousands, and lie for several hours in front of it basking in the sun, and return into their cave before the coldness of the evening approaches.

"Why, that's the 'Rattlesnakes' Den,' that I have heard my father talk about."

"Yes," said Darrow, "the 'Rattlesnakes' Den;' it's in the top of Steele's Mountain, back of Hilbourns, under the high ledge looking off into Hemlock Hollow. About ten years ago these devils got to be so bad, that Joe Snidigar, Atwill, and myself, and several others, went out in a spring day and thrashed about three hundred of them to death whilst they lay sunning themselves in front of their den; and they are now getting to be so bad again, that you and I must make another row among 'em, George. Say nothing of it yet, but on Sunday, if it should be a sunny day, when neither of us have any work to do, we'll go and merely take a peep at them, and lay our plans as to the time and mode of attack."

Sunday came, and it was a fine and sunny day; and though I had difficulties of a very peculiar and embarrassing kind to contend with, I met Darrow as arranged, "in the lower barn," with my little single-barrelled fowling-piece, and he in his hunting shirt and fox-skin cap, and rifle in hand, a model to which my whole soul aspired.

My dear mother was a Methodist, and a devout and professing Christian, and my father a philosopher, professing no particular creed, but keeping and teaching the Commandments. My incurable propensity for trout-fishing, under the unfortunate conviction that they "took the fly" better on Sunday than on other days, had gained me the condemnation of those good parents, and on several occasions severe floggings, for disobeying their positive commands as to fishing and shooting on that day.

It had been a long time since I had had one of these, and though, old as I was getting, I still was under the injunction, and with the certain conviction that the penalty would be inflicted in case of disobedience.

Darrow assured me that our mission was one for the public good, offering to plead my case with my father; and leaving the "lower barn" with our pieces trailed, and following the bed of the "Big Creek," so as not to be seen from the house, we soon reached, through my father's meadows, the riverside, where we got a canoe to land us on the other shore, at the foot of the mountain, into the thick forest of which we were soon ensconced, am our day's enjoyment (whatever might come after it! was now secure before us.

We sat down upon a large log, and whilst Darrow was knocking the priming out of the pan and repriming his gun, which he always did on entering upon promising hunting-ground, he said:

"George, we are now going to pass through one of my best ranges. Many a fine buck "Old Ben" [2] has knocked over on this side of the ridge, and we have full two miles to go before we reach the "Rattlesnakes' Den." Keep some five or six rods behind me, George, and don't break a stick; watch me close, and if you see me on my hand and knees (or on my belly, which is sometimes necessary) don't move an inch. On the first ledge we shall rise, about half a mile from here, is a famous buck who always lies chewing his cud from nine or ten in the morning until near sundown. I've tried him several times, but he's always too wide-awake for me. I've let fly at him two or three times, when nothing but his white flag was seen bounding through the bushes'; but those were random shots, only sent for amusement. I'll give him a call, however, as we pass up the hill; and a little beyond that, at the foot of the second ridge, I'll show you, George, the spot where I shot the beautiful painter, whose skin, you know, lies on the floor in your father's hall, in front of the parlour-door."

At this, with his rifle trailed in his right hand, and his wiper [3] in the left, and an extra bullet in his mouth, more quickly handled than if drawn from his pouch, and his body was seen gliding through the bushes and between the rocks without moving a leaf. Oh, how beautiful to my young and aspiring vision the cautious and graceful movements of this stalking teacher! What pupil ever watched the magic touches of his master's pencil with more admiration than I watched the movements of this master-hunter as he led me through the forests and rocks and ravines of the mountain's side? No time or circumstances have ever yet effaced the slightest impression then made upon my youthful mind, nor will they leave me while recollections last.

We passed the lair of "Old Golden" (as the famous "Big Buck" was called) without finding him at home; and getting near to the top of the last ridge, I saw Darrow carefully sinking down upon his left knee, with his rifle drawn to his face. What a palpitation! I heard my heart distinctly beat! Was it a panther, or an Indian (for reports were that they were still lurking about)? Was he to fire, or not? And if he did, and should miss, or should wound I was charged with small shot only, and what might the next moment disclose?

Darrow held his position without moving for a minute or two, when he gradually lowered his body to the ground, and, getting his face around so as to see me, beckoned with his hand for me to come on my hands and knees to him. I applied my first ideas of stalking as well as I could in my agitated state, and getting by the side of him, with a large log before us, which screened us from its view, he whispered to me:

"George! it's a fine large doe. What a pity to harm the poor thing! She's big, and I haint the heart to draw a bead [4] upon her. Look at her, but be cautious."

I raised my forehead above the log as gradually and cautiously as I could; and at the instant that my eyes were above the surface of the log, I discovered the deer about a hundred yards from us, lying down, and with nose and ears pointed, looking me full in the face! She sprang upon her feet, and bounded off, and "Old Golden," lying behind a bunch of fern at a few paces distant, rising as it were into the air, and waving his white flag to and fro, accompanied her!

"Zounds! what a fool I've been, George!" exclaimed Darrow, "that old fellow has played me many a trick, but I never expected him in company with his wife at this season of the year. He don't get off in that way another time, I assure you."

Poor Darrow (I never shall forget it), how he was chapfallen; his face became wrinkled and creviced in a minute, and he sighed and groaned as he contemplated the beautiful position in which "Old Golden" had laid under the range of his rifle, "if he only had known.it." However, the misfortune was irreparable, and we moved on towards the "Rattlesnakes' Den."

On the top of the mountain, which was barren and level for a long distance, Darrow shouldered his rifle, and said:

"George, we can talk here as much as we please - no game lives here." He then said, "We are now close to the 'Den.' That tall pine you see yonder stands right upon the rock where the snakes come out; and probably they go under the rocks as far as where we now stand. There's not another word to be said, but you keep a little back of me, and watch my signs."

Darrow advanced on his hands and knees towards the brink of the precipice, and, getting within a few yards of it, laid down his rifle, and then, lying closer to the ground, and advancing more slowly, got so as to look over and down upon the level platform of rock below. After gazing for a minute or so, by reaching back with his right hand he made signs for me to come to him, which I did, creeping in the same manner he had done, and leaving my gun behind. Getting by the side of him, and both of us permanently fixed and motionless, we had together the strange view of some five or eight hundred of the reptiles (devils, as he called them) spread out on the surface of a level rock of some four or five rods in diameter, and twenty-five feet below us, in coils, in knots and bunches, basking in the sun, and all were motionless, and apparently asleep. Their scales, fresh from their damp cavern, and not yet soiled by their summer's travels, were glistening in the sun, of all colours - yellow, black, and white, and the breathing motions of their bodies gave them the sparkling effect of moving diamonds.

In the midst of these groups were here and there harmless black snakes of some ten or twelve feet in length, intertwined and coiled with them as if members of the same venomous family. There were rattlesnakes of all sizes - some were black, some brown, and others of a bright yellow. Some were lying on their backs, perfectly straight, and others were hanging from the limbs of the adjoining trees, and others coiled around their trunks. Oh! what a beautiful sight, and what a perdition, if, by a slip of the foot, one were to have been launched into the midst of it!

Darrow at length gave the signal, and slowly withdrawing his head, and I following, we were in a moment beyond their view, and safe for the remarks which Darrow was prepared to extemporise and I to ejaculate. I have no sort of recollection what they were, but whilst we were descending the mountain, on our way home, and had got about halfway down, Darrow said, "There, George, we are now at the 'Devil's Pulpit.'"

I had some vague recollections of stories I had heard about the "Devil's Pulpit," and being just old enough to know the meaning of a pulpit, I was curious to know what the devil had to do with a pulpit.

"Well," said Darrow, "George, I don't exactly know the whole history of the place myself, but that rock you see standing out in front of the wall there is shaped like a pulpit, and has just room for a man to stand in it and make a speech or preach a sarment. And I've heard say that when the Indians had made the 'Massacre of Wyoming,' the great Mohawk chief Brant held his army of 2000 Indian warriors here encamped, on the very ground where we now stand, in front of the pulpit, to guard the narrows below, in case the Pennsylvania militia attempted to follow the Indians through. Brant was a terrible warrior, though only a half-Indian: he had brought a number of white prisoners to this place who had been taken in the battle of Tunkhannock, and some of them who afterwards escaped said that he every morning preached a sarment to his warriors from this pulpit, and everybody, knowing him to be a very devil, called the rock the 'Devil's Pulpit.' But your father, George, can tell you more about it."

We were, in a little time, from the "Pulpit Rock" down to the river's side, which we crossed, and entered my father's fields. Now was approaching the tribunal, the awful retribution for me. Darrow had engaged to plead my cause with my parents, and Sunday not yet being passed, we halted awhile at the "lower barn," where my little fowling-piece was secreted; and Darrow fearlessly shouldering his rifle, we successfully entered my mother's kitchen, without being noticed by any one.

Darrow, after waiting awhile for my trial to come on, gave me these consoling words, -

"I don't believe your father is going to say anything about it to-night, George, and I shall see him early in the morning."

He then departed for his own home, half a mile distant, where he was living with his family; and I soon after slipped into bed. Before I had got to sleep, however, a light entered my room. It was my father, with a candle in his hand. He took a seat by the side of my bed. Oh what a moment!

"My dear son," said he, "you never tell me a falsehood. I have looked everywhere to-day, and your mother also, for the 'little musket.' Do you know anything about it? Where is it?"

"It's at the 'lower barn,' father."

"How came it there, George?"

"I left it there, father."

"It was missing this morning at an early hour, and you have been absent all day with it?"

"Yes, father."

"You recollect what I promised you if you ever broke the Sabbath again in that way, old as you now are?"

"Yes, my dear father."

"You never knew me to break my promise, George?"

"No, father."

"Would you wish me to break a promise, my dear son?"

"No, dear father."

"Then get up and put on your clothes, and go down to the bank of the creek, below the wheatstacks, and cut a good bunch of water-beech sprouts, [5] about three feet long, and lay them in your mother's cheese-room until morning, which will give you time to reflect upon the truant you have been playing this day."

Trusting to my advocate to speak for me, and my mind overloaded with what I had seen during the day, I failed to make any defence, and started off for the "beech sprouts," which I procured, and went to bed. In vain I attempted to lie in bed in the morning until I could hear Darrow's voice below, for I was called up at an early hour; and my father waiting for me at the bottom of the stairs, with the "beech sprouts" in his hand, said to me, as I came down, "Walk this way, George," as he went through the kitchen and into the woodhouse, where we were alone together.

"My dear son," said he, "you are old enough now to know the meaning of this, and the painful necessity of it; that I do it not because I hate you, but because I love you; and I am sure it will be the last time."

"It *shall* be, dear, *dear* father."

*****

Darrow came in, but too late; my case had been tried judgment, sentence, and retribution! How much and what he said to my father, and how far he succeeded in exciting any repentant feeling, I never learned, though I thought for several days I discovered a sort of *ex post facto* signs of a partial forgiveness, arising from the plea that my friend and master, Darrow, had put in for me, the public importance of our expedition, which had led us to the "Rattlesnakes' Den" on Sunday, and now admitted by all.

However, I was silent, and determined to be so, though Darrow, with the countenance of my father and all the neighbours, was proceeding with his plans for a grand onslaught on the "devils," in the course of a few days. Darrow was everywhere listened to in his descriptions of what we had seen, and I was called on as a witness to the facts, but I was *mum,* having resolved to have no further hand in the affair.

But when my father said to me,

"George, my dear son, did you see, with Darrow, at the 'Rattlesnakes' Den,' what he has described?"

"Yes, dear father," (I said it in a sort of convulsion, and before I willed it), "I saw it all, father; it is all true."

"Then, my dear boy, you shall go with us. We shall have a grand holiday on Wednesday, if the weather is fine. Captain Brush is going, and Medad, and Jonas. The Snidigars are going Rowley and O'Neil, and half-a-dozen others, and you shall join us, and carry the little musket for your weapon."

What a concession! I soon forgot the ordeal I had passed, and was inflated with the most impatient ambition for the catastrophe that was pre paring. Wednesday (after a long time) came; a fine sunny day. The Snidigars (old hunters) were on the spot, Atwill was there, and Heth, and Captain Brush, and all assembled at my father's house at ten o'clock in the morning, and all, in Heth's ferry-boat, crossed the river, and Darrow (with me by his side) taking the lead, we penetrated the forest on the mountain side, and soon arrived at the "Devil's Pulpit," which was considered halfway.

My father, to make it a real holiday, had freighted Johnny O'Neil, his faithful hired man, with a number of bottles of cognac brandy from his cellar, and a good boiled ham, and other accompaniments for a comfortable lunch after the grand feat should be accomplished, and we should be on our return march. A bottle of this being used at the halt, and Johnny having safely secreted the rest in the "Devil's Pulpit," for our return, the party were about resuming their march, when Darrow said, -

"Hold on, my friends; 'Old Golden' sleeps only a little above here, and right in our way."

This required no explanation for any one present, for "Old Golden" was a famous deer of an enormous size, known to all the hunters of the valley, who had each in their turn followed him, and been foiled in all their attempts to come round him. The name of "Old Golden" had also been for years in the mouths of even the women and children of the valley, and many had seen his tracks, nearly the size of those of an ox. He had been followed from one side of the valley to the other, sleeping on the mountains on one side or the other, just as his security might demand it, and now had established his lair a little above the "Devil's Pulpit."

"Hold on a bit," said Darrow; "the cunning old fellow played George and me a shabby trick last Sunday, and I want to see if he will do the same thing to-day. You know him well, Snidigar?"

"That I do. The old fellow has slipped through my fingers often enough. I know exactly where he lies, Darrow."

Darrow had his plans all laid, and now, assuming the spokesman, he said to my father, -

"Squire, I want you to take charge of the party, and keep them all where they are, and without much noise, for about a quarter of an hour; and if 'Old Golden' is in his bed to-day, it is gone case with him: he will make fools of us no longer. Snidigar and I both know where he sleeps, and we know exactly where he runs when put up. George and I will go round and take our stand at the foot of the 'Eagle's Nest,' close to which he generally runs; and Snidigar will go round and stand at the 'South Pass.' One or t'other of those places he must go out at; and we will see to-day what he is made of. Wait here about a quarter of an hour, Squire, giving us time to get to our stands, and then At-will, who knows the way, will lead you up the hill."

Darrow and I swung around a mile or so to get to our stand, and Snidigar started for the "South Pass," a famous run-way, known to the hunters, and often used by them for driving the deer through.

Darrow took a tree, and placed me behind another close by, charging me to keep my body hidden whilst looking around the tree; and if I saw the deer coming in the distance, not to stir an inch, as the deer pay little attention to a man if he stands still. He had directed my attention to the quarter where the deer would first be seen, if he came.

We had not stood many minutes before I heard the heavy tramp of his feet amongst the leaves and sticks, as he was bounding over the logs, and was approaching; and at length the dodging of his white flag amongst the bushes showed that he was close at hand, and in an instant leap, his full and frightful figure plunged out of the thicket into the open timber; and just before he was to have passed us, "Ma!" said Darrow, in an under and tender tone, and he stopped, with his legs braced out, ready for another spring; but it was too late, for bang! went Darrow's rifle, and that spring he never made, but reeled backwards and fell, and was dead in an instant! Darrow ran up to him as quick as he could, and drawing his long knife from his belt, cut his throat, whilst I was cautiously advancing up.

"That's the way, George!" said he. "'Old Golden' don't play any more of his tricks."

A place has been kept clear on my retina for the impression of that picture then made, which nothing in the whole course of my life has effaced or in the least obscured.

The horns of this noble buck, which at that sea son were growing, were in the velvet, and, when running, they looked like a chair carried on his head.

Darrow had set his rifle against a tree, and, with his knife in his hand, was giving me some lessons for my future guidance in deer-hunting.

"To stop a deer, George, when running, always call "Ma!" they are sure to stop; if you whistle, it is apt to frighten them, and make them run faster. And when your deer is down, always cut its throat as quick as possible, to bleed it properly; if you don't, you have the blood all inside, which is awkward in dressing it, and hurts the meat also." And pointing to the mark of his bullet, "The old fellow stopped with his head and shoulders right behind that beech-tree, so I took him in the kidneys. The best place to aim, George, is always at the heart, just back of the fore-shoulders, and rather low down; and next to that the kidney; it's a small mark; but if you can hit it, it is just as fatal as to strike the heart. It's just forward of the hip-bone, and a little above the centre."

Darrow now went a little around the point of rocks, and sounded his whistle, the hunter's call, which he always carried, and in a little time Snidigar, who had heard his rifle, and now knew what was the result, soon came up, and soon followed Atwill, with the whole of the party. "Old Golden" down was a splendid sight for all, and in a few minutes his skin was off, and his heavy quarters were on the hunters' shoulders, and were carried and suspended in our route to the "Rattlesnakes' Den," to be taken up on our return from that enterprise.

On our route again; we were soon on the top of the mountain, where a sort of council of war was held, when Darrow and Jo. Snidigar, who had been parties in the onslaught ten years before, laid the plans of attack and took the lead.

I was to creep cautiously up to the brink of the precipice from which Darrow and I had viewed the reptiles a few days before, and getting into my position, to be perfectly still and ready to fire; until Darrow, and Snidigar, and Atwill, and the rest of them, had got round on the hill-side below the den, and below the level platform on which the reptiles were sleeping.

From that point the hill descended with a steep declivity, up which the invading parties were cautiously to advance, unseen, except by me, and within a few paces of where the snakes were lying; each armed with a heavy club of six or eight feet in length, to be wielded with both hands, and paid on to the group when the concerted signal should be given. For this Darrow had ordered me to watch his fox-skin cap, and when he gave the signal of "ready," I was to fire into the thickest of them, and the discharge of my gun was to be the signal for all to rush on.

Though my father had indicated that I might carry the "little musket," a light one-barrelled fowling-piece belonging to me, I had, without his knowledge, designed something more destructive for this particular occasion, and had borrowed of Captain Beebe, our nearest neighbour, an old Revolutionary rusty musket, of larger calibre and of greater power, and charged it before starting with an exorbitant charge of duck-shot; and just before getting to the brink of the precipice, to be sure that my explosion should lack nothing, had rammed down an extra charge of shot on top of the others. And with this, which required my utmost strength to elevate, I was peeping over the brink of the precipice. (Plate No. 2).

The Rattlesnakes' Den

To my astonishment and ecstatic delight, in the midst of the group there was a knot of these reptiles the size of a bushel basket, wound, twisted, and interlocked together, with their heads standing out, just the mark I wanted for the old musket. I got exceedingly timid and nervous while waiting for the signal, but when it came I "let fly!"

I knew nothing, for some time afterwards (when I was picked up), what had transpired from that moment. I saw nothing of the grand *melee* that ensued, nor ever knew anything of it, except what I got from tradition.

The old Revolutionary musket, doubly (if not trebly) charged, and filled with the rust of many years, and pointed *downhill* when I fired, had made a tremendous rebound, slapping me on the side of my head, and pitching over, a rod or so behind me. I was found lying on my back after the *fracas* was over, by several of the party, who had gone around and ascended the ledge to where I was. I was put upon my legs, but covered with blood, which was running quite into my shoes! However, I was soon on the battle-field, and helped to count the scalps. My double charge of shot had cut the knotted mass (perhaps from fifty to one hundred) to pieces, and the party rushing on with their clubs, had thrashed some hundreds more to death, whilst hundreds were saving themselves by running under the rocks into their den.

In a council of war again held on the battle field, while counting the scalps of some five or six hundred slain, and whilst Darrow and Snidigar and Atwill, and others, were pulling off the glistening skins and rattles of some of the most beautifully coloured of them, the rattle of one was heard, which, in the death-struggle, had escaped over the edge of the rock, and slid down the mountain-side for a considerable distance. It was a huge specimen; and Snidigar cut a pole with a crotch at the end of it, which was put upon the reptile's neck, when Darrow took it by the throat with his hand, and brought it alive on to the battle-ground.

An instant thought struck me, and I said, "Father, if a horn of powder was fastened to the fellow's tail, and a slow match applied to it, and he allowed to drag it into the den, wouldn't the whole lot of them be destroyed?"

"Good!" said Darrow. "George, you are now the best hunter in the valley of the Ocquago." Snidigar took the idea, and my father also, and the rest of the party. Snidigar had an immense powder-horn attached to his bullet-pouch, which was taken off for the purpose, and the other hunters emptying their horns into it, filled it to the brim. A string of four or five feet in length was tied to the rattlesnake's tail, and at the end of it the powder-horn, with a slow match of a yard or more in length, which Snidigar made of some wetted and twisted tow, filled with powder, dragging after it.

This fatal appendage all ready, and Darrow still holding the reptile by the neck, laid it upon the ground near the mouth of the den. When all hands, excepting Snidigar and Darrow, ran down the hill some distance, and most of them, like myself, took positions behind large trees. Snidigar set fire to the fuse, and Darrow let go, and both ran for secure quarters, when the powder-horn could be heard, rattling amongst the rocks, as the snake was carrying it home to its defeated comrades.

A breathless silence of a minute or so, and bang!! (like an instant clap of thunder) went the horn of powder, shaking the very earth on which we stood, and sending up blue streams of smoke through the crevices opened in the solid rock of twenty-five feet in thickness overlaying the den! The smoke rose in clouds amongst the trees, and when cleared away all hands ventured again on the scene of action, where not the sound of a rattle, even in distress, could be heard, and where no mortal being could have escaped destruction.

"I'll be blathered, Squeer Cathlin" (as he called my father), said Johnny O'Neil, "if iver thase var mints mahks us iny mare troobie, they've all gan to the Divil, Squeer!" - and turning to me - "They've cast you a lackin, Garge, and a bloody noase, but that's nathin."

A look of approbation from my father was even more encouraging than the speech of Johnny; and, what was still more satisfactory to my pride, was the unanimous applause of the model hunters, Darrow and Snidigar, and which all the rest of the party gave me, as the inventor of the scheme by which the pests and the terror of the inhabitants of the flourishing and happy little valley of the Ocquago were disposed of, undoubtedly, for several years to come.

Before commencing to descend the mountain, I recollect all hands were for a while seated in the shade of some large oaks, when several pipes were lit, and a bundle of cigars distributed, which my father had brought in his pocket. From the spot where we sat, we had an extensive view to the East, overlooking the *"Sturrukker"* and the *"Hemlock Hollow."*

The "Sturrukker" (or "bloody run"), a large and dashing stream, emptying into the Susquehana at Hilbourns, three or four miles distant from where we were sitting, said to have "run red with blood" during the Indian war, waged but a few years before; and since, equally famous for the incredible quantity of trout taken in its black waters, and in the taking of which several lives were said to have been recently taken by the Indians of Hemlock Hollow, in which dark and dreary solitude the stream rises.

During our ascent of the mountain, and even when taking off the skin of "Old Golden," from remarks made by Darrow and Snidigar, I learned that the party were ascending these mountains under a sort of presentiment that their day's sport might be intercepted by lurking and revengeful Indians, said to be still hanging about the Ocquago and Randolph Mountains; and the fact seemed to be well known by Darrow and Snidigar, and other hunters, that, since the defeat and expulsion of Brant, a lingering and marauding party of *Oneidas* were still remaining ensconced in the dark and almost impenetrable forest of the *"Hemlock Hollow"* a constant terror to the border inhabitants, and game, occasionally, for the rifles of the hunters which they had to contend with.

Though nothing as yet had transpired to affect the nerves or apprehensions of the party as to Indians, and whilst they were enjoying their tobacco, I saw Snidigar's corrugator muscles drawn down, and his long forefinger of the left hand pointing to the dark green "Hemlock Hollow "which lay beneath us, and to which Darrow's eye was being directed, "There," said he, "there are those devils again - there's their smoke rising above the hemlocks! 'Red Feather' is there, Darrow, and 'Yellow Mocasins;' I'll be bound those fellows are back again, and very likely a party with them - the poor people at Hilbourn's Landing are in great danger - they may all be cut off."

"I know," said Darrow, "we'll have to give it to those chaps again."

"And I howp," said Johnny O'Neil, who was listening to the conversation, "I howp, gintlemin, ye'll nat be dowen of it to-day. I thank we'd batter be gangin' tow-ards howm, for won't the thunder and the smohk we've been a raisin' bring thase divils upon us?"

The party seemed mostly to incline to Johnny's opinion, and were soon on the march, descending the mountain, as they were evidently not prepared for an Indian fight.

Poor Johnny was no doubt influenced by a double thought - of the smoke of the Indians in "Hemlock Hollow," on the east side of the mountain, and the "bottles of brandy" he had secreted at the "Devil's Pulpit," on the west side, towards which we were all now progressing.

On our way, the quarters and skin of "Old Golden" were again taken on to the shoulders of the hunters; and, arrived at the "Devil's Pulpit," the party were seated on some large logs on a level plain in front of the pulpit, and ever good-natured, Johnny brought forth with great alacrity and some grace, his hidden bottles of brandy, and his boiled ham, &c.

As in the celebrations of most great victories, where jocose hilarity, boasting, threatening, and defying are mixed with the cup that's passing around, so with Johnny's tin cups of brandy and slices of ham, which were dealt about, were ejaculated the most unqualified exultations for the conquest of "Old Golden," the most unfeeling huzzas for the fate of the poor rattlesnakes, and boasts of the unerring truth of "Old Ben" and "Long Polly," [6] and fearless contempt for the "Red Feather" and his party of marauders, whom Johnny O'Neil had "supposed" might be coming upon them from "Hemlock Hollow."

In the midst of this jubilee lunch, in which some were seated on logs and others upon the ground, and the conversation was, of course, on rattlesnakes and Indians, bang! went a rifle on our left, and at a distance of some twenty-five or thirty rods, the smoke of which was seen amongst a thicket of bushes, and the ball of which was heard as it went whizzing over our heads.

Darrow at the time was sitting on a log, somewhat higher than the rest of us. All of us sprang to our feet, or on to our hands and feet, and amongst the last were Darrow, Snidigar, and Atwill, the only ones who had rifles with them.

"That's a close shave," said Darrow; "he knows my old fox-skin cap, but it was only a graze, any how."

"That's 'Red Feather,'" said Snidigar. "No doubt of it," said Darrow. "I know the crack of his rifle; it's not the first time that I have heard it. He's snatched many a fine buck out of my hands on these mountains, and you and I know the music of his rifle, Snidigar, and we shall have more of it. Look wild!"

"Lie close there, every one of you," said Snidigar, as Darrow was creeping forward on the ground,' as close as a rattlesnake would crawl, to the roots of a large beech tree, poising his rifle in his left hand before him in a horizontal position.

"Take the pine-log there, near its root," said Darrow to Snidigar, "and see every leaf that stirs in that direction."

The rest of the party were dropped under or by the side of the logs, and as whist as mice, all except Johnny O'Neil, who had also been flat, but had conceived the plan of pushing down a handful of buck-shot into my old musket, and which he was doing by resting on one elbow.

I got my head sufficiently raised to see my friend and master, Darrow, whose every motion I was still studying, as important to the education I was receiving. His motions at that time were all so slow as to be almost imperceptible, and on either side of the tree, before advancing his head far enough to see, his fox-skin cap was held a little in advance, so as to receive the bullet when it should come. I saw him at length lying perfectly still for a 'minute or so, when his cap was lowered down, and his rifle gradually raised to his face. He didn't fire, and in a moment lowered it again, but before taking up his cap, he raised it quickly up and fired; and instantly, from amongst the logs, with a tremendous crash, Johnny O'Neil let off the old musket with its charge of buck-shot in the same direction.

Darrow at this time was flat on his back, and with his wiper was pushing down another ball, when in a low whisper he said, "It's nothing it was only a shaking leaf." Johnny O'Neil, however, *actually saw an Indian, and saw him quail before the handful of buck-shot!*

"I've kilt one of the divils!" said Johnny.

Snidigar whispered to him to hold his tongue, and he could shoot no more, for his buck-shot had given out.

Darrow was on the lookout again, and all the party resting in breathless anxiety, when "spang!" said another rifle behind us (and exactly in the opposite direction, the Indians' mode precisely, and on the level platform on which we were resting, below, and in front of the pulpit rock), and whew! - went the ball over our heads.

Snidigar, from the beginning of the fight, had placed Atwill on the lookout in that direction, apprehending, from Indian modes of warfare, that we should be attacked on both sides simultaneously.

Atwill could see nothing to "draw a bead" upon, though the smoke of the Indian's gun, as in the other case, was seen rising out of the bushes. Darrow was steady at his post, and looking out, and Snidigar's eagle eyes were roaming about in all directions, and not a leaf moved without his seeing it.

The Indians had decidedly the advantage, being sheltered by the thickets on each side of us, when our warriors were obliged to stand exposed, comparatively in open ground.

The most of our party being unarmed, and we being surrounded, it was evident that our best chance was to lie as still and close as possible, and meet what might come in the best manner we could, with the three rifles of famous hunters to protect us.

There was no use in advancing, which would only expose us to the Indians' fire, and the suspense became awful, waiting for the attack to be resumed. In the midst and silence of this, I heard my father whispering to Johnny O'Neil, on the other side of the log, and, from what I could understand, he was sending Johnny off into the valley for help: "From the very first leap that you make," said my father, "don't even turn your head to look back, but go straight to the river - to Atwill's house! - tell his brother - and tell him to bring the Hilbourns! Send someone to Heths! - Take Atwill's canoe and cross over - tell Rowley and the other men in the field! - jump on to the sorrel mare in the south stable - and go up the valley at the utmost speed! Go to the Buels! - go to the Smiths! At the Devil's Pulpit - the Devil's Pulpit! Mind!" - as I saw Johnny taking his tremendous kangaroo leaps down the hill, when I peeped over the log.

Johnny was out of sight in an instant, and, for *one,* out of danger; and the instant thought came that *I too,* in the like way, could save *one,* and perhaps help in bringing succour to the besieged and doomed party. And as quick as thought, a bound and a leap or two took *me* out of the sight and hail of the party, and, like a rolling hoop, I was bounding and rebounding down the mountain side for a mile or more.

Atwill's wife, where Johnny had been and reported as he passed that "Squeer Cathlin" (no doubt to make the alarm more exciting) was "kilt," and to Mrs. Atwill and others whom I met, that "Garge" was wounded (for I was still covered with blood from the bruise of the old musket, and had no time then to explain the cause of), and that he had himself "kilt one of the divils."

Johnny was soon across the river, and, astride of the sorrel mare, was electrifying the people of the valley as he advanced towards its head, and rallying the rifles into the field. Men were everywhere seen running, some on horseback and others on foot; and in a little time the river was spotted with canoes, with their glistening paddles and rifles, on their hurried way to the scene of action, to land at Atwill's, as Johnny had said, and proceed to the "Devil's Pulpit," where the battle was waging.

Horsemen were started across the mountains for the rifles of Randolph Valley; and horns were blowing, women were screaming, and dogs were howling, and even the very atmosphere of the little valley seemed to be aware of the horrid scene that was transpiring at the "Devil's Pulpit," and to breathe, in unison with the voices of the living, "Death to the Indian devils, every one of them!"

What a piece of good luck for Johnny O'Neil and I that in an instant's thought we bounded off and escaped as we did! And how little, two hours before, was dreamed of in this quiet little valley, and by the jovial party at the "Rattlesnakes' Den," of the scenes *now* to be related! I would stop here if I could, but the whole must be told. Who had expected the dread sound of the frightful war-whoop, and the relentless blows of the tomahawk and scalping-knife? Who had thought that these things were to be unburied, and stained again with the blood of the innocent and quiet inhabitants of the little valley of the Ocquago?

What reader who has ever read the history of the ill-fated valley of Wyoming, of its "Indian Massacre," the battles at "Bloody Run," of "Oosterhouts Narrows," and of "Tunkhannock," will lack the patience to bear with me a few moments until we can arrive at the end of this gathering storm, or lack the means of appreciating its anticipated horrors when they are made known? The mind shudders at scenes of blood, of massacres, and murder when they transpire, and that is enough; and therefore the *finale* of these descriptions must await the result.

I, as I have said, luckily scaled the mountain's side, crossed the river, and got home. My dear mother met me with screams, as I was covered yet with blood; and learning from me that "Squeer Cathlin" was not yet "kilt," she washed off the blood, and put me into a clean shirt. And gallant Johnny O'Neil at this time was galloping down the valley with his scattered volunteers, and the canoes of the river were landing their heroic cargoes at "Atwill's Landing," where Johnny and myself had first arrived in our stampede from the "Devil's Pulpit."

There had been no Devil to preach to the poor affrighted group packed away under the logs, or watching, with their rifles, on their hands and knees, or bellies, for the show of a red feather or a string of wampum.

Whilst weary and nearly exhausted, and impatient for the battle or a rescue, the awful silence was at last broken by a *terrible,* a *wicked,* and a *cruel* laugh that broke out from the summit of the rock above the Pulpit, higher up than the affrighted group had been looking, from the stretched mouths of two giggling country lasses of their familiar acquaintance, who sat overlooking the unhappy and imprisoned group, having their two sweethearts seated behind them, and joining in the laugh, with their rifles on their shoulders.

The prostrate group gradually arose from their painful lairs, and Darrow, rising upon one knee, and bringing his rifle to his face, exclaimed, "Bogard, you'll not play that trick again." But Bogard's head was lowered out of sight, and that of Trowbridge, his companion, and their damsels departed with them.

The Indian battle, of course, with all its horrors, terminated here. Bogard and Lyman Trowbridge had been engaged to join the party to the "Rattle snakes' Den," but mustering their sweethearts to accompany them, were behind time, and left behind. They had followed on the trail, and travelling slow, with petticoats, through the thickets, had met the returning party, without being themselves discovered, near the "Devil's Pulpit," and resolved to give them a "sensation," which had been done in the manner described; one firing his rifle over their heads from the right, and the other from the left, from which points, unseen, they had mounted the precipice and joined their damsels, and with them sat amusing themselves by overlooking the splendid and warlike maneuvers, transpiring below, of pre paring for an Indian battle.

Darrow had laid until his legs were stiff, and the strained eyes of Snidigar had become bloodshot. The rest of the party, stowed away under the logs, came forth in better condition, and in the midst of an excited dialogue as to the infamous trick, and the manner in which it should be eventually punished, the undevoured crumbs were gathered up, and a bottle or two of brandy yet remaining, their suddenly broken lunch was resumed with increased appetites.

In the midst of this, Snidigar's long forefinger was seen pointing down the hill. "Look! there's Bill" (his brother, also a celebrated hunter), "there's a fellow always ready." Bill Snidigar was a man six feet and a half high, and with his head and shoulders rising out of the fern (for he was on his hands and knees), with his rifle in his hand, and at thirty or forty rods distance, where he had arrived, he was ready for the fight, for the rescue.

At a less distance, and further to the right, and from behind an oak tree, "Tom Ely" gradually showed out his ugly face; and within a few rods, and further to the left, appearing like mermaids looking out of the sea, were discovered the uncovered foreheads of "Jake and Jim Seeley," never behind; their bodies hidden in the mass of fern in which they were embedded. These were the foremost for the rescue, and first on the ground, like serpents, silent and unseen, they were on the spot, and ready for action.

The "up river boys" had landed at Atwill's ferry, and were now spread out, and entering the forest in position, and ready for a tree fight, sounding the frightful war-whoop, and advancing from tree to tree, as the forest rang with the echo of their yells a-head of them.

The besieged party at this time were gathered up, with their rattlesnakes' skins bandaging their hats, their waists, and their arms, and others were carried on poles as flags and trophies.

The beautiful and silent vanguards then rose from their hidden lairs in the fern all around, came up, got a drink of cognac brandy, raised the war-whoop over the saddle of "Old Golden," with whom all had been acquainted, helped to transport his remains, and meeting the advancing columns, turned them, and all together descended the mountain's side to the river shore, where boats were ready to cross them over, and other boats of riflemen were just arriving.

Across, all hands met upon my father's meadows, and my father taking the lead, the little army was soon upon the lawn of my father's house, on which all were seated. A bottle or two more of brandy added to the merriment of that picturesque scene, in which I was put forward in a white shirt, and with a clean face, as the *hero* of the day.

At this moment two poor young men came up from "down the river," each one bringing a string of several dozens of fine trout. "Jo Still," who was spokesman for the two, said, "Squire Catlin, what will you give?" holding them up.

"Do you mean for all?"

"Yes, squire."

"What do you expect for them?"

"Well, we'll take a dollar, squire."

There it is, said my father. "Still" (inquired my father, as all the party were listening), "where did you catch these?"

"In *Hemlock Hollow,* squire. The Sturrukker is full on 'em there, and yesterday bein a showery day, they bit uncommonly well."

"But I thought there were Indians there?"

"We thought we saw their smoke there to-day. We feared that *'Red Feather'* and *'Yellow Moccasin'* were there."

"No," (said the second fisherman, as he advanced forward, and drew his shirt-sleeve from his elbow to his wrist of each arm across his face, beneath his nose), "no, squire, I'll be darned if that's so, there haint been an Ingin there these five years! *'Jo Still'* and I has each on us got a nice little farm a cummin on there in 'Hemlock Holler.' We've been burnin logs there for some days, and I think that was the smoke you seed, squire. We was gitten a little afraid this mornin howsomsever, when we saw a smoke on Steele's mountain, or somear thar abouts, and thinkin it might be Ingins (though I think they dasent come to Hemlock Holler any more), we still thought twas best to take our wives and little ones down to Hilbourn's landing for a day or two, and from there we've just cummed up here, squire."

My father explained to these men the cause of the smoke they had" seen on Steele's mountain, and twilight approaching, with a few united warwhoops, the party dispersed, giving "three cheers for 'Garge'" (which Johnny O'Niel proposed), "who has been *lacked,* and been *kacked,* but has blawn the pison manufactury to the divil!"

So much, and nothing would have answered short of it, for the affair of the "Rattlesnakes' Den," a legend not before known in history, but rife with the name of its *hero* in Susquehanna lore.

[1] An open shed, in which wood for the winter is stored.
[2] His rifle.
[3] An extra ramrod, which hunters carry in their left hand, for facility in loading and cleaning their rifles.

[4] To take sight.
[5] Water-beech, a sort of beech that grows by the water's edge, and is very wiry and tough.
[6] Barrow's and Snidigar's rifles.

Chapter Two - Gold Hunting in the Crystal Mountains

In the past chapter we have halted a little, and I hope not too long, amongst the scenes of my boyish life; in this, I shall retrace some of the interesting steps of my elder days; and stopping occasionally for scenes which I too hurriedly passed by in the first volume of this work, will bring the reader to where that left off, with a field vast and boundless before us, in which again to view the Indians and the incidents of Indian life.

In the first volume the reader learned that I had travelled eight years amongst the tribes of North America, east of the Rocky Mountains, and made a collection of more than 600 portraits of Indians and paintings illustrating their modes of life; and that I made an Exhibition of the same in New York, in Paris, and in London.

That Exhibition was very popular, and gained me great applause, and money also; but, like too many fast men, I was led into unfortunate speculations, and, like them, suffered injurious consequences.

At that time, however, the Senate of the United States was considering a Bill for the purchase of my collection, for the sum of 65,000 dollars. A committee had reported a bill in favour of the purchase, and in their report had stated that they considered the price of 65,000 dollars to be a moderate compensation for it; and I had encouraging assurances of its success.

Messrs. Webster, Seward, Foote, and the other Federal members were in favour of the appropriation, and voted for it; and the democratic members voted against it. Mr. Webster advocated the purchase, in a long and eloquent speech, of which the following is a brief extract:

EXTRACT FROM THE SPEECH OF THE HON. DANIEL WEBSTER, ON A MOTION IN THE SENATE OF THE UNITED STATES, FOR THE PURCHASE OF "CATLIN'S INDIAN COLLECTION," IN 1849.

"MR. PRESIDENT: *The question is, whether it does not become us, as an useful thing, to possess in the United States this collection of paintings, etc. made amongst the Indian tribes? Whether it is not a case for the exercise of large liberality - I will not say* bounty, *but policy? These tribes, sir, that have preceded us, to whose lands we have succeeded, and who have no written memorials of their laws, their habits, and their manners, are all passing away to the world of forgetfulness. Their likeness, manners, and customs, are portrayed with more accuracy and truth in this collection by Catlin than in all the other drawings and representations on the face of the earth. Somebody in this country ought to possess this collection - that is my opinion; and I do not know who there is, or where there is to be found, any society or any individual, who, or which, can with so much propriety possess himself, or itself, of it, as the Government of the United States. For my part, then, I do think that the preservation of "Catlin's Indian Collection" in this country is an important public act. I think it properly belongs to those accumulations of historical matters respecting our predecessors on this continent, which it is very proper for the government of the United States to maintain. As I have said, this race is going into forgetfulness. They track the continuation of mankind in the present age, and call recollection back to them. And here they are better exhibited, in my judgment, better set forth and presented to the mind, and the taste and the curiosity of mankind, than in all other collections in the world. I go for this as an* American subject *- as a thing belonging to us - to our history - to the history of a race whose lands we till, and over whose obscure graves and bones we tread every day. I look upon it as a thing more appropriate for us than the ascertaining of the South Pole, or anything that can be discovered in the Dead Sea or the River Jordan. These are the grounds, sir, upon which I propose to proceed, and I shall vote for the appropriation with great pleasure*"

The following letter also, which I received at that time, I have a right to introduce in this place:

LETTER FROM GENERAL CASS, SECRETARY OF STATE OF THE UNITED STATES OF AMERICA

"Dear Sir: *No man can appreciate better than myself the admirable fidelity of your* Indian Collection *and Indian book, which I have lately examined. They are equally spirited and accurate: they are true to nature. Things that are - are not sacrificed, as they too often are by the painter, to things as (in his judgment) they should be.*

"During eighteen years of my life I was superintendent of Indian affairs in the north-western territory of the United States; and during more than five I was Secretary of War, to which department belongs the general control of Indian concerns. I know the Indians thoroughly. I have spent many a month in their camps, council-houses, villages, and hunting grounds; I have fought with them, and against them; and I have negotiated seventeen treaties of peace or of cession with them. I mention these circumstances to show you that I have a good right to speak confidently upon the subject of your drawings. Among them I recognize many of my old acquaintances, and everywhere I am stuck with the vivid representations of them and their customs, of their peculiar features, and of their costumes. Unfortunately, they are receding before the advancing tide of our population, and are probably destined, at no distant day, wholly to disappear; but your collection will preserve them, as far as human art can do, and will form the most perfect monument of an extinguished race that the world has ever seen.

"To Geo. Catlin."   "LEWIS CASS.

Mr. "Jefferson Davis," at that time (previous to the Rebellion), a member of the Senate, before giving his vote, made, in a speech of two newspaper columns in length, and now matter of record, the most complimentary eulogy that has ever been passed on my works, stating that I was "the only artist who ever had painted, or could paint, an American Indian; that he had been a campaigner with me for several months amongst the Osages, the Comanches, Pawnee Picts, &c, whilst he was an officer in the 1st Regiment of mounted Dragoons, - that he had sat by me and seen me paint many of my portraits from the life, and knew their accuracy, that the collection was one of great interest and value to our country, and that it would be a shame if it were sold in a foreign land." And yet, when the stage of the voting showed that his vote was to turn the scale, stated that, "from *principle,* he was bound to vote against the appropriation," which he did, and defeated the bill.

This unexplained *"principle,"* I construed to be clearly the principle adopted and proclaimed by President Jackson many years before, of removing all the southern tribes of Indians west of the Mississippi River, that their two hundred and fifty millions of rich cotton lands might be covered with slave labourers; and which principle, with an accompanying hostility to everything Indian, had been and was being carried out by the successive ad ministrations, convincing me that I had nothing further to expect or to claim from my country for the labours I had expended and the collections I had made in the Indian countries.

This discouragement, and the explosion of my pecuniary affairs in London, came upon me together, and both contributed to impede my return to my native country, which I had contemplated at that time; and, as will be seen, to my subsequent wanderings, to be briefly narrated in the following pages. In this dilemma I was lost; but *my collection* was saved to my country by an American gentleman, - an act so noble and so patriotic that I cannot believe my country will forget it.

My "occupation gone," and with no other means on earth than my hands and my brush, and less than half of a life, at best, before me, as with all that is human and mortal, my thoughts tended towards Dame Fortune, to know if there was there anything yet in store for me. The thought was an extremely unpromising and visionary one, and yet, without a superstition, seemed worthy of a trial.

In this state of mind, therefore, into one of the eccentric adventures of my chequered life I was easily led at that time, by the information got by a friend of mine, a reader in the Bibliothèque Impériale of Paris, from an ancient Spanish work, relative to gold mines of marvellous richness, said to have been worked by Spanish miners some 300 years since, in the Tumucumache (or Crystal) mountains, in the northern part of Brazil.

According to this tradition the Spanish miners, after having accumulated great riches, were attacked by the Indians and massacred in their houses, or driven out of the country, leaving their gold behind them. This wonderful relation, with other corroborating legends I had received, had enough of probability (with the additional circumstances already narrated) to excite my cupidity, and what follows is a brief account of my singular enterprise entered upon at that time.

In my wandering contemplations, ten years, at least, of solitudes in voluntary exile, with my pencils and sketch-books, were before me as agreeable realities. Nuggets of gold of all sizes appeared in my dreams, and in my waking hours I had allowed a half superstition to intimate to me that Dame Fortune might have something precious in store for me, and which she could not bestow without the suitable opportunity. As traditions had said that the gold miners of the Crystal Mountains had accumulated vast amounts in gold dust and nuggets, imagination naturally and easily depicted these riches left behind, buried within the walls of their adobe houses when the miners were destroyed, or obliged to flee from their villages.

The wealth of London was to be at my command if I succeeded; a company, with unbounded capital, was to be formed, and a concession was to be obtained from the government of Brazil for the right of working the mines and *carting* the gold away; and I had yet the stimulus of an unexplored country before me.

With such reflections and anticipations I started, in 1852 - fourteen years ago - for the Crystal Mountains, in Brazil. I sailed to Havannah; from thence I went to Carraccas, in Venezuela, to see the wonderful "Silla," described by Baron de Humboldt. From Carraccas to the Orinoco and Demerara, designing to ascend the Essequibo to the base of the Crystal Mountains.

Learning from friends in Demerara the jealousy with which the unsettled boundary between British Guiana and Brazil was at that time guarded, and the consequent difficulty, if not impossibility, of passing the frontier post at the Grand Rapids of the Essequibo, I obtained a British passport for Brazil, and an incognito cognomen, as kings and emperors sometimes do, resolved to leave the river below the "Sabo" or great cataract, and approach the mountains by a land route, taking a guide and escort from some of the Arowak or Taruma villages I should have to pass through.

Having previously met my old acquaintance, Sir Robert Shombergk, returning from his second exploring expedition to the sources of the Essequibo, he also had explained to me the uncertainty of getting permission from the post-holder to pass the Grand Rapids, and also of the extreme difficulty of ascending the Essequibo from that to the mountains, owing to the numerous rapids, requiring a strong force of men He approved my plan of taking the eastern route; and having learned from me the object I had in view, stated that he had long since heard legends of the Spanish gold mines in those mountains, and that were it not that he was at that time executing a special command of Her Majesty the Queen, he would have accompanied me in the enterprise.

Joined in Georgetown by an enterprising young man by the name of Smyth, an Englishman, a good shot, and carrying a first-rate minié rifle; and, armed myself with Colt's revolving carabine, we left the Essequibo below the grand cataract, and after a desperate encounter with rivers and swamps, reached an Arowak village. Received in this village with great kindness (as has been described in the first volume), we procured hired horses and mules, on which, with an Indian guide, passing several Indian villages, and a country of three or four hundred miles, we reached the base of the mountains, and then, with a half-caste interpreter and guide, who knew the route, and a mule to carry our packs, we trusted to our legs for a passage across the mountains into the valley of the Amazon, which we accomplished, but with great fatigue and some distress, to the forks of the Trombutas, from which we descended in an Indian pirogue to the Amazon, to Santarem, and to Para, as has been more fully narrated in the first volume of this work. Instead of finding the Tumucamache (or Acarai) a single mountain ridge, which I had contemplated, we found ourselves in the midst of a *series* of mountains of palaeozoic rocks of the most frowning and defying aspect for a breadth of fifty or sixty miles. In the midst of these our poor mule gave out, and we were obliged to leave it and most of our packs, and trust to our weapons for subsistence. Food and life and progress now became subjects of more importance than gold; and in our jaded and exhausted condition we were but miserable nugget hunters. We *hunted,* however, passing over extensive beds of auriferous quartz, and in some instances distinctly exhibiting to the naked eye the precious metal.

In a beautiful valley amongst the mountain ranges we struck upon an ancient waggon-road, which we followed for several miles, intelligible proofs of mining operations. This, however, we lost, from the thick overgrowth of a sort of thorn, not unlike a compact hedge, extending in some places for miles together, and entirely impenetrable to man or horse, until cut away.

From such causes all my nugget fever for the time passed away, and I was happy to be again at my old vocation, and safe and sound in the valley of the Amazon.

Near the close of the first volume, I gave some account of the valley of the Amazon, its rivers, its forests, and inhabitants; but, for want of space, was obliged to make it brief and very incomplete. Other features of it, which I was then obliged to pass by, will now be taken up, and the end of this chapter will bring us to the Pacific, where we will have a new region to pass into.

In my boarding-house in Para I made the agree able acquaintance of Señor L___, to whom I gave
a description of my long voyage, and the object I had had in crossing the Crystal Mountains. He told me he had long heard traditions of those gold mines; and the massacre of the miners by the Indians; and he added that he had no doubt of the facts, nor any doubt but that great wealth had been left concealed in or about the miners' adobe houses.

He informed me that he lived on an island in the Amazon, some hundreds of miles above Santarem, which he had stocked with several thousand head of cattle and horses; that he was returning by steamer in a few days; and that if I would accompany him, he would fit out another expedition at his own house, and at his expense, approaching the mountains from a different direction, and in a different place; and, he thought, with a better chance of success.

I accepted this gentleman's kind offer, and in three days we were prepared for our coming campaign. At Para we obtained each a tunique and leggings of strong buckskin, and other articles necessary for our tour, and various trinkets and other presents for the Indians.

I had at the time in my employment a first-rate negro man (a maroon), six feet and two inches in height, *"Caesar Bolla,"* who had freed himself from bondage by leaving his master, Señor Bolla, in Havannah, and had proved to me his value in a tour of five or six weeks which we had just made together amongst the Xingu Indians, on the river by that name.

My former companion, Smyth, having left me in Para, I purchased of him his minié rifle, which I had put into Caesar's hands, and of which he was very proud. Señor L___ proposed to take two of his own negroes, and employ a couple of friendly Indians living in the vicinity of his residence, as guides and interpreters, making in all a party of seven.

This hospitable gentleman had on his island ten thousand cattle and horses, and fifteen negroes. He told me before starting, that, as we were going into a section of country known to be rich in minerals, and guarded with great jealousy by the Government, we should be more or less liable to fall into the hands of one of three garrisons of bare-footed soldiers, stationed at the Barra and at the base of the mountains; and that in such an event he should much rather answer to the name of Señor Novello than that of Señor L___.

His motive for this he knew I could correctly appreciate when I showed him my passport, and at the same time told him my real name, with which (when he heard it) he said he had been for some years familiar. He spoke the Portugais, the Spanish, and the "lingua geral" (the language of the country), and Caesar spoke the Spanish and the English, and our two Indian guides spoke the "geral," and the Indian language of the tribes where we were going; so that on the score of languages we had nothing to fear.

The route proposed was to descend the Amazon some fifteen or twenty miles in a huge and unwieldy pirogue; then ascend a small and sluggish stream some twenty or thirty miles, leave the pirogue, and traverse the vast and gloomy forest until we reached the llanos (prairies), where we would hire mules of the Indians to take us to the mountains.

We were several days -making the necessary preparations; laying in salt and dried meats, coffee, sugar, biscuits, tea, salt, &c, and a few culinary articles; and amongst them a large tin pan from his wife's pantry, for washing gold, and a heavy hammer for breaking the rocks, and a cold chisel for cutting the nuggets which we might find, too large to be transported entire!

Embarked in our heavy pirogue, with all our stores and equipments laid in, we were venturing on a tour which probably no white man had ever made before (and of which we had no knowledge except that obtained from our two Indians, who had traversed it several times before), of wading, of creeping and crawling, through the vast and sunless and pathless solitudes which lie between the Amazon and the llanos that spread out at the foot of the Tumucamache, or Crystal Mountains. And those who would appreciate the grandeur, the vastness, the intricacy, and the mysteries of the Amazon forests without seeing them, now listen! -

Gently and easily we floated down the northern shore of the river for the distance of fifteen or twenty miles; most of the way, the banks, the shore, and the trunks of the lofty trees were entirely hidden by the outrolling and outstretching masses of foliage of various hues and various patterns, which seemed to be tumbling over our heads into the river.

Without discovering the least appearance of a landing-place, or mouth of a river or stream, "Ya-ka, ya-ka" (there it is, there it is), cried out one of our Indians, and pointing to it, when our pirogue was steered about, and plunged by force of paddles amidst the hanging boughs that were dipping in the water. In a moment we were out of sight of the mighty Amazon, and ascending a deep and sluggish stream of unknown width, for the hanging foliage was everywhere bathing in the stream, and hiding the muddy shores and the trunks of the trees from our view.

A sort of *"Lingua-geral"* boat-song was now raised as the negroes were plying the paddles; and the two Indians, in the bow, with their paddles were dividing and lifting the drooping boughs out of the water and passing them over our heads as the boat moved on. When raised, they were struck with the paddle, and most of their water discharged, but enough still filled the air, like a mist or a gentle shower of rain.

The little Indians, with their entirely naked bodies, who were thus nicely and comfortably cooled, were laughing at our buckskins, in which we were completely drenched.

The song progressed, the paddles were plied, and we still went on, whilst the artificial rain was falling, and the sun was shining. Night approached; and we found a comfortable landing-shore, where our hammocks were slung, and between two tremendous fires we passed the night, amidst the howling of monkeys and hooting and screaming of nocturnal birds.

The third day of this perpetual shower-bath brought us to the head of navigation of this little river without a name, where there were lying three other pirogues belonging to Indians, each one fastened to the shore with a thong of raw hide, and claimed by the owner's totem and the figure of a knife drawn on a piece of bark with blood-red paint and fastened to the raw hide thong.

Here was a little spot of open timber, comfortable for an encampment, and we remained two days, arranging our packs, and preparing for our march through the forest, leaving our canoe for our return, labelled and claimed in the manner of those of the Indians; and our Indian guides assured us that no Indians would ever remove it.

Now our mighty task began. So far the pirogue had carried our "bags and baggage," but now we had to divide them amongst ourselves; each one carrying his load upon his back as he squeezed and crept through the mazy network of shrubbery and twisted vines. Our Indian guides professed to be "following a road;" but what a road! A road here, is where the Indians have with their knives cut away the vines and made an opening large enough for a man's body, as he stoops, to pass through; and this, in a few months or weeks, requires the same process repeated to make it pass able again.

Strapped upon Caesar's back was always my large portfolio, containing a large number of cartoon portraits of North American Indians, and blank cartoons for other portraits to be made, protected by a waterproof covering. Over that was fastened the tin pan for gold washing. On his left shoulder his minié rifle, and in his right hand the sledge-hammer for getting at large nuggets, for which my cupidity was now, for a second time, becoming roused.

Señor N___ and myself carried our rifles, and each his knapsack of provisions, &c; and the other articles were divided amongst the two negroes and the two Indians, the two last of whom were armed with their *sarbacanes* (or blow-guns) with poisoned arrows.

Thus freighted, and thus equipped, we started on our long and painful campaign, little knowing of, and little caring for, the toils and difficulties ahead of us those of an *Amazon forest,* and yet to be described. The earth, shrouded with an endless impenetrable mass of green leaves, of twisting vines, and wild flowers of various hues, penetrated, where we walk, or stand, or creep, by the trunks of the stately moras, hackeas, and palms, and fifty other sorts of trees, but whose tops, and even branches, are lost in the chaotic mass of foliage that embraces them.

Man wanders under and through these vast canopies without finding a log or a stone, or even the roots of a tree, to rest his weaned limbs upon. No tree, even in its natural decline, falls to the ground, but, like the masts of vessels with their cordage, they are held and braced up by twisting vines, whilst their decaying trunks are wasting away in the moist alluvion, and they gradually settle down (as they arose) to the earth from which they came.

No stone has been dropped here from a drifting iceberg, or tumbled along in a mountain torrent, and the roots of trees, to be seen, must be dug for, so rapid is the accumulation of soil around them, that the trunks of trees have the shape of piles driven into the ground.

Owing to the shade and perpetual dampness of those solitudes, fire never makes any progress, and the heaviest showers of rain generally fail to reach the ground, otherwise than in a light mist, or by creeping down the branches, trunks, and twisting vines by which it is broken and conducted.

In the fresh air and sunshine at the tops of the trees, which we never can see, there is a busy and chattering neighbourhood of parrots and monkeys, but all below is a dark and silent matted solitude, in which a falling leaf, for want of wind, may be a month in reaching the ground, and where a man may be tracked by the broken cobwebs he leaves behind him.

On, on we go, from day to day, in "Indian file," cutting our way, without the slightest change, encamping at night between our fires, always serenaded by the frightful ariguatos (howling monkeys), whilst we are beating off the mosquitos, or shaving our legs to the knees with our knives to destroy the thousands of red ticks that fasten their heads in the skin.

Our progress is slow, perhaps some ten or twelve miles per day. If man were but knee high, or, like a serpent, could crawl upon his belly, he might travel further. Not only are we impeded by the vines that are twisting about our necks and our legs, but the ground we walk on is painful and fatiguing owing to the vast quantity of leaves that fall, which have neither winds nor heavy rains to flatten them down, or fire to burn them.

Nuts, and shells of nuts, are dropping on our heads, disengaged by monkeys and birds engaged in the tops of the trees, the chattering of which we constantly hear, though we don't see them. The falling nuts are lost to the eye when they reach the ground, owing to the depth and looseness of the leaves amongst which they are hidden. The peccaries, in search of these, throw up the leaves around their sides until they are often nearly lost sight of, but the troupe thus engaged always keep sentinels on the look out, to give the alarm when an enemy is approaching.

On the fifth day of our march, getting into a region a little elevated, and with more open timber, we passed a large gang of these little fellows busy in their furrows; and a short time after, our little Indian "Bok-ar" announced that they had taken up the line of march, and were following us, and that we were in great danger unless we could reach a small stream that was a few miles ahead of us. At his request we relieved him of as much of his load as we could, and he went back to meet them, and keep them at bay by some sort of charm that he was master of, and which I did not learn, the same, he told us, that the jaguar uses to decoy them up to a leaning tree or other place where he can pounce upon the fattest of the herd, and, with it, leap to a nook above their reach.

About three or four o'clock in the afternoon we reached the anticipated stream, and forded it, the mud and water reaching to our waistbands. All hands safe over, we came to a halt, and laid our packs upon the ground, the Indians assuring us that our enemies would not enter the water for us.

Our daring little *Bok-ar* was in full view, dancing backwards towards us, singing, and now and then squeaking like a young peccary, but staring at them as they were advancing in a solid phalanx upon him, chafing their tusks and preparing for battle.

Bok-ar waded the stream, and joined the party, whilst the band of nut-gatherers advanced to the edge of the stream, and in a body as thick as they could stand, little else being seen than their heads, with their noses pointed towards us.

Thus they stood, chafing their ivory, the sound of which was like that in a marble yard when stone cutters are chipping marble; their eyes were blood-red with rage, and a white froth was dropping from their jowls.

As near as I could judge, there were from five to six hundred of these bristly little warriors in the group, and the reader will easily imagine that so wild and savage a spectacle could not escape a place in my sketch-book.

This done, we were resolving to give them a broadside with our rifles, when I saw the little *Bok-ar* slipping a poisoned arrow into his blow-gun. We lowered our rifles, and gave the two Indians a chance to exhibit the powers of their insignificant looking weapons. They seemed very proud of the compliment thus paid them, and smiled as they slipped the fatal knitting-needles into the slender reeds.

The distance across the stream was some twelve or fifteen yards. The little *Bok-ar* asked me which one he should hit, and I pointed to one of the largest, standing with its feet at the water's edge, and with its head elevated, exposing its breast and the veins of its neck. A sudden whiff! and the deadly missiles were off.

Bok-ar's pig pitched forward into the mud, and never moved, the arrow having struck the jugular vein; the other victim, shot in the side, wheeled about, and after reeling and staggering for two or three seconds, gave a squeak or two and fell, when a scene commenced that baffled all description. The sagacious group around the falling animal seemed to know that it was dying, when they pitched upon it, ripped and tore it, and tossed it in all directions.

I ordered Caesar to fire his minié rifle over their heads, when the whole group took fright and disappeared in an instant, and we saw no more of them.

The Indians waded the stream, and both recovered their arrows, and returned them to their quivers, and (as they told me) as ready and efficient for battle as if they had not been fired! How wonderful this poison, and what can it be? Some have thought it extracted from the rattlesnake's tooth, but that can't be, for the poison of a serpent's tooth produces immense swelling - the poisoned arrow's victim never swells at all.

Attacked by Peccaries

In the first volume of this work I have given a fuller account of this wonderful weapon and its effects, from experiments I witnessed and made while amongst the Connibo Indians. When the Indian requires for such deadly effects but an almost imperceptible quantity of the poison on the point of his needle-arrow, I would ask what awful havoc would be produced in war if an army or regiment of men were armed with the ancient bell-muzzled arquebuses charged with duck-shot that had been rolled in this liquid and dried, and driven by powder instead of the Indian's feeble breath? - or if small field-pieces were charged with such missiles? No surgeons would need to follow, no wounded would be left upon the field of battle, for where one drop of blood is drawn, death *must* ensue.

A conique rifle-ball, charged at its point with this poison, entering the body of an ox, a tiger, or an elephant, would, in my opinion, produce death as instantaneous as the flash of a gun. [1]

To proceed on our voyage. The surface of the country over which we were now passing was beginning evidently to rise, and after some five or six days' further march the forest became more open, its twisting vines and other impediments in a measure disappeared, and its true grandeur and beauty more fully developed, showed us that we were on the divide between water-sheds, and that we were consequently approaching the llanos (prairies), which we should soon meet, pointing into the forest.

Encouraged, we marched easier and further each day, and on the eleventh day from our start we beheld the opening to the prairie the sun shining upon it, the smoke from a Zurumati village and the blue Acarai (or Crystal) Mountains in the distance. Our Indians soon found their acquaintances; our views were made known to them, and we were received with hospitality and kindness. Caesar soon got my portfolio open in a suitable place, and began his usual lectures on the portraits of their *"Red bredren"* in North America, as he held them up one by one to their view. Great excitement and amusement were produced by the pictures, but all were afraid to be painted when it was proposed, and no one would consent to the operation.

The women had not yet come forward, and one of the chiefs very respectfully inquired if the women could be allowed to look at the portraits. He said he knew that the white men did not like to see women naked, for he had been in some of the white men's large villages, and he saw that they kept their women all covered; and if their women could be allowed to look at the portraits the next day, they should be dressed properly for the occasion.

The next day about noon, some fifteen or twenty of them came, mostly young and unmarried girls. They had no clothing whatever on them, though their ordinary habit is to wear a sort of apron of skins or of bark, extending from the waist down nearly to the knees.

On this occasion, to be, as they had proposed, in full dress, they had left off their aprons, and very curiously (and, indeed, in some cases very beautifully) painted their round and pretty limbs with vermilion and other bright colours, and ornamented their bodies and limbs with long and sweet-scented grass, parts of it plaited in beautiful braids, forming kilts that extended from the waist to the knee. Braids of this grass also ornamented their ankles, their wrists, and their necks; and wreaths of evergreen boughs tastefully arranged encircled their heads and waists, enlivened with orchids and other wild blossoms of the richest hues and odours, whilst their long and glossy black hair, which is generally kept in braids, was loosened and spread in beautiful waves over their naked breasts and shoulders.

Gaiety, modesty, and pride were imprinted on every one of their faces, and evinced in all their movements, which were natural and exceedingly graceful. And oh, that a photographic impression could have been taken of this singular and pretty group, which would have vanished like a flock of antelopes had I attempted to have made a sketch of it. Caesar was embarrassed, but with his *Lingua Geral,* which these Indians partially understood, he got along tolerably well in showing them the pictures.

With a dozen or two of knitting-needles for arrows to their blow-guns, and some other little presents, we easily engaged men with mules to convey us with our packs to the base of the mountains, a distance of forty or fifty miles; and, if anything on the face of the earth could properly be called a paradise, it was the beautifully rolling prairies, with their copses and bunches of graceful leaning palms and palmettos, encircled with flowers of all colours, spotted here and there with herds of wild cattle and horses, and hedged in a hundred directions with the beautiful foliage bordering the rivulets and rivers wending their serpentine courses through them.

We had no time or disposition for the chase, and the only gun fired in our course was fired by myself, and much to my regret. A wild cow, lying directly before me, shook her head and seemed to dispute the right of way with me. I raised my rifle and shot her dead; and, on approaching, found the poor creature had been watching over the body of her calf, which had been some days dead, and, from its swollen condition, we supposed from the bite of a snake.

In this ride we forded several streams, and, amongst them, the west fork of the Trombutas; and, if the Indians informed us rightly, something like one hundred miles from its junction with the eastern branch, where I struck it six months before, as related in the first volume of this work.

After two days' ride, the blue of the mountains became grey, and green as we were at their base. In some places, for many miles together, they were in perpendicular palisades, like shore cliffs of ancient seas, with higher mountains rising above and behind them; and, at their base, sloping descents of clay, with gullies of great depth and a thousand curious forms winding down and blending with the prairies.

With no instruments to determine our meridian or latitude, we supposed we were here directly under the equator, and something like two hundred miles north-east of the Barra, at the mouth of the Rio Negro.

The "nugget fever" was now raging on us. Our Indian *employees,* with their mules and with our hammocks and other packs which we should not want, went back, as they were afraid of the Woy-a-way Indians in the mountains, and their mules being of no further service to us amongst the rocks, which we were obliged to scale on our own bones and muscles.

A sad occurrence here embarrassed us very much. One of the mules, on the night before they left, had, by accident, stepped its foot into our "tin pan," our only gold-washer, and completely broke its bottom through, and rendering it irreparably useless, and narrowing our "golden" prospects to the chances there might be of *nuggets* alone.

Gates were here and there opening into these mountain escarpments, into one of which we entered, and found ourselves in one of the most beautiful valleys in the world, surrounded by high ridges on the north, the east, and the west, the slopes of which were beautifully ornamented with vines, and with natural orchards of orange and fig trees, bending down with their fruit.

Here we established our headquarters, building a sort of cabin with rocks and covering it with palm leaves. This valley, of some six or eight miles in length, and varying from two to three in breadth, was filled with boulders of granite, and gneiss, and quartz, not transported by icebergs from foreign sources, but descended from the mountain slopes around it, and which were consequently an unerring index to the minerals of the beds from which they came.

Several days were spent amongst these by Señor N___ and myself, but with no success. A few days' rest, and our next expedition was to strike for the ancient road which I had before discovered and crossed, or to meet the Woy-a-way or other Indians of the mountains, from whom we might obtain some information of the ancient mines and the remains of the adobe houses to which I have before alluded.

For this, leaving in *Cache* a part of our provisions to fall back upon in case of emergency, we started, with our knapsacks on our backs, in a north-easterly direction. We scaled the rugged mountain behind us to get a glance at the country beyond it, but then a deep and desolate ravine succeeded, and beyond that another mountain range of greater height than the one we had ascended. We gained the summit of this, and then beheld the field for all our labours spread out before us.

Not a "crystal mountain," but a succession of mountains - hills peeping o'er "hills - and Alps on Alps arising," until they were blue and lost in the distance. Their summits were capped, not with snow, but some with naked granite, and others with grass and rhododendrons, their sloping sides and deep ravines seeming to sink down, down, far below the earth's surface, were covered with evergreen thickets that tried the nerves of the boldest and bravest who undertook to penetrate them.

In this pictured landscape, long and broad valleys were seen, and lakes reflecting the white Equatorial sky that was over them; and glistening waterfalls and cascades were seen in various directions: but not the smoke of an Indian's wigwam could be discovered with the most patient telescopic examination. How desolate! and yet how beautiful!

We kept on our course for several days, crossing ravine and ravine, and mountain and mountain, having nothing but a pocket-compass and mountain landmarks to guide us. As the naked rocks were chiefly granite and gneiss, and the others covered with impenetrable vegetation, and our means of washing in the earthy deposits were gone, our only remaining chances for discoveries were in the beds of the deep ravines, where the rocks descended from the mountain sides were exposed and washed by the running streams.

Many of these streams we traced for long distances with various success. One of these, a large and dashing stream - its course, where we struck it, from east to west, and probably one of the sources of the Essequibo - presented us many huge blocks of a greyish rose-coloured quartz, containing frequent speculae of gold, easily apparent to the naked eye.

These blocks were undoubtedly from a vein of quartz in the slope of the mountain above, but which we were too feeble to uncover, or even to get sight of.

In one of these blocks of several hundred tons weight, lying in the bed of the stream, I discovered a cluster of nuggets, from the size of a pin's head to the size of a pea, washed bare and polished by the action of the water. We now believed we had arrived at or near our "El Dorado:" all hands were gathered around it, until these, by chisels, screwdrivers, &c, were extracted, when Caesar set to work with the sledge-hammer, in hopes to make an opening into further and richer discoveries.

In one of his tremendous swings, when all hopes were high (as if Dame Fortune was set against us), the hammer slipped from its handle and plunged into the foaming stream, dashing amongst the rocks below us! Every possible search was made for its recovery, but from the depth and maddening force of the water amongst the rocks, our efforts were in vain. Various smaller nuggets were afterwards secured with our lighter tools, and others were picked up in the sands and gravel of the stream.

The beds of several other streams presented us similar quartz rocks, and in some instances lesser evidences of their auriferous character.

Nuggets having been our only chance for the last few days, and that chance now reduced to a failure, and our supplies running low, we swung around for two or three days in desperate marches, in hopes still to re-discover the "ancient road," or to strike upon some Indian villages or Indian paths, but none of which could we discover; when we turned our faces again towards the valley of the Amazon, which we entered some forty or fifty miles from where we had left it.

We reached our hidden stores in a few days in a starving condition; after that the friendly Zurumati village, our pirogue, and at last the mighty Amazon, more ragged than Falstaff's men, and actually richer in gold than when we started, two months before, by *just two ounces!*

MORAL. - In this wise Dame Fortune's kind favours were solicited; and if she bestowed not upon me the visioned mines of gold, should I complain? She has given me what is better - life, and health, and wisdom, and greatly added to my only wealth, my portfolios, to which she has long been a liberal and kind contributor.

[1] Six or seven years after my adventures in that country, a correspondent in Para states in one of his letters:- "Since your visit to the Upper Amazon, several agents have been traversing the whole country, both on the Amazon and in Guiana, and buying up all the Indian poison, at any price, but for what purpose no person has been able to ascertain, God forbid that it should be used for the advancement of civilization, for the Indians themselves have long since ceased to use it in Indian warfare."

Chapter Three - Descent of the Yucayali

The "gold fever" having thus been cured, and two weeks of delightful convalescence passed in the hospitable hacienda, of Señor N___, an ascending steamer snatched Caesar and myself, with scarcely a moment to shake hands, from this scene of enchantment to the "Barra," at the mouth of the Rio Negro;

from thence we went to Tabatinga, and to Nauta; and after visiting the surrounding tribes, the *Muras,* the *Marahuas,* the *Yahuas,* the *Orejones,* the *Angusturas,* the *Mayoroonas,* the *Iquitos,* the *Omaguas,* the *Ccocomas,* the *Ticunas,* the *Connibos,* the *Sepibos,* the *Chetibos,* and a dozen other *"bos"* and *"guas"* of the Yucayali and Upper Amazon, we crossed by the mail route, with many jovial and agreeable passengers, the rocks, the snows, the ravines, and the frightful dug-ways of the Andes, to Lima, where I took leave of my readers in my first volume, and said I was in "the most beautiful" city of the world."

We have now a starting-point, and here this volume begins. But, before we proceed, let us halt a little; the steamer is not ready to start. In the last chapter I was bringing up incidents passed by in the first volume, as I have said, for want of space to recite them; and of the hundreds and thousands that are yet left, those of the shores of the Yucayali demand our attention yet for a few moments, and we will go back.

After our ride on the Pampa del Sacramento, and our visit to the Connibos, where we saw them manufacturing the beautiful pottery described in the first volume, and where the facetious and troublesome old medicine-man contended that my painting of their portraits was "only an ingenious mode of getting their skins for museums." Caesar and I, with a faithful Indian canoeman, who knew the river, and a young man by the name of Goiau, a Spaniard, from one of the missions on the head waters of the Yucayali, and on his way to Para, started in a pirogue for Nauta, on the Amazon, near the mouth of the Yucayali, a distance of 300 miles.

In our down-river voyage we went at a rapid rate, and keeping in the middle of the current, to get greater speed, exposed us so constantly to the rays of the sun, that I became sick, and slinging my hammock on a high bank, and under a tremendous and open forest, we remained for a week, with provisions enough, and a great variety of fish, taken whenever we required them.

The crumbs of hard biscuit that I was in the habit of throwing to some monkeys from my hammock, while eating, seemed to be telegraphed in some mysterious way, for in a day or two the hordes of these begging and beseeching creatures became so numerous and so extorting, that we were somewhat alarmed, and were about to change our encampment; but a circumstance, droll enough, at length afforded us relief.

One of the animals, of tremendous size, and, in fact, the first one which had introduced himself to us, was in the habit of approaching a little and a little nearer every morning to my hammock, whilst I was taking my coffee, and receiving the bits of biscuit, dipped in coffee, which I was in the habit of tossing to him, became so jealous of the uninvited flocks that were gathering around us, that he pitched upon the nearest of them, and from tree to tree leaped and bolted on to them, till the whole multitude fled and stood aghast at his bristled and frightful aspect! It was a complete *"coup de singe!"* - a *déroute* - a *victory,* and he had for the rest of the time the ground to himself.

I applauded him for his gallant services, and rewarded him by larger bits of biscuit, which he seemed perfectly to understand. His adversaries were afterwards always more or less in sight, but in the distance; and if anyone attempted to come nearer, the hair on his ugly face and on his back stood on end, the meaning of which they evidently understood; and turning his face towards me, every hair was laid smoothly down; and as he approached me, the motions of his mouth and his lips seemed as if he was talking, but in a language that had no sounds.

This rational creature was present regularly at all of my meals, and particularly docile and agreeable in the morning, when his crumbs were dipped in coffee, and the sweeter the better.

At every meal he ventured a little nearer, and got so at length as to reach up and catch the crumbs from my hand as I dropped them; and at length, to be more familiar, and probably to feel more secure from Caesar, (as they were occasionally showing their teeth at each other), he took his position in the crotch of a little sapling tree to which the headrope of my hammock was fastened, and there, a little above, and within arm's reach of me, sat, and took his crumbs from my hand, and evidently either as an expression of gratitude, or for the sugar on them, licked the ends of the fingers that gave them.

Caesar and the other men, cooking and eating at a little distance, tried him in vain with food of various kinds; and when Caesar even looked at him he showed his teeth, and seemed to take it as an insult. I must say I felt somewhat vain of his exclusive attachment, and I believed (and I still believe) that a few days more would have enabled me to have got the fellow into my arms, and a harmless bed-fellow in my hammock, but for an unfortunate occurrence that I could not explain to him, and which led to a different result. My dried biscuits gave out; and as he neither ate fish nor meat, mutuality of sympathy was at a standstill.

I offered him coffee, but he knew not how to drink it, and tendering to him a piece of boiled meat, of which he smelled, the creature stepped backwards into the crotch of the tree, and looking me full in the face for a minute, without the movement of a muscle, made an instant spring upon me with all his force, breaking my hammock-rope, and falling with me to the ground, and with a horrid growl and a snap, bit me through the joint of my thumb on my right hand; and in a leap or two, was among the trees and out of sight, with screams, and afterwards howlings, so frightful and so horrible at every leap, that neither itself nor a monkey of any grade or caste showed itself again whilst we remained in our camp!

(How acceptable are kindnesses and caresses whilst they last; and how disastrous they are apt to be when stopped)

My *compagnons de voyage,* moved, I believe, by jealousy, rather than anything else, were very merry at the sudden termination of our growing intimacy, not knowing that I was suffering everything but lock jaw itself, from the severed joint. My Indian guide, who seemed to be somewhat of a medicine man, told me he had feared from day to day that our intimacy would come to that; and tracing the river shore, he collected some herbs, of which he made and applied a poultice, which soon gave me relief.

A Visit from an Anteater

Our little camp seemed to be destined to the intrusions of inquisitive visitors, and the next morning, whilst I lay dozing in my hammock, and Caesar was boiling the coffee and frying some fish and Senor Goyau and the Indian were fishing in the canoe, I was instantly alarmed by Caesar's vehement and startling exclamation, -

"Well, de Lord o' massie! wot you call dis, Massa Catlin?"

I looked out, and he was startling back from the fire, where he had been sitting, with one hand on the ground, and holding his frying-pan, in the other, whilst a huge ant-eater was advancing upon the other side of the fire, with its long nose almost in the embers.

My rifle, which was hanging over my hammock, I took down, and shot the stupid beast through the heart. Poor Caesar, who never had been in museums, had never even imagined so curious a creature, was agitated at first by fear; but his nerves were still more convulsed after fear was over, by the inexpressible drollness of this outlandish animal, which anyone may laugh half an hour at without an effort; and as soon as he got his nerves in a condition to express anything, he exclaimed, -

"Well now, affer dat, I wonder wat de Lord eber make nex!"

I took the measure of this ugly, stupid, and harmless creature, and found its length, from the end of its nose to the end of its long, bushy tail, to be twelve feet!

After our encampment of a week we took to our canoe again, and after paddling a few hours, I was taken again excessively ill with vertigo and vomiting. We went ashore, and landed again in a noble forest, and were preparing our encampment, though in a thick undergrowth of grass and weeds.

I was too helpless, from vertigo, to walk, and being assisted up the bank, had laid down on a mass of long grass and weeds, that bent down as I reclined back upon them. Whilst in this position I was rendered doubly sick by a stench that was evidently rising from under me, and which I at first attributed to some noxious weeds that I had crushed. It became so bad, however, that I could bear it no longer, and I called Caesar to help me move to some other spot.

Our Indian companion, seeing my distress, came with Caesar, and the moment he got over me he exclaimed, - *"Buccare-hul-be, buccare-hul-be!"* "A rattlesnake, a rattlesnake!" They lifted me up, and by the direction of the Indian's eyes and the expression of his face, I saw that he considered the snake which he smelled, but had not seen, was under the grass and weeds, and that I had been lying on it.

I got seated on a bare piece of ground at a little distance, when the Indian, with his paddle lifted up the weeds, and showed me a huge rattlesnake that I had been lying on! nearly suffocated, I suppose, from my weight, and of course ready for the most deadly battle.

Caesar sprang for his rifle, and was going to shoot it, when the poor Indian threw himself forward, and in so imploring an attitude, begged for its life, that I told Caesar not to fire or to harm it, knowing the superstitions of most of the tribes of Indians, who never kill a rattlesnake, but, on the contrary, pay it a sort of devotion, lest their heels may be in danger from some of its surviving relations.

This was new to Caesar, and when I had explained it to him, he exclaimed, - "Well, I don't wonder; dat berry good reason."

Señor Goyau, who was at this time overhauling some of his luggage in the canoe, and who under stood the language of the Indian, learned from his excited remarks, and from seeing Caesar with his rifle in his arms, that something was wrong on shore, came running up the bank,, and pitching down by the side of me, exclaimed, in Spanish and in Indian, - "I am bitten by a rattlesnake!"

All got around him, and his half-boot, apparently of sheepskin, and reaching half-way to his knee, being taken off, the wounds by two fangs were easily perceptible in the lower part of the calf of his leg, but apparently in the fleshy part only, without striking a vein or artery.

The Indian, in a moment, was flat upon his belly, and seizing the calf of the leg a few inches above and below the wounds, in both hands, as tight as he could possibly grip them, commenced sucking the wound, and spitting the blood from his mouth at short intervals.

Between his two hands and around the wounds the flesh of the leg became the same colour, and bore the same marks as the skin of a rattlesnake itself;

but after an operation of a quarter of an hour in this manner, without letting go with his hands, or ceasing his suctions, the flesh took again its natural colour, when the Indian let go of his patient, and triumphantly exclaimed, -

"It is all done; there is no more danger."

Goyau seemed convinced of this, though I had still some fears. The snake that I had laid upon was still coiled and ready for battle, and emitting the most sickening odour imaginable.

Goyau had not seen the snake that had struck him as he was rising the bank, nor had he the least disposition to go and look it up; for I found that his superstition was the same as that of the Indian. And he told me that both he and the Indian knew from the smell that we were in the midst of a nest of these creatures, and the sooner we were off the better.

Either from inhaling the poisonous effluvia arising from these reptiles, or from the excitement, my vertigo had at this time entirely left me, and I could walk as straight as ever; and taking the Indian's paddle, and annoying the snake that I had laid on, and which was in no way disposed to retreat, it began a most frightful shaking of its rattles, when we heard several others in the grass and weeds in different directions, answering it, which convinced all that we were in bad company, and that, as Goyau had said, "the sooner we were off the better." And not to wound any superstitious feeling, Caesar and I agreed (and possibly, on my part, in a measure, from recollections of the wholesale murder at the "Rattlesnakes' Den") to bruise no serpents' heads on this occasion.

My disease seemed completely cured by this day's excitements, but poor Goyau was sick all the way to Nauta, and we left him sick there when the steamer took us from that place, though apparently not in any danger.

Now we start. The field is new, and vast, and fresh, before us. Between Lima and San Francisco there are many Indians inhabiting the coast, but we go by sea, and necessarily must leave them, at least till we come back.

San Francisco is a highly civilized place, so we have little interest there. There are a plenty of books written about it. They are all for gold there, and I am *shy of gold,* having just recovered from it. Some straggling Apachee Indians come in there at times; but we will probably see better specimens of them by-and-bye, on our return. We are now on our way to Oregon, the mouth of the Columbia. Our craft is small, and sails slow; and when the sea is smooth, gives me a good chance to finish up my sketches, and to prepare my cartoons for others to be made.

The schooner *Sally Anne* (she was built in New York) doubled Cape Horn in 1843, and is now sailed by Señor Pedro Pasto, a Spaniard, who goes once a year to Astoria, to Victoria, to Queen Charlotte's, to the Alaeutian Islands, and to Kamskatka, and returns with sheepskins, wool, dried fish, and other products of those countries.

J. Paulding, of New York, L. Simms, of Missouri, J. Stevens, of Ohio, then living in San Francisco, (who had got an idea in their heads that *nuggets of gold* were. larger on the Columbia coast, and perhaps in the Alaeutian Islands), and I (who was quite sure that *Indian portraits* in any quantity could be got there), agreed to pay to Captain Pasto 200 dollars each to take us safe to Queen Charlotte's Island - to Liska, on the Alaeutian Islands - and to Kamskatka, and back to Victoria, on Vancouver's! Island (my man Caesar to be carried free, but a servant to all, when required). And did Captain Pasto do it, and what did we find, and what did we see?

Before we enter further upon this, it will be well for the reader to understand upon what conditions we sallied forth on the broad ocean for so long and so critical a voyage. An *"understanding"* (as agreements are called in that country) was definitely agreed to, and an off-hand article for all to sign was drawn up in the following form and words, by Simms, whose extraordinary tact and dispatch in draughting contracts and other documents of those countries, to be executed by revolvers and bowie-knives, if not otherwise, will be visible on the face of it.

"Understanding.

"Agreed - the *Sally Anne,* Captain Pasto, bound for Nishnee Kamskatk, to take us 4, and found, whole way and back to Queen Charlotte's Sound and Victoria, at 200 dols. each, one half down; salt pork and beans to last; owner's risque; arid Catlin's nigger to go free."

"(Signed)" J. Paulding., V. Simms., J. Stevens., Geo. Catlin.,
Pedro Pasto, Capt. *Sally Anne."*

Each contracting party, armed with a copy of the above "agreement," a six-shot revolver, a rifle, and a bowie-knife in the belt, in a country where there are no courts of justice, or even magistrates, feels abundantly able to defend his rights, and to enforce the performance of all engagements so solemnly and *definitely* undertaken as this.

These documents pocketed (which, by the way, were not rights, but only *indications* of rights), we move on; all is jocularity, mutual confidence, and good fellowship, or sure *to be* so, at least, in the outstart.

A long voyage, with no other absolute misfortunes than the total exhaustion of all our "salt pork and beans," and alarming symptoms of scurvy, brought our little bark to the mouth of the Columbia, with the safe harbour of Astoria close before us. Here, however, when the dangers of the sea seemed over, our difficulties began.

Captain Pedro Pasto (for the owner was captain of his own craft), about to glide from the rough waves of the ocean into the smooth waters of the Columbia, ran his ship upon the bar her bow in the sand, and the waves dashing against her stern, and driving her farther on, as the tide was rising.

Night approaching, our position was critical; but morning showed us, at full tide, driven quite over the bar, and at anchor in the quiet water of the river, with loss of rudder only.

Captain Pasto, with Paulding and Stevens, in a small craft, went up the river to Astoria for ship-carpenters to make repairs, and to replenish the exhausted requisite of "salt pork and beans," and other provisions, and Simms and myself remained on board.

At low tide the schooner laid upon her side on the sands, and Simms, with his hawk-eye, in walking around her, discovered that the name of the vessel, the *Santa* (I forget what) *de Callao,* in large yellow-ochre letters, was chiefly all washed off by the force of the driving waves against her stern, and the remainder of them peeling off under the rays of the sun, and underneath them, covered with a thin coat of paint, the *"Sally Anne, of N. York,"* was quite conspicuous.

I opened my paint-box, and with a brush, and a tube of yellow chrome spread upon my palette, I touched the letters up a little.

When the captain returned, the vessel was afloat, and Simms, taking him around astern in the yawl, said to him, "Look there! by the eternal, sir, I can disfranchise you, when we get back, for changing the name of your vessel when at sea. It is a very grave offence."

Getting on deck, Simms said, "We have no idea, captain, that you stole the vessel, and *Sally Anne* being a favourite Yankee name of ours, we shall christen her so, for this voyage at least, and you bringing out a couple of bottles of wine for the occasion, we will agree to say nothing about it."

With his wine, the good-natured captain brought on to the table his papers, showing that he bought his schooner of a couple of Americans in the port of Callao; and it was at this moment that the famous *"understanding"* on the previous page was first reduced to writing and signed.

A few days making the necessary repairs, and we sailed out, all in good humour, passing outside of Vancouver, and coasting along its western shore of huge rocks and pine-covered mountains, towards Queen Charlotte's Sound, the grand anticipated field for the gold-hunters, and also for the operations of my brush.

Nootka Sound took us up. A strong north-west wind, increasing to a gale, held our schooner three days wind-bound in this snug and quiet little shelter, with the picturesque island of Nootka on one side of us, and the dark green pine forests and over-towering black piles of upheaved rocks, and blue, and then snow-covered mountain peaks of Vancouver, on the other.

Nothing ever surprised me more than the information I here got, and demonstrated to my eyes, that mountains covered with perpetual snows were standing in the island of Vancouver! And nothing that I ever before heard, or ever should have heard, would have conveyed to me an adequate idea of the singular appearance (and beauty, I may say) of its vast and ever-changing (in form, but not in colour) hills, and mountains, and ravines, not only *clothed,* but *robed,* and *mantled,* and *belted,* with dark green and gloomy pines and cedars, throwing out their long and drooping arms over rocks and streams,' and even over the waves of the ocean.

The first day that we laid here we had amusement enough on deck of our little vessel in studying the scenery around us, and the darting (and seemingly *leaping*) canoes that were passing around, and the *Klah-o-quat* Indians, and their wives and little pappooses, that we invited on board.

A remarkably fine looking man, whom I supposed, from his appearance, was a chief; with his wife, carrying her infant in its cradle on her back, and their daughter, came on board, after getting permission, for which he was asking by smiles and intelligible signs. His manner was that of an intelligent man and a gentleman; and when he raised his hand and presented its palm towards the throng that was endeavouring to follow him, I was convinced that he was a chief, and was going to use his authority to protect us from an uncomfortable crowd on deck.

It was but half an hour's sail from here to the place where the *"Tonquin,"* John Jacob Astor's brig, was destroyed, some years before, by the Indians, and the crew destroyed, and Captain Pasto began to feel fears for ourselves and his vessel. The chief seemed evidently to be aware of this from the captain's manner, and leading his wife and daughter up to me, easily explained by signs that he would leave them with me until he would go in his canoe and bring someone who could talk with me. And I said to Caesar, -

"This is a fine old fellow; jump into his canoe with him, and take the wife's paddle, and help him; and if he runs away with you, I will hold on to his wife and daughter, and easily get you exchanged after a while."

"Agreed, massa! I no fea!"

They paddled off rapidly, and soon turned round a point and were out of sight. And in half an hour they came back, with a brigade of canoes following them, and bringing with them an intelligent mulatto boy, who spoke English very well, and also the *Klah-o-quat,* and several other Indian languages of the coast.

This young man told me that he swam ashore there from a whaling vessel, two years before, because they flogged him too much, and was now making his living by interpreting for the Indians, and for vessels coming into the Sound; and that he lived most of the time in one of the Indian villages; and that the Indian who had come for him was the chief, and a very good man.

Then, said I, the first thing I wish you to tell him is, that I knew by his actions that he was a chief, and by the expression of his face, that he was a good man. And tell him that I am very much obliged to him for going in search of you. This being interpreted, a hearty shake of the hand took place all around.

My three gold-seeking companions, who had rather shunned him at first, now came forward, and shook hands with him also, and Simms went to his luggage, and brought and gave to him a bundle of about a dozen cigars. The chief was so pleased with the pre sent, that he seized hold of Simms, and embraced him in his arms. "Well, by G__, Catlin," said Simms, "that's a very fine old fellow that man is a gentle man! I'd trust myself anywhere with that man!"

Always carrying with me a quantity of little trinkets and ornaments for the Indians, on such occasions, I went to my trunk and got a handsome string of blue and white beads, which I placed on his daughter's neck; and a little looking-glass, which I gave to his wife in return for his kindness in going for the interpreter. This explained to the chief we were all friends, and under a sudden and tolerably good understanding.

There were at this time a great number of canoes from the Vancouver shore around the vessel, and the crowds that were in them were generally a poor-looking set - poor-looking as to clothing, weapons, &c, but at the same time with faces full of sprightliness and intelligence. A great proportion of the women had their heads flattened; and occasionally a man was seen with a flattened head, but very seldom.

They were beckoning and whining, and some of them were crying to be allowed to come on board; but the chief, by showing them the palm of his hand, quieted them, and kept them back. I told the interpreter to say to him, that if there were any whom he would like to indulge by permitting them to come on board, he could do so, as the captain of the vessel had agreed to it.

He then called to several whom he thought deserved the privilege, and they came on board, and amongst those there came several with baskets of dried salmon, whale blubber, and oysters, to barter, and the captain and mate at once had something to do in replenishing our larder.

The interpreter I engaged to be with us as long as we should remain in the harbour, and he agreed to take us the next day to the Klah-o-quat village, where the chief had invited us to go.

Leaving Caesar to amuse the Indians on deck and in their canoes around the vessel, I got the chief, with his wife and daughter, and the interpreter, below, and as each of us *compagnons de voyage* had laid in at San Francisco a certain number of bottles of cognac brandy for emergencies, I uncorked one of these on this especial occasion. I explained to the chief that we were all temperate men, but that we carried a few bottles for medicine if we get sick, and, once in a while, to those whom we loved, not to make them drunk, but to give them a pleasant drink, as a mark of respect.

He replied, through the interpreter, that he perfectly understood my meaning, and, taking up his glass, took me by the hand, and bowing his head, "My friend, I drink your love." This was a little different from the usual form of salutation; but what could be better? more expressive? Simms, whose heart was always ready for anything *from the heart,* was quite touched at this, and swore it was something "new, and ten times better than the old and hackneyed and worn-out expression."

I learned from this intelligent man, to my great surprise, that there were about twenty different tribes of Indians on the island of Vancouver, and containing some six or seven thousand persons, though, after all, they are but different bands of the great flat-head tribe, and speaking languages, though dialectic, oftentimes almost entirely different.

The greater portion of these practise the abominable custom of flattening the head, which will be described anon.

"On that western coast of Vancouver," the chief continued, "besides the *Klah-o-quats,* there are the *To-quahts* living in Barclay Sound, further south;

and several other tribes living on the coast between Nootka Island, and Cape Scott, the northern cape of Vancouver that they all believe in a Great Spirit, who created them and all things, and that they all have times and places when and where they pray to that Spirit, that He may not be angry with them. That they live chiefly on fish of various sorts, salmon, halibut, blubber of whales, oysters, clams, &c., which they can always get in abundance; and that they had but one fear, that was that 'King George,' as they had been told, was soon going to drive them all from the coast into the mountains and rocks, and in that case," he said "they would all get sick, and soon starve to death."

I told him "King George" had long been dead, and that there was a queen in England, who was kind-hearted and good, and I knew she never would allow her Red children to be treated so cruelly; which seemed to please him very much; and his wife, hearing it translated, cried out in a most expressive tone, "la-la-la-a," (good, good, good).

After the chief had drunk about half of his wine glass of brandy, and which he told me he never had tasted before (though he had sometimes drunk whisky), I took a large glass, and with brandy and water, and sugar, made a "brandy toddy," which he said he liked much better, and which I got him to share with the old lady, and her daughter. All were delighted with it, and after that I opened my portfolio of cartoon portraits of Indians. These surprised and amused them very much, and after an hour or so the interpreter took canoe with them, and paddled towards their village, as night was approaching, the interpreter having promised to come on board the next morning, and conduct Caesar and me to their village.

The next morning, if we were still wind-bound, the captain had promised me the use of the yawl; but at the hour appointed, the chief himself came with the interpreter, paddling his own canoe, which was a compliment that I could not decline; and Caesar and I got into it, taking the portfolio and my sketching apparatus, and leaving my gold-hunting companions at cards with Captain Pasto, and the gale outside of the Sound still blowing.

The *canoe* - the canoe of the chief, in which we were riding - *floating,* not flying, though it seemed so. A *shell,* apparently as thin and as light as bark, and made from the trunk of a huge cedar - a "dug-out" yes, *strictly* a dug-out. And I must tell you *how* it was dug out. Large enough and strong enough to carry thirty men, yet its sides so thin and light that the paddles of two men, with us four in it, sent it like a bird flying through the air. The gala-boat, the gondola, the water-phaeton of a nobleman, kept dry except on fete days, saluted by the multitude when it passed, and a beautiful ornament for a palace park, or a royal museum.

"Dug-out," I have said; but how? not from the patriarchal cedar as it *stands* in the forest, on the mountain's side - it must lie prostrate on the ground for that; it must be "chopped down." But how? These people have no axes! Listen, and say if there is not industry and tact in this? Wapiti, a noble animal and shy, with immense horns, feeds under those stately cedars on the mountain sides; *they* must be brought down to bring the *cedar* down. And how? not with rifles (these people know nothing of gunpowder and of rifles) but by motive power *sinewy* - not explosive. Missiles are designed and shaped in wood, made light and steered in the air by feathers on their sides, and their points of flint or bone one about as good as the other. Bows are made to throw them, and strained by sinews, not by gunpowder. The stately elk (or wapiti) falls before them. His horns - the broadest, hardest parts - are cut with knives and hatchets of flint into the form of chisels. With these chisels in the left hand, and a heavy mallet made of a stone encompassed in a withe for its handle, the axe-*men* and axe-*women,* on their knees, set to with "hammer and chisel" at the trunks of these stupendous trees; and doomed, they are cut near to the centre, and left; and, when the wind is in the right direction to lay them on the ground best suited for their excavation, a few blows with the hammer and chisel send them tumbling to the ground.

The monster tree is down! What next? Why, a hundred labourers, both men and women, with the same tools and others, mount upon it, and work at the same time. The bark is stripped off, and the work laid out and marked by master workmen, and all - even women and children - dig, and cut, and drill to the lines marked out, and no further.

For digging out, a species of mussel-shell of a large size, found in the various inlets where fresh and salt water meet, are sharpened at the edge and set in withes of tough wood, forming a sort of adze, which is used with one hand or both, according to its size, and the flying chips show the facility with which the excavation is made in the soft and yielding cedar, no doubt designed and made for infant man to work and ride in.

But, felled and dug out, this is but brute force and industry. The beaver can do this, and all Indians; but the architect, the naval constructor who conceives in the log and lays out those beautiful lines that are to balance and ease it through the water - those "lines of beauty" - what artist? Where did he get his art? And where is he? Is he gone? He can't be a savage. And the soft, and smooth, and polished finish, outside and in, how done? And the painter the artist who designed and drew those ornamental lines and figures on its sides, its bow, and its stern; and for what, and what do they mean? Maybe we shall find out. [1] At present we get in and we ride; and a chief who "drinks my love" paddles me to his house - his humble dwelling. What is it? It is a shed made of heavy posts standing in the ground, with long and immense timbers resting on their tops, and covered with planks for a roof. Its floor is the ground; trodden and swept, it becomes hard, and dry, and polished. The fireplace is a circular enclosure of stones in the centre, and the chimney the raising of a short plank in the roof directly over it. Their food is served and eaten on the floor, and their beds - without feathers - cribs eighteen inches above the ground, made of small elastic poles and covered with rush mats; and pillows made of a solid block of wood excavated so as to receive the head, with soft matting underneath; the best sleeping contrivance ever yet invented, as it holds the head elevated and inclined forward, and keeps a man, in his sleep, always on his back, as he ought to be.

This chief, not like the chiefs of the Crows, the Sioux, or Mandans, clad in skins fringed with scalplocks and ermine, with painted robes of buffalo skins, and headdresses of war-eagles' quills - but with a simple breech-cloth around his waist, and a blanket over his shoulders, his hair parted on his forehead and falling over his shoulders without ornament. He is quite their equal in war or in councils, and no less the gentleman.

What evidence of this? In his hospitable wigwam, where he had invited me, he had assembled the worthiest of his tribe who were at the time near him; and when I entered he brought them to me one by one and presented them, not according to ribands, or medals, or other decorations, for they have none; but according to their rank for honour able deeds, which he explained to me as he introduced them. What could be more gentlemanly than this? And he gave us a humble feast. It was the best he had; and, whilst we ate, he ate no thing, but waited upon us as we were eating, and charged and lit the pipe for us to smoke when we had done. Humble and unpretending, but what could be more polite, more gentlemanly than this? Is such a man, who has had none but nature to teach him, a brute?

He had invited a dozen or more of his friends to see me, and to see my portraits of Indians, which were now opened, to their astonishment and amusement.

The wigwam of this man was an immense thing, one hundred feet or more in length, and twenty-five feet in width, in several apartments, with intervening partitions of planks, lodging the different branches of his numerous family.

As our time was to be very short, I set Caesar at work in a corner of the wigwam, amusing them with the portfolio, and the interpreter to explain, whilst I went to work upon a sketch of the chief and his wife and child, which I got tolerably well before night; and just at the time when I had got about through, an instant excitement arose, which I was at a loss to understand, and which I must say, for a few seconds, gave me a degree of *alarm,* accustomed as I have been to Indian modes. I heard the shouts first in the village, at a distance, and the next moment bursting forth from the whole multitude in the house and around it. All sprang upon their feet; some leaped in the air, and others clapped their hands and danced, and I then instantly saw, by the expressions of their faces, that it was a jubilee rather than an alarm; that there was no bad news, for every face, even in its astonishment, teemed with joy, and vociferated and echoed in all parts (though in Indian), "A whale ashore! a whale ashore!" The interpreter ran to me, and echoed again, "A whale ashore!" News had just arrived that the north-west gale had landed a sperm-whale on the sands, near the entrance of "Hope Canal," at the head of Nootka Island.

Here was a "Godsend" for these poor people, and every throat was stretched with "A whale ashore! a whale ashore!" and all was "helter-skelter."

The wigwams were all emptied, for "out doors" was a larger and freer space for the circulation of the mutual expressions of joy that rang from every mouth. The dogs caught the excitement and howled, and knew as well as their masters that *something* had happened, but probably knew not *what*.

The chief came to me with the interpreter, and told me that news had just arrived that a whale was struggling on the sands at the head of the strait, and that every canoe of the village would be in a few minutes on the way to the spot to secure it.

He had told me in the morning that the north west gale would drive many fine fish into the sound, and in the inlets and coves, where the water was calm, there would be fine spearing that night by torchlight; that salmon and halibut would be taken in great quantities, and it had been arranged that I should go and see the sport; but the sudden news of "a whale ashore" silenced every other excitement for the time, and engrossed everybody and everything that could be handled or moved.

Every canoe was starting off, filled with men, women, and children, and with harpoons, and cords, and spears, and everything that their wigwams contained that could be used in securing the monster on the sands. The wind was still blowing a gale outside, and yet their flying canoes were starting off and up the strait, through which, a distance of fifteen or twenty miles to the spot, they could creep along the shore, and in quiet water.

"A whale ashore" is surely a gift from Heaven for these poor people, and they receive it and use it as such. They believe it is sent to them to be received and used by all alike, and, no matter how many tribes assemble on the occasion, all share alike in their efforts to secure it, and all share equally of its flesh, its sinews, and bones when it is dissected. A great proportion of its flesh is eaten; other parts produce oil for their lamps, sinews, bones, skin, and fifty other things useful for Indian existence.

Not only the canoes from this little village were on their way, but the coves and inlets of the sound were alive with canoes darting about, and wending their way to the whale wreck.

The chief sent the interpreter with us in a canoe to our vessel, and, night arriving, we lost sight of the Indians. The next morning the wind had so much abated that Captain Pasto put his schooner in motion, and sailing out of the Sound, and outside of the island, we were on our course, and had Hope Canal, at the head of the island, before us, and almost exactly in our route.

Getting off the northern cape of the island, with glasses we had at once a view, at several miles distance, of the monster lying high and dry on the beach, and the group of Indians, like ants around a sugar-bowl, moving in all directions about it. We were all curious alike, and prevailed on Captain Pasto to steer in towards the shore, and to give us his yawl for landing.

He ran us within two or three hundred yards of the shore, and, the yawl manned, Simms and Levens and Caesar and myself got in, and Captain Pasto agreed to lie off and wait for us.

The beach looked smooth and sandy and the sea calm, but it being ebb-tide, and a current running off, we had a tremendous hard pull to reach the sands, and a tremendous sea-bath in landing. We got ashore, however, but drenched, and pulled our boat on to the sands.

Then the sight! - the spectacle! The monster lay embedded in the sand, yet a long distance from us, and we started towards it. On our way we met our mulatto boy interpreter and several Indians coming to meet us. We approached the monster on the sea side, and in the immense furrow which in its struggles it had grooved out in the sand, as the waves of the rising tide had forced it towards the land, the sight was imposing when we came near to it, but not until we came around it on the shore side had I any idea of the scene we were to witness.

Some hundreds, if not thousands of Indians of all ages and sexes, and in all colours, were gathered around it, and others constantly arriving. Some were lying, some standing and sitting in groups; some were asleep, and others eating and drinking, and others were singing and dancing.

At our approach the women commenced crying, and a mournful murmur ran through the crowd; eating and dancing and sleeping were all stopped. The women covered their mouths with their hands, and cried and howled in piteous tones, and the men were silent. I asked our fine little interpreter if the chief whom we had seen the day before was there, and he said that he had not yet arrived, but that he would be there in a little time. I asked him what the women were crying about, and he said they had seen us coming from the ship, and they knew that we were some of "King George's" men coming to claim the whale. I asked him if he thought he could interpret what I wanted to say, so that they could all hear and understand it, and he said yes.

"That's right," said Simms, "make a speech to them, Catlin."

Several immense baskets which had been brought to carry blubber, &c. in were lying near, and placing two or three of these one within the other, and bot tom side upwards, our little interpreter we lifted on to them, so that all could see and hear him.

I stood upon another by the side of him, but not quite so high, and began, making significant signs which they all understood, that what I should say I spoke from my heart.

I told them that I was sorry to learn that their women were crying because they thought we had come from our ship to claim the whale; and if that was what they were crying for they need not cry any more, or have any fears of us; that we were not "King George's" men, as they had thought, but that we were all friends of the Indians, and had come to see the whale, and to shake hands with them if they wished.

"Tell them," I said to Joseph, "that I consider the Great Spirit loves them, and has sent this large fish to them as an evidence of it; that it therefore belongs to them, and to nobody else."

This interpreted to them, there was a shout of applause from the whole crowd with uplifted hands.

"Tell them, Joseph, that we are only passing by on the ocean, never to see them again, and that we shall leave here in a few minutes, and wish them well."

Another uproar of applause, and Joseph got down. A great many of the chiefs came up and shook hands with us, and all troubles were ended.

The scene was now curious. No stones, no timbers, or anything of the sort were placed about the monster to secure it; but on the shore side some twenty or thirty harpoons had been thrown into its side during its struggles on the rising tide by the first who were on the spot, and with long cords, some reaching to the trunks of the trees on the shore, and others fastened to stakes driven into the ground. These were watched, and at every lift of a wave moving the monster nearer the shore, they were tightened on the harpoons, and at low tide the carcass is left on dry land, a great distance from the water.

The whale, to Simms and Levens, was the curiosity; and they took the measure length and breadth of it; to me, the curiosity was the crowd of poor *humans* who were gathered about it, and of them I could take no other measure than by the naked eye; for though I had put a sketch-book in my paletot-pocket, in the drenching which we got in landing every leaf of it, like everything else upon us, was soaked.

The dissection of this monstrous creature, and its distribution amongst the thousands who would yet be a day or two in getting together, the interpreter informed us would not be commenced until all the claimants arrived, and I therefore lost one of the curious scenes of my life which I should have been glad to have witnessed.

Their mode of slaughtering such a beast and dividing it would have been curious in the extreme. A *per capitum* division is always the mode of the Indians in such cases - the poorest of the tribe and the youngest infant drawing the same as a chief.

I could have studied for hours, without pencil or sketch-book, amongst the curious group, and those studies I never could forget. The beach, for half a mile, was almost literally covered with something - with reclining groups of women and children - with baskets, and bags, and cribs, and pouches, and every sort of vehicle they possessed, for transporting their respective proportions of the prize, and the drying of blankets, red, blue, and green, and white, wet like ourselves in landing their canoes, made a carpet for the sands in the distance of the most extraordinary hues.

Not like the Sioux, or the Crows, or the Chayennes, covered, and plumed, and mocasined in full and handsome dresses, but poor, and naked, excepting their breech-cloths and blankets, they were yet human - painted in a thousand forms and of all colours, and thus were subjects for a picture, and subjects for a sermon or a lecture.

Our drenched condition and signals from Captain Pasto terminated our visit here. A crowd of these poor people followed us to our boat, took it up bodily, and entered the water with it, and took us up in their arms one by one, and waded through the surf with us, and put us into it, and bade us a civil and affectionate farewell.

Sailing out of Nootka Sound, and again on our way to the visioned fields of gold and Indians, maps and charts' were mustered out upon the table, correspondences relating to nuggets of fabulous sizes that had been seen amongst the Nayas Indians, and supposed localities in which they had been found, were brought out and referred to, and the second and last great effort to raise another "gold fever" on me was strenuously tried, but decidedly failed.

This, however, in no way impaired my influence in the consolidated strength of the expedition at that place, for the very field which was soon to become the scene of action for them, the actual *"El Dorado"* of America, was the very point to which my ambition led me, that coast being thickly inhabited by tribes of Indians of the most interesting character, and as yet but little known or appreciated.

Passing the picturesque shores of Vancouver, we were soon in Queen Charlotte's Sound, and gliding along in front of the ever-varying mountain barriers of the mainland, covered alternately with rhododendrons and honeysuckles, or capped with moss-covered rocks enclosed by deep and dark ravines shooting up their tall and pointed pines and cedars.

At the shore of the sea, huge blocks from the mountain tops stood in relief, like houses, and sometimes like immense ramparts and castles rising out of the water, and behind and around them quiet glades overshadowed by outstretched arms of pines and hemlocks, and overhung by long-leafed laurel, under, and through, and around which, brigades of the Nayas' painted canoes, with their cargoes of red shoulders, and glistening paddles, were darting, and easily keeping us opposite company.

On our left, and towards the setting sun, and blue and purple in the distance, rose the shining summits of Queen Charlotte's island; and near its base, a blotched mass of deep green (its pines and cedars), underlined by a streak of white, the sands of its shore, at ebb-tide. No imagination could paint, and few artists' pencils ever have painted, scenes so grand and so picturesque as these.

We are gliding along from day to day, with our glasses beholding the "rocks that are doubtless full of gold," and my Indian subjects flying about in their light canoes, and the smokes of their villages on the shore, which, by our "agreements," we are bound to pass by, and leave for our homeward voyage. What temptations, and what glorious fields were beckoning us back!

These left behind, what then is before us? Liska is the chief town of the Alaeutian islands; a little village of some sixty or eighty Russian and Indian houses and huts, where Captain Pasto goes once a year, gets skins, gets wool, and other products, for which he trades cotton and woollen cloths, hard ware, cutlery, &c. The Russians here are half Indians, and the Indians are Americans, not Kamskatkans, nor Mongol Tartars; not an expression or feature of either, as my portraits will show.

What next? The captain's business done, we are on the sea, and a few days' sail brings us to the coast of Siberia, and the river Kamskatka, of twenty miles, transports us to the town of Nishna-Kamskatk, or Petropolovski. What a town! How droll. Russian houses built of pine poles and mud, adobes and mud! and huts of Koriak Indians, somewhat like the Mandan wigwams, earth-covered, but the doors in their tops - how strange - men, women, and dogs walk down a ladder to get into them!

There's Che-nish-ka Wabe (a mountain on fire), the volcano of Avatcha; its smoke stands up in a vast column leaning to the right, and softening away in the distance in a long and straight cloud towards the western horizon. The mountain is blue in the distance, and yet we must look into its sulphurous crater. Mud, and then snow, and then the most frowning and defiant rocks are in our way, but we go on. We get to the brink of the awful and boiling lake, when nature is completely exhausted.

Sulphur is glazed over everything we touch and everything we see. Excepting smoke, we see nought but rocks; we tread upon them, and lean against their slippery sides, and tremble at the awful sight that is before us; and rage and fret too, for all beyond, below, and all around us is smoke, smoke! and nothing else.

Hissing like a thousand furnaces at work is constant; a hollow and consumptive cough is frequent; and now and then a sneezing, ejecting jets of stones and gravel, coated with liquid, blazing sulphur, whizzing past our heads, and rattling amongst the rocks around and over us. These significant monitors determine us to retrace our steps and get a view from the valley several miles below, for nothing of the Avatcha can be seen, at this season, from Its fumy head and sides above.

What a day of toil was spent to see a sight unseen! And yet, as we are sailing off, upon the green waters of the bay, how splendid to gaze upon the snow-clad sides (yet blue in the distance), and the rising clouds from the crater of the Avatcha. Good bye, ye icy, muddy, willowy, cedared, rocky coast of Siberia, and ye *Koriaks,* fine fellows, whose portraits I slipped into my portfolio!

"Back to Queen Charlotte's," said the captain, and so said our "agreements;" "but stop - a codicil!" said our attorney, Simms. "Captain, we have agreed to see Petropetrovski, the Russian capital, and you must run us to it; and then we will sail for Queen Charlotte's, and not before. And we four have agreed to give you thirty dollars each."

"I can't do it," said Captain Pasto. "You have all seen my papers, and you know if I leave my track I risk my insurance." "Curse the risk and curse the insurance," said Simms; "we will insure your vessel, and a better insurance you can't find on the face of the earth. Bring forward your agreements, all hands," said he; and in ten minutes the following "codicil" was appended: -

"**Codicil,** off the Coast of Kamskatka, 1853.

"*Further agreed,* to run the Sally Anne to Petropetrovski, and thence to Queen Charlotte's Sound; no risques; enough to eat, and nigger free.

"Signed, J. Paulding, V. Simms, J. Levens, Geo. Catlin, Capt. Pasto, of the Sally Anne."

The thirty dollars each were put down, and the vessel headed for Petropetrovski. "You do things quick," said Captain Pasto to (Squire) Simms, as we called him. "Yes, by G__, sir, when I know I am right I go ahead. I've been a Missouri attorney for ten years - I take but little time to do up such things as this. I have sat three times as Judge Lynch, and signed death warrants in half the time. Brevity is the life and strength of all business, and when I know I'm right I lose no time."

Each one pocketed his agreement again, and the captain went to the deck, evidently under a strong conviction of the necessity of following to the letter the meaning and intention of the document he had put in his pocket.

Petropetrovski had very little interest for any of us; the captain had no business there; and the prospect of "gold" was a dead one. I saw, however, during the four days that we remained there, a group of Esquimaux Indians, and a number of Athapascas, who come in there occasionally. These were interesting to me, and I got my sketches of them.

My gold-hunting companions were getting impatient; and all hands, the captain included, were sighing for wind, as we were sailing down the coast and aiming for Queen Charlotte's.

There was now another overhauling of papers between my fellow voyagers; who, it seems, had before but partially informed me on the subject of their grand design, and the excitements which had turned their attention to it.

"Catlin," said Levens (as they had got me to the table), "you must know all about our plans before we go any further." A number of letters were read to me, and amongst them one from a brother of Levens, in New Orleans, who had drawn from a sailor, some years before, something like the following extraordinary narrative: -

"After a fatal shipwreck in Queen Charlotte's Sound, in 1825, he and one other sailor succeeded in reaching the land, on the mainland shore, and in a state of starvation got into an Indian village, where they wore large round blocks of wood in their lips, and were very kind and friendly to them.

"That they remained there two years, when one of them died, and the other one, who gave the narrative, got permission to go with a party of Indians, in their canoes, to Nootka Sound, where he got on board of a vessel sailing for Panama."

The surprising and only supposed available part of this narrative was the astounding description of lumps and masses of pure gold which he had seen in the possession of the Nayas Indians; and amongst these, belonging to the chief, "a solid block, the full size of a man's head, and as much as one man could lift!"

What a cause for an epidemic or a contagion! Who would not catch the gold fever - unless he had had a touch of it before - at a recital like this?

No precise locality for this wonderful discovery was given; nothing more definite than that it belonged to one of the great chiefs, and was seen amongst the Nayas Indians, on the mainland side of Queen Charlotte's Sound, which has an extent of several hundreds of miles on the coast and some hundreds of miles in the rear.

The "gold fever," however, has the wonderful power of shortening distances and of solving the most embarrassing difficulties. "Such wonderful nuggets as this," I was informed, "must be known throughout the tribe, and the way, therefore, could easily be found to it; and the bed from whence it came must be known also to 'the Indians. That's what we want, Catlin, more than the big nuggets; but we'll get at them both, you may rely upon it."

The cool and perfect state of health I was in as to "gold" seemed to check a little the fever that was raging around me, but not to allay it, for I said, "Gentlemen, I am yours for any expedition we can agree upon into the interior of this interesting country; there are many things in it which I have heard of, and which I want. But, hold," said I, "do you know that the whole of this country and its populations have been for these fifty years in the possession and under the control of, the Hudson's Bay Company, who are gold-hunters as well as yourselves? They have their trading houses amongst these people; and has it occurred to you that such a wonderful nugget would probably have found its way into their hands before this, if it actually existed amongst the Nayas Indians? I do not suggest this to discourage you, but I will go ashore with you and use all my endeavours to assist you in discovering these wonderful treasures."

The third day of sailing brought us into the Sound, and nearing the coast, the smoke of an Indian village was soon in view; and getting near to it, the roofs of houses, which at once informed us that we were in front and in full view of one of the Hudson's Bay Company's factories. All hands suggested, and I agreed, that we had better proceed further down the coast, and land at some of the villages which we had passed on our northward passage.

My comrades seemed evidently surprised at the information I had given them as to the Hudson's Bay Company, and their influence in that country, and began to show symptoms of fear lest they should excite an enemy more fatal to their enterprise than the Indians themselves. They evidently were approaching a country that they had known little about, and which, they had believed, with all its treasures, lay open and free to all comers.

I explained to them as near as I could the vast influence the Company had over the whole of that country, from the Rocky Mountains to the Pacific Ocean - the great number of trading houses they had, that one or more of their *employees* would probably be found in every Indian village, and that the present existence amongst the Indians of such a block of gold as had been described was a matter of impossibility, or that rich mines of gold known to the Indians could have escaped their acquisitive investigations.

My advice and suggestions, which were less patiently listened to at first, were now being more thankfully received, as I reiterated with them my intention to use my best efforts and all my influence, under any circumstances, to promote their views, whilst any chance of success remained.

We were running on, and sundown and twilight approaching, we ran into a deep cove, sheltered by a high and precipitous rock escarpment, and the "Sally Anne" cast anchor and laid till morning. At sunrise, and before coming on deck, I heard distinctly Caesar's loud voice and broad laugh, as he was ejaculating English, Spanish, and the Lingua Geral, all in rapid succession, convincing me that we had visitors on board. I got on deck (the gold hunters yet fast asleep), and found our forward deck half covered with a party of Indians, and double the number resting on their paddles, in their painted canoes, lying around us. Fresh salmon and dried, in great abundance, and oysters and whortleberries, were brought on board for barter, and the captain and mate were busily engaged in laying in supplies, while Caesar, a head taller than all the group, and the sun shining on his glistening cheek-bones and forehead, stood, with his rifle in his arms, a model, vainly endeavouring by his Lingua Geral and Spanish to get some clue to conversation with the curious group around him; but all in vain, and for the first time I had seen him put to his trumps completely.

All eyes were upon him, and the Indians were as much surprised and perplexed at his sudden advent and novel appearance as he was perplexed with the total unintelligibility of their language. It required but a *coup d'oeil* to see that shining, glistening black Caesar was to be the lion, the paragon of the enterprise. The Indians on deck all shook hands with him, and, in total default of his Spanish and Geral, he had got into a partial conversation with them by signs manual, of which he was master, and which (a curious fact) are much the same amongst all the tribes, both in North and South America; and by the time I got on deck he was becoming a tolerable interpreter for me.

"Well, dear me, Massa Catliri," said Caesar, "dem dar berry curious people. I b'lieve dey berry good. I guess you go ashore, Massa?"

"Yes, Caesar; we are going to land here for a while, after the other gentlemen get up."

We were lying about four hundred yards from the shore at this time, and though no signs of a village could be seen, their light and bounding canoes were constantly putting out from the nooks and crevices in the rocks overhung with cedar and impenetrable masses of red, and white, and purple rhododendrons, and gathering in a gay and dancing fleet around us.

Though I had heard of the beauty of their canoes, and their dexterous mode of handling them, I had formed but an ignorant notion of them. The sluggish logs and tubs that Caesar and I had been knocked about in on the Amazon and the Xingu, gave us no clue to the light, the gay, the painted gondolas now dancing on the ocean's waves about us. Excavated from the trunks of the immense cedars of that country, they were fashioned with grace and lightness, and painted of all colours, and so were the naked shoulders that were seen within them.

Like a flock of goats playing up and down upon a group of hillocks, upon the rising and sinking waves they were sporting and vaulting in all directions, and seemed, at times, actually rearing, as if to leap upon the deck. Their paddles were all painted with similar designs as those upon their boats, and their robes, when worn, showed characters the same, and all seemed like some system of hieroglyphic signs yet to be understood.

In Plate No. 5, two of these canoes, with paddles, are represented.

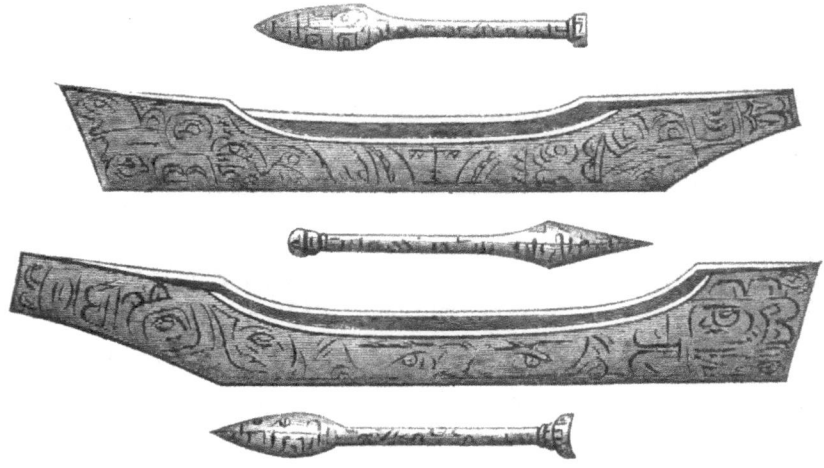

In the midst of the group now assembled on the deck, our attorney, Simms, emerged from the cabin below, exclaiming

"Good God, Catlin, we are prisoners!"

"Oh, no; we are in the midst of one of the most friendly receptions, and it is a great pity that you, and Paulding, and Levens, should lose any part of it. We are in the midst of the Nayas Indians, and their largest village is just around the point ahead of us."

"Halloa, below there, fellows!" exclaimed Simms, putting his head as far down the hatchway as he could. "You are losing everything!"

Half-awake, and misunderstanding the two last words, and hearing the voices of Indians on deck, and catching a glimpse of the group through the sky-lights, they advanced most bravely, and at a jump were on the deck, with their rifles up and their revolvers ready! Simms sprang at one, and I at the other, and, just in time, saved the carnage that was at the instant of commencing.

The Indians, unarmed, flew to the bow of the vessel, and a number of them overboard. And well they might, from the frightful aspect of the two gladiators, but half dressed, and rising, like demons, from below, at the signal call, for their extermination.

I spread my hands forward and over the Indians, and made signs for them to come back, whilst Simms and myself were cooling down the two firebrands; when Caesar threw himself between the two groups, and, a figure like the Colossus of Rhodes, he stood, explaining by signs to one party, and by tolerably good English to the other, that "it was only a little mistake, and dat we were all berry good friends."

This little sensation over, others of the Indians began climbing on board from their canoes, and, last of all, some half a dozen of their women, whose eyes were riveted on Caesar; and he began to loom up, as he used to do amongst the Muras, the Connibos, and the Chetibos, and other tribes of the Amazon.

He was naturally a tremendous gallant, and, stimulated by the gaze of these fair, and oftentimes half and three-fourths naked, beauties, he was frequently in the clouds, and almost beyond the reach of all control.

Frequent instances showed me that his sympathies, at last, were with the damsels; and the singular appearance of one of them, whom he had observed, brought him to me at this instant.

"Well, de Lord be praised, Massa Catlin. I berry sorry for dat poor gal dar, she got mighty soalip!"

"Yes, Caesar, it's a great pity; for she seems, from her dress and manners, to be a very nice girl; I should say, the belle of the village."

Breakfast was ready below, and Caesar and the hands of the vessel amused the group on deck whilst we were taking our coffee, and discussing the movements of the day, to be made on the land.

Caesar had learned that their village was just around the point, and, at the request of the mate, the Indians were returning to their village, where they were informed we should follow them when our breakfast was over.

About nine o'clock we four, with Captain Pasto (with only our revolvers, our rifles being left on board), and Caesar, carrying my portfolio on his back, and his minié rifle in his hand, got into the yawl and went ashore, and were conducted to the village, which was at the head of a little cove, a half a mile or so from the shore.

The Indians, informed of our visit, had all gathered into their huts, and the chief, a very dignified man, was seated in his wigwam and ready, with his pipe lit, to receive us. We were seated on mats spread upon the ground, and whilst the pipe was being passed around, the first ceremony on all such occasions, the Indian dogs (half wolves), of which there were some hundreds, got upon our tracks, and completely invested the chief's wigwam, and set up the most hideous and doleful chorus of yells, and howls, and barks. The sentinel whom the chief had placed at the door of his wigwam, to prevent all access except by his permission, drew his bow upon one of the foremost of the gang, and shot it through the heart, when the throng was silenced and dispersed by the Indian women, who set upon them with their paddles.

Our position was rather awkward, having no other interpretation than the imperfect knowledge of signs named, of Caesar and myself, brought from South America and the valley of the Missouri. However, we effected a general understanding, and learned from the chief that he had sent to another village not far off, and would have an excellent interpreter in a little time.

I told my companions I thought they had better not say a word of their object in visiting the country until the interpreter arrived, when it could be clearly explained without being misunderstood, and in the mean time I would not lose a moment's time in making a sensation, and of exciting a friendly interest.

"Good," said Simms, "I know what it is, Catlin, go a-head! Show him your pictures."

I had beckoned Caesar, who was at that moment unstrapping the portfolio from his back, and advancing towards me. I opened it before the chief, and sat by the side of him explaining the portraits, as I turned them over. He was a very deliberate and dignified man, and exhibited no surprise whatever, but at the same time evidently took a deep interest in them.

I showed him several chiefs of the Amazon, and also several of the Sioux, Osages, and Pawnees, and the last one turned up, a portrait, full length, of Caesar Bolla. He could not hold his muscles still any longer, but burst out in the most uncontrollable and vociferous laugh, and turning around to Caesar, who was sitting at the further side of the lodge, extended his hand, which Caesar advanced and shook, and at the chief's request, took a seat by the side of him.

The book of portraits was creating such an excitement, that three or four sub-chiefs came in and took their seats. And the wigwam being in two sections, and divided by a door made by a hanging bearskin, which was put aside, two women and a young man entered, and also took their seats on the ground, to get a peep at the portraits; one of these was the wife of the chief, and the other his daughter, an unmarried girl.

Caesar had his attention at this time fixed upon one of the men who had taken his seat, with the block of wood in his under lip, and the chief's daughter was decorated in the same way.

"Caesar," said I, "here are more sore lips."

"Well, now, I do deck, Massa Catlin, *dea* me, I think it is ketchin!"

I turned the portfolio through again, to the amusement and astonishment of all, and when Caesar Bolla was turned up, there was a roar of laughter again, all eyes were upon him, and turning his face one side, and a little down, he whispered to me, "Well now, Massa Catlin, I neber felt so shame in all my life afoa." And when he had mustered courage to raise his head, and cast his eyes around, I said, "Caesar, your portrait has cured the sore lips" (the two wearing blocks of wood in their lips having slipped them out in order to enable them to laugh).

About the instant that Caesar had observed that the blocks were out, and the broad laugh was over, they were slipped in again, when he exclaimed, "Well, Massa Catlin, affer dat, I neber know wat I will see nex."

Though this curious and unaccountable custom was known to me, my companions had been as ignorant of it as Caesar was, and evidently were regarding it with equal astonishment. I said to them and to Caesar, "Of the 'sore lips' take no more notice until the interpreter comes, and then we will learn all about it."

My attention was then fixed on a beautiful mantle worn by the chief's daughter, made, as I learned, of mountain sheeps' wool and wild dogs' hair, wonderfully knitted with spun-yarn of beautiful colours, and so assembled as to exhibit the most eccentric and intricate figures, and bordered with a fringe of eighteen inches in length, the work of three women for one year, I was told, and its price, five horses.

The bowl of the pipe which the chief had been passing around was full fourteen inches in length of pot stone, jet black, and highly polished, the whole, a group of figures, human and animal, interlocked and carved in the most ingenious manner.

Of these pot-stone pipes I saw many, and obtained several, and the eccentric designs on them, on their robes, their canoes, their paddles, their leggings, and even the paintings on their faces and limbs, are peculiarly tribal, and their own, differing from anything seen in the other tribes of the continent.

The same extraordinary characters are written on their spoons, their bowls, their vases, their war-clubs; on their pottery, of which they make great quantities, and on everything else that they manufacture, and seeming to be a system of hieroglyphics not yet explained, and which for the archaeologist and ethnologist may yet be a subject of peculiar interest.

Instead of the stupid, superstitious fears and objections which generally stood in the way of my painting their portraits in the valley of the Amazon and other parts of South America, this intelligent and rational man at once said, when I asked him -

"Yes; if you find any of us worthy of so great an honour, and handsome enough, we will all be ready to be painted."

"Good!" said I (by intelligible signs); "I love such a man. Caesar, bring my painting-box and easel from the vessel, and I will begin this noble fellow's portrait this afternoon."

"Catlin!" said Simms, "you are getting altogether ahead of us."

"Never mind," said I, "I am on the right track - the right vein. I know these people better than you do; they must be pleased first, amused, complimented; and the compliment I am now paying to the chief will make him the friend of all. I will secure his goodwill first for the whole party, and when the interpreter comes to-morrow, you may put in your claims in the best manner you can devise."

The afternoon came, and my paint-box and the chief were before me, and with him his lovely daughter. He told me he loved her, and always made it a rule to have her by him, and he thought I had better place them both in the same picture. I told him I loved him for that; it was natural and noble.

Vanity is the same all the world over, both in savage and civilized societies. Good looks in portraiture and fashions, whatever they are - crinoline of the lip or crinoline of the waist (and one is just as beautiful and reasonable as the other), or rings in the nose or rings in the ears, they are all the same.

Night came, and my picture was taken on board.

"Catlin," said my companions, "you are leaving us all in the background."

"Never mind," said I again, "I am introducing you where you never could have got a foothold for an hour. We will have a council to-morrow in the chief's lodge, and, his interpreter present, your plans will progress as well as mine."

During the night the wind veered about, and, very nearly being driven on to the rocks, the captain set sail, and crossing the sound, got shelter under the lee of Queen Charlotte's Island. The wind abating the next day, we were able in the afternoon to return to our anchorage in front of the Indian village.

The Indians were all on the shore, and received us with shouts, and many in their canoes gathered around us whilst we were coming to anchor; and amongst them came on board the interpreter who had been sent for by the chief. He was a young man, a Frenchman, by the name of Frénié, an *employee* in the fur company, and met us with much civility.

From him we soon got an account of the numerous tribes of Indians along the coast, and on Queen Charlotte's Island, over which also the fur company's business extended. The interpreter had learned from the chief that I had painted his portrait, and it being brought on deck, he was excessively delighted with it, holding it up over the gun wale and showing it to the Indians paddling about in their canoes.

Caesar was on the spot with my cartoon portraits, and ready to make a further sensation. "Yes," said I, "Caesar, bring it forward." We had a look at the portraits, and the interpreter then asked my name. When I wrote it for him with my pencil, he said my name had been familiar to him for ten years past, and that there was not a man in the Hudson's Bay Company nor an Indian between the Rocky Mountains and the Pacific coast who had not heard my name, and of the collection of Indian paintings I was making, though he believed I never was in that part of the country before.

He told us that the chief expected myself and my companions to eat and to smoke with him in his wigwam that afternoon, and that at night the doctors were going to give us a medicine dance. Simms agreed with me that "all was going right," and that it would be best not to start the inquiries about gold until these festivities were over.

We were soon ashore, all excepting Captain Pasto and his crew, he having hinted to me that there might be a plot in all this to get all ashore, and then take possession of his vessel. I was quite agreed to this, as the festivities would now be tendered to us alone who could appreciate them.

As we approached the village a great throng came out to meet us, and I observed the mass (and particularly the women) were siding up to Caesar, who was marching at his fullest height, with the portfolio of portraits strapped on his back.

The concourse of people seeming to me too large for so small a village, led me to make the suggestion to the interpreter, who replied that "the news of our arrival and the masquerade dance to be given that evening had brought a great number from Jaurna's village, and that others were coming."

"Soa lips" now began to thicken around Caesar, who had got the portfolio off from his back, and was carrying it under his left arm, whilst the other was constantly employed in answering the questions put by signs. He was evidently the lion, and as soon as I could I got him and his portfolio into the chiefs lodge, to be subject to the chief's orders.

My companions found enough for their amusement amongst the throng whilst I was sketching two other portraits, and at sundown we sat down to a feast of venison in the chief's wigwam. This and "a smoke" kept us till sometime after dark, when a dozen or more flaming torches, with yelping, and barking, and singing, approached his wigwam, and in front of it commenced the masquerade dance.

Bizarre is but a lame word for the startling eccentricity and drollery that were then before us. Caesar was not in the midst of it, but by the side of it, and overlooking it. I had serious apprehensions that I should lose him, from the hysterical bursts and explosions of laughter that fell in bolts and half-strangled hiccups from his broad mouth.

Some fifteen or twenty, all men, were engaged in in this singular affair, all masked and otherwise dressed in the most strange and curious taste, and many of the lookers-on, in the front ranks, both men and women, were masked and dressed in a similar manner.

The leader of the dance, *a medicine man*, the drollest of the droll, was the *"King of the Bustards;"* another was *"King of the Loons;"* another was the *"Doctor of the Rabbits;"* one was the *"Devil's Brother,"* one *was "the Maker of the Thunder,"* one was *"the White Crow,"* one was *"the Bear that travels in the night,"* and another *"the Cariboo's Ghost,"* &c. &c. until the names of the animal and feathered tribes were chiefly exhausted.

A Medicine Dance

The masks which the dancers wore (and of which I procured several), were works of extraordinary ingenuity. Carved in a solid block of wood, excavated in such a manner as closely to fit the face, and held to the dancer's face by a transverse strap of leather, from corner to corner of the mouth of the mask, inside, so that when the mask was on, and close to the face, the strap of leather was taken between the teeth, counterfeiting thereby, not only the face, but the voice, a perfection in masking yet to be learned in the masquerades of civilized frolickings.

Besides the ingenuity exhibited in the forms and expressions of these masks, they were all painted of various colours, and with the most eccentric designs. These masks (with the exception of that worn by the leader of the dance), were all made to imitate the mode of the people, of wearing a block of wood in the under-lip.

The custom of masking and of masquerade dancing is by no means peculiar to the Nayas Indians, for in many of the tribes, both in South and North America, I have witnessed similar amusements.

In plate (No, 9), copies of two of my portraits illustrate the mode of wearing the blocks of wood in the under-lip, and also of slitting and elongating the cartilage and lobes of the ears, in which large blocks also are worn as ornaments.

The ornament of the lip is a mode belonging chiefly to the women, though there are some eccentric men who also practise it. And of the women, it is but a portion of them who perforate the lip, and even by them it is only on particular occasions that they wear the blocks, to be seen, as they term it, in full dress. When eating and sleeping the blocks are removed, and also when much use of their tongues is required; for, with the block in the mouth there are many words not pronounced.

(*a*) A block worn by a child of three or four years' old.
(*b*) A block worn at the age of seven or eight years.
(*c*) A block worn by a young woman at maturity.
(*d*) A block worn by the men only, in the cartilage of the ear.

In Plate (No. 10), I have given the exact dimensions and shapes of three blocks for the lip and one for the ear, which I procured of the people whilst amongst them.

The perforation for the block in the lip is made at a very early age, and is kept open through life, and is scarcely perceptible when the block is out.

For inserting the block, the thumb of the left hand is forced upwards through the aperture, and by the side of it the thumb of the right hand, and the block is delivered into its place by the fingers, from above, as the thumbs are withdrawn.

The whole of the next day after the masquerade I was painting, and Caesar was showing and des canting on the portfolio; and my three companions, with the interpreter, were discussing gold nuggets and gold placers; and as near as I could ever learn it, the total of their discoveries led to this: that there had been, about two years before, a party of gold-hunters from California in that country, having heard marvellous accounts of gold nuggets in the possession of the Indians, and that they had been ordered out of the country by the Hudson's Bay Company, and were obliged to leave in a great hurry; that there had, no doubt, been some nuggets in the hands of some of the Indians, but that they had been found at a great distance off, near the mountains, on the bank of a great river (supposed to be Frazer's river, where the rich mines are now being worked).

The Frazer River mines, at that time, were just becoming known; and my companions very judiciously decided that their best way would be to return to Victoria, and take the track of the flood of Frazer River miners at that time ascending the Frazer's river.

This resolution suited the captain of our little craft exactly, as time was precious to him, and his vessel more or less at risk whilst lying along the coast. Victoria, which was then but a town of some forty or fifty houses, was our next aim; and stopping a day or two in several villages of *Hydas* and *Bella Bellas,* on the coast, we were safe at anchor in Smith's Inlet, opposite to the northern cape of Vancouver's Island. Its shores were alive with the smokes of Indian villages, and there was no need of leaving the vessel to see Indians. We were at all hours of the day surrounded by their bounding and galloping pirogues, and often had more than the captain was disposed to accommodate on deck, mostly a miserable, almost naked and squalid-looking multitude, bringing fish and oysters to barter for rum or whatever else they could get. Amongst these were *Skidegates, Stickeens, Bella Bellas, Hydas,* and several other tribes inhabiting the coast and islands in the vicinity. Some were flat heads, and others were not.

It mattered little to me what the shapes of their heads were, and for a couple of days I was gathering them into my portfolio, whilst Caesar kept all comers, and of all languages, amused with the portraits, which he was lecturing on alternately in English, in Spanish, and Lingua Geral, from which they learned just as much as they would have learned from the squalling of a paroquet or cockatoo.

It seemed a perfect mystery to my impatient companions, "how I could sit out two whole days without my dinner, painting those ill-looking Indians." They killed time, below the deck, with the captain, at cards; and during the third night sails were up to pass the straits and run to Victoria, which our chart showed us was but a short run.

Morning came, and where were we? not in the harbour of Victoria, nor near it, but in front of Nootka Island, where we had been before, off the west coast of Vancouver, and its tall pines and rocky peaks but just discernible! And for what? nobody could tell, unless the captain's reasons were correct, that the shape and character of the winds made it hazardous to run the Strait and the Sound, and that an open sea and fair sailing, which he was making, was apt to be the quickest and the safest.

A forty-eight hours' run brought us around the southern cape of the island, and into the Strait of Juan de Fuca, and hugging the shore, and heading towards Victoria. And hugging a little too close, at low tide, the keel of the *Sally Anne* was rubbing on the sands, and losing her headway, and hitching in wards a little at every wave, as the tide was rising. She was hitched up, and hitched up, until, at high tide, she was lying, and was left, broadside upon the sands in a little sandy cove, between huge and frowning rocks.

We remained on board until another flood tide, which only lifted us higher up and left us again, a few rods further on to the island, and, of course, a few rods nearer to Victoria. All chances of getting his little craft nearer to Victoria harbour being now apparently ended, and with due sympathy for the poor captain, which we all felt, as we were taking leave, we each agreed to leave him a *bonus* of thirty dollars, and each signed his "agreement" to take us to Victoria, *"executed."* We got some Flathead Indians on the shore to carry our luggage, and at their guidance we trudged through the forest to Victoria.

In Victoria all was confusion, complete pell-mell; houses were filled, steamers and vessels were full, and men and women were sleeping in carts and wagons in the streets, and others were not sleeping at all, but, with bonfires built upon the bank, or under the pines, were dancing away the nights in wild and frantic whirls.

Frazer River had just *débuted* as the *El Dorado* of the world, and it seemed as if California had emptied itself, "neck and heels" its men, its mules, and its steamers into the Sound of Vancouver.

Reports were hourly arriving from the mines, and all was - on - on! "pull Dick and pull Devil," and "bad luck to the hindmost." The "Celestials" were there, with two oblique sabre cuts and two gimlet holes for eyes; New Yorkers and Londoners were there, and all the nations of the earth seemed to be assembling. The Omnipotent hand had spread nuggets and sands of gold in such profusion over the new-discovered fields, that it required but the hand of industrious man to pick and scrape it up, and load his pockets with it.

The midst of this grand *mêlée* was the place exactly for my three impatient companions, and the mere hurried "Good-bye, and God bless you, Cat.," was about all that I could get from them as they disappeared; and all that I can say of them, unless in a more appropriate place, and in a more advanced part of this little book, I may be able to do it.

The poor Indians living in the vicinity of Victoria, on Vancouver's Island, and all belonging to the Flathead family, seemed alarmed, and withdrew their encampments into the forests.

In the midst of such an epidemic, after having had the fever myself, one can easily imagine my position anything but agreeable, and in a few days, by a returning San Francisco steamer, Caesar and I got a passage to Astoria, and from thence, by another craft, to Portland, the head of navigation on the Columbia River.

This thrifty little beginning of a town has the prospect of wealth and greatness before it. [2]

The "Dalles" (and we soon made it) was the next and the last destination foreshadowed in that direction, thirty miles above, and on the same river. This famous place, from time immemorial the living, the life, and support of tens of thousands of surrounding Indians, from the endless quantities of salmon taken in it, is a bold and furious rapid, for several miles dashing and foaming through compressed channels in the rocks, in the eddies of which the fatigued fish, in their laborious ascent, stop to rest, and are pierced by the harpoon arrows of the overleaning and overlooking Indian, and lifted out.

The fresh fish for current food, and the dried fish for their winter consumption, which had been from time immemorial a good and certain living for the surrounding tribes, like everything else of value belonging to the poor Indian, has attracted the cupidity of the "better class," and is now being "turned into money," whilst the ancient and real owners of it may be said to be starving to death; dying in sight of what they have lost, and in a country where there is actually nothing else to eat.

[1] This beautiful canoe was a present from a Nayas chief, of Queen Charlotte's Island, to the Klah-o-quat chief; though the interpreter informed me that, amongst the Klah-o-quats and the To-quahts, there were others of their own make, quite as handsome.

[2] Whilst halting a few days in this little seaport town, I learned by accident that Captain Pasto had got his schooner afloat, and had put out to sea.

Chapter Four - The Flathead Indians

Just at this time another epidemic was raging, and not less prolific in its victims than the scourge of the country I had just escaped from; the crusade from the States across the Rocky Mountains to Oregon, by wagons, by ox-carts, and by wheelbarrows, spot ting the prairies and mountains with recent graves, and strewing the wayside with carcasses of oxen and horses, and broken wagons and abandoned house hold furniture.

The greater portion of this disastrous and almost fanatic pilgrimage crossed the mountains at what is known as the "south pass," that is, south of the terrible and impassable piles of twice-upheaved rocks where the Salmon River Mountain traverses the Rocky Mountain range, and over, or through, the mountains, descended through the valley of the Shoshonee (or Snake) River to the Columbia.

Learning by some of the most recent of these arrivals that the Paunch (Grosventres), a band of the Crow Indians, had crossed the mountains north of the Salmon River Mountain, and were encamped in the Salmon River Valley near its sources, I made the instant and desperate resolve to reach them, if impossibility were not in the way.

I asked Caesar how he would like to take a trip on horseback and see the Rocky Mountains.

"Well, dat ar just wat suit me now, zactly. Lor me! you guess you go?"

"Yes, if I can get a horse and a couple of good mules. This I can't do here, Caesar, but at Fort Walla Walla, further up the river, I think it can be done."

Flatheads we were now in the midst of, and for the time I had my work to do. The *Klatsops,* the *Chinooks,* the *Clickatats,* the *Walla Wallas,* and the *Nez Perces* and *Spokans,* constituting the principal bands of 'the Flathead family, I was there in the midst of, and had enough to do. Some of these flatten the head, and others do not, yet all speak the Flathead language, or dialects of it.

(11)

(12)

The Flathead tribe, so called from their singular practice of flattening the head, is one of the most numerous (if not the most numerous) west of the Rocky Mountains, occupying the whole country about the lower Columbia, including the island of Vancouver. It is altogether a canoe race, living in a country where there is little else than fish to live upon. The tribe is divided into something like thirty bands, speaking nearly the same language, and generally spoken of (but erroneously) as so many different tribes, the names of the principal of which I have already mentioned.

The strange and unaccountable custom of flattening the head in this tribe is confined mostly to the women, and amongst them it is by no means general, and ornamentation, singular as it may seem, appears to be the sole object of it. In Plate No. 11 I have given copies of two of my portraits of women, showing the artificial shapes produced by that strange custom; and in Plate No. 12 portraits of a Flathead chief curiously wrapped in his blanket, and his wife, with her infant in its crib (or cradle) on her back, undergoing the process of flattening. The infant, at its birth, is placed in its cradle dug out of a solid log of wood, and fastened down with bandages, so that it cannot move, and the frontal process is pressed down by an elastic lever, which is tightened daily by strings fastened to the sides of the cradle. The bones of that part of the head, at that period, being cartilaginous, are easily pressed into that unnatural form, and after two or three months of this pressure the required shape is obtained, which lasts through life. By pressing the frontal region back, the head is pressed out on the sides to an unnatural extent, as seen in the illustration (No. 11). If this were a natural deformity, stultility would undoubtedly be the result; but as it is an artificial deformation, no such result is produced, nor need it to be looked for, as it is only a change in the *form* and *position* of the mental organs, without interfering with their natural functions. The evidence of this is, that those with their heads flattened are found to be quite as intelligent as the others in the tribe; and it would be a monstrous supposition to believe that the fathers of families and chiefs would subject their infants to a process that was to stultify them.

Near Fort Walla Walla, for the first time in my life, I procured a tolerable horse, a stout mule for Caesar, and a pack-mule, at a fair and honest price; and in company with three young men who had recently arrived from the States, and were going back to meet and aid the sick and disabled of their party that had been left behind, we started, with our faces towards the mountains.

After five days' march together, their course being to the right, and through the Snake River Valley, we were obliged to part company, and Caesar and I, with an Indian guide, took to the left, hugging as near as we could the ragged and frightful, and all but impassable, southern bank of the Salmon River, until, at length, after many days of deep repentance, we entered the more calm and beautiful meadows and prairies of the Salmon River Valley.

Our ride (or rather walk, for we had to walk and climb most of the way, leading our horses) was one which I deeply regretted from day to day, but which I never have regretted since it was finished. The eighth day opened to our view one of the most verdant and beautiful valleys in the world; and on the tenth a distant smoke was observed, and under it the skin-tents, which I at once recognized as of a Crow village.

I was again amongst my old friends, the Crows! men whose beautiful forms and native, gentlemanly grace had not been deformed by squatting in canoes, nor eyes bridled by scowling on the glistening sun reflected on the water, or heads squeezed into wedges, or lips stretched around blocks of wood.

As soon as we were dismounted, and in the midst of the crowd around us, I was struck more forcibly than ever with the monstrous and pitiable deformities of man which the peculiar necessities of life often drive him to, as seen amongst the squatted, paddling tribes of the Amazon, Vancouver, and the Columbia coast and river.

It was a pleasure that I cannot describe to find myself again amongst mankind as Nature made them, the Crows, whom I had long since thought I had seen for the last time.

The Crows (as they are called by their neighbours), *Belantsea,* of whom I gave some account in the first volume of this work, are probably the most unbroken, unchanged part of the original stock of North American Man. Their numbers, at the time when I was amongst them, in 1832, were about 10,000, living on the head waters of the Yellow Stone River and in the Rocky Mountains.

From their traditions, which are very distinct, they formerly occupied the whole range of the Rocky Mountains and the beautiful valleys on each side, from the sources of the Saskatchewan in the north, and as far south (their traditions say) as the mountains continue: that would be to the Straits of Panama.

They say that their people were a great nation before the Flood, and that a few who reached the summits of the mountains were saved when all the tribes of the valleys were destroyed by the waters.

That they were the most ancient American stock, and the unique, original American type, I believe; and that they were the original Toltecs and Aztecs, who, history and traditions tell us, poured down from the mountains of the north-west, founding the cities of Mexico, Palenque, and Uxmal.

My portraits of Crows, made in my first series of voyages, in 1832, and exhibited in London, from their striking resemblance to those on the sculptured stones of Mexico and Yucatan, excited suggestions to that effect by many of my friends; and the first of these, and the most enthusiastic, my untiring and faithful friend, Captain Shippard, an indefatigable reader amongst the ancient archives of the British Museum; and of my friend the Baron de Humboldt, who told me also that the subject was one of profound interest to science, and well worthy of my further study.

These reiterated suggestions, added to my own intelligence, have kept alive, for many years, my anxiety on that subject, and undoubtedly were the uncombatible arguments which determined me, when hearing, at the Dalles, of a band of Crows encamped in the Salmon River Valley, west of the Rocky Mountains, to "make shift" (*coute qui coute*), and with Caesar, to throw myself amongst them.

I have said that "we were there," and whatever I found amongst them in customs and contour, and traditions, as well as amongst other tribes that I visited in more southern latitudes, between them and the Straits of Panama, tending to establish the belief above advanced, that they were the Toltecs and Aztecs of Mexico and Yucatan, will be noticed in a subsequent part of this work.

The Crow-village that we were in, consisting of some forty or fifty skin tents, had crossed the mountains on to the head waters of Salmon River, to take and dry salmon, there being no salmon on the east side of the Rocky Mountains.

The chief of the band, a sub-chief, called the *"Yellow Mocasin,"* was a very intelligent man, and gave me a clear, and, no doubt, a true account of the recent history of the tribe, as he had received it from his father and grandfather. According to this, the Crows were originally confined to the mountains and their valleys, from which their enemies of the plains could never dislodge them; but that since horses have made their appearance in the plains, a great portion of their people have descended into the prairies, where they have been cut to pieces by the Sioux, the Blackfeet, and other tribes, and their former great strength destroyed.

I was received with great kindness by these people, and told by the chief that I should be welcome, and that his young men should watch and guard my horses. The incidents here, enough in themselves for a small book, must be passed over, for there are yet many adventures a-head of us.

One thing, however, cannot be passed by. Whilst seated in the chief's lodge, where there were some six or eight men besides the chief, and endeavouring, as the necessary preliminary in all first interviews with Indians, to make the object of my visit distinctly known, I opened the portfolio of cartoon portraits, which all were examining with great interest and astonishment, and on turning up the fifth or sixth portrait, one of the party gave a sudden piercing yelp, and sprang upon his feet and commenced dancing in the most violent jumps and starts, and vociferating, *"Bi-eets-e-cure! Bi-eets-e-cure!"* (the name of the young man), whose portrait I had painted at the mouth of the Yellow Stone twenty years before, and was now holding up.

The portrait was recognized by all, and on their feet, and darting out of the wigwam, were three or four of the party, and through the village to where the women were drying fish, on the bank of the river, and back, re-entered the chief's wigwam, and with them, out of breath, and walking as if he was coming to the gallows, entered *Bi-eets-e-cure* (the very sweet man).

I instantly recognized him, and rising up, he took about half a minute to look me full in the eyes, without moving a muscle or winking, when he exclaimed, *"how! how!"* (yes, yes), and shook me heartily by the hand. I took up his portrait, and showing it to him, got the interpreter to say to him that I had "kept his face clean!"

The reader can more easily and more correctly imagine the pleasurable excitement, and the curious remarks amongst the party at this singular occurrence, than I can explain them; for, not knowing their language, I was ignorant of much that passed, myself.

"One thing, I'm *sua,* Massa Catlin," suddenly exclaimed Caesar, who had not before opened his broad mouth, "I quite *sua* dat ar man knows you, Massa!"

All eyes were now turned for a moment upon Caesar, who was sitting a little back, and evidently looked upon by most of the party as some great chief, until the interpreter explained that he was my servant.

During this interlude, and which required some little exchange of feelings and recollections between the *"very sweet man"* and myself, I had shut the portfolio, to begin again where we left off; and proceeding again with the portraits, after showing them several of their enemies, the Sioux and Blackfeet, *Ba-da-ah-chon-du* (the Jumper), one of the chiefs of the Crows, whose portrait also was painted at Yellow Stone twenty years before, turned up! All recognized him, and *Bi-eets-e-cure* told them that he saw me when I was painting that picture twenty years before.

Through the interpreter, I told them that more than 100,000 white people had seen the chief's face, and, as they could see, there was not a scratch upon it! The chief then arose upon his feet, and making signs for me to rise, embraced me in his arms, and each one of the party saluted me in the same affectionate manner.

See Ba-da-ah-chon-du (the Jumper, Plate No. 13). His head-dress of wareagles' quills his robe the skin of a buffalo, with his battles painted on it, his lance in his hand, his shield and quiver slung on his back, his tobacco-sac suspended from his belt, and his leggings fringed with scalp-locks.

In conversation which I had with *Bi-eets-e-cure,* he informed me that the chief *Ba-da-ah-chon-du,* whose portrait we had just seen, was dead - that he died soon after I painted his portrait, and many of his friends and relations believed that the painting of the portrait was the cause of his death; "But," said he, "I told them they were very foolish - that I had no fears when mine was painted, and here I am alive, after so many years!"

I told them that no man of good sense could see any way in which the painting could do them an injury, and that amongst the white people we all had our portraits made, and it did us no harm. They all gave their assent in a "How, how, how!" and the next day I slipped off the "skin," as they called it, of two or three of them; and, amongst them, and the first, 'that of the young chief whose hospitality I was enjoying. Plate No. 14.

I painted him at his toilette, as he was letting down his long hair and oiling it with bear's-grease, which his wife was pouring into his hand from a skin bottle; and she, poor woman, from a custom of the country, not to compete with her husband in a feature so ornamental, was obliged to have *her* hair cropped close to the head.

In the first volume of this work I have given a more detailed account of this striking peculiarity of the Crow tribe, in which there are many men who trail two and three feet of their natural hair on the ground as they walk.

Reader, our journey is yet long, and our halts must be short. What else transpired during the ten days that I remained in the Crow-village must await the appearance of a larger work which is in progress.

The day before I left, a report was brought, by one of the Hudson's Bay Company's men, that a party of Blackfeet - their deadly enemies - was preparing to march upon them from the north. All, of course, was excitement and confusion; and they were preparing to move into a defile in the mountains, where they could protect themselves if attacked; and whatever was the result of this movement I never heard.

With a faithful guide, who knew the route, recommended by the chief, we started to cross the Salmon River Mountain into the Snake River Valley - a pass difficult to traverse, and requiring the most desperate resolution. Ravine after ravine, amidst the most frowning and defiant rocks of all sizes, which had tumbled down from the snow-capped summits on either side of us. Our guide entered us well into them, and, sleeping with us one night, instructed us how to proceed, and left us to our fate, returning to his village.

We had an ample supply of dried salmon for our five or six days' march, which was to bring us to Fort Hall, one of the Company's fur factories, near the source of the Snake River. We might have returned to the Dalles by the same route by which we had come, and escaped the terrible task we were now performing, but for two reasons I had for not doing it - the first, that in all the travels of my life I have had a repugnance to return by the same route; and the second, that I had an unconquerable desire to cross this range of Palaeozoic rocks, and to examine the strange confusion produced by a mountain lifted by a rising mountain.

This mountain range, running from west to east, traversing the Rocky Mountains, and becoming the "Black Hills" on the Eastern side, is known to geologists to have been a mountain under the sea before the continent of America arose, and to have been relifted up at the intersection by the Rocky Mountains rising underneath at a later date. How sublime! A stupendous mountain with its hidden treasures, from the bottom of the sea, lifted up to the heavens and crumbling to pieces, is tumbling into the valley and ravines below! And what a field for the geologist to get at the deepest productions of the earth's hidden material!

Gneiss and granites, from their deepest beds in the earth, raised in stupendous mountain piles under the sea, and, risen with a continent, have again been shoved up by deeper beds of granite underneath, until their subaqueous, cavern-formed limestones of all colours - of snow-white, of green, and blue, and grey, and their associated felspathic rocks and massive blocks of felspar - are turned out upon their tops and tumbled down their sides.

What a field for geologists, and why are they not there?

Amongst these immense and never-ending blocks I was reading an instructive book, and making notes, which Caesar could not understand; he had enough to do to take care of the horses, whilst I was sometimes for hours out of his sight and hearing; and coming back, and waking him and the mules from their sleep, all I would hear was: "Well, Massa Catlin, you bery strange man, dat's all I got to say." He was getting sick on dried salmon and no excitement; and our poor animals were all but starving to death, there being some times, for miles together, not one solitary blade of grass for them to crop. What a time to study geology!

We had a sort of a path - a track - to follow, which we could keep to only with the greatest difficulty. The tracks of horses shod convinced me that the men of the trading houses were in the habit of passing from one trading post to another by it, and it was our only confidence that we should sooner or later discover the valley of the Snake river.

This we did on the fifth day; and even our poor and jaded animals neighed and brayed when we saw, through a ravine, the blue of the valley, and the *"Trois Buttes"* - three beautiful and stupendous natural pyramids - though blue in the distance, standing in the centre of it.

Getting out, and upon the flank of the mountain, green grass was in abundance and shady trees; and I spent several hours in revising and re-writing my hasty notes on the rocks and the minerals we had passed, whilst our poor animals were luxuriating, and Caesar was sleeping.

At a great distance, and before us, where a forest of shrubbery seemed evident, a smoke was seen rising, which I decided was Fort Hall, to which we were aiming, and minuting its bearing by my pocket compass, we launched off into the (not grass, but sand covered) valley towards it.

We started at noon, and hoped to reach it before night. The Trois Buttes, three conical hills of granite, and of great height, standing in a group, and at many miles distance, were on our right. We travelled slow and night overtook us, and we encamped, not in sand, but in cinders and pulverized pumice, and without vegetation for our horses.

The valley, though beautiful to look into, like too many things in this world, when seen at a distance, is anything but beautiful when we get into it. The surface is generally without grass and without timber, or even bushes, excepting here and there bunches of artemisia, and everywhere covered with volcanic ashes and pumice, which are wafted by the winds; and all roads, and all tracks of living beings before us are obliterated before we see them.

No living animal or fowl is seen, to afford us food; not even a rabbit or a prairie hen; and the tail of our last dried salmon for *us,* and nothing for our poor horses, put us to sleep upon this barren and desolate waste.

Our course was continued in the morning, and about noon we came upon the bank of a small stream covered with luxuriant grass; and here we were *obliged* to stop, for our poor animals would have gone no further; and who could have had the heart to push them beyond it? But *we* had nothing to eat, and our only chance to get anything was to lay down and quietly wait till our animals were satisfied, and able to carry us, and then move on, which we did; and a little before sundown we approached the patch of timber we had seen, and soon after (not Fort Hall, but) the encampment of some twenty or twenty-five emigrants from the States, who had crossed the Rocky Mountains at the South pass, and were on their way to Oregon.

When we rode up to their tents, or wagons and carts (for these were mostly used for tents), they seemed as much surprised as ourselves; and if not the first sentence that I pronounced (certainly the *second* was), "Have you got anything to eat?" "Well, neighbour," (said one of them, a middle-aged man, who stepped forward as spokesman), "we are pretty hard up; our flour has long since gin out; but we have a plenty of hard biscuits, and some good salt pork." "Don't say any more, my dear sir," said I, "that's enough; we are just starving to death."

"*Oh, dear* ME," said his tidy and red-cheeked wife, as she jumped down from one of the wagons and came up to my stirrup, her face beaming with sympathy, "Dear *sir,* if you had come a little sooner! We had a nice pot of boiled beans and pork to-day, and I don't know - Sally! my *dear,* look into the iron pot and see if any of them beans is left!" Sally, without running to look, came to her mother, ejaculating, with a sort of a hiccup, "Oh *yes,* mother; I *know* there is a *heap* left; we didn't eat a *half* on 'em; and there's a *large lot* o' pork, too!"

Here my young readers must again *imagine* (to save space), how comfortable Caesar and I were made when there was a pot of boiled pork and beans all ready, and a plenty of hard biscuits, and good grazing for our horses; and in the midst of twenty-five intelligent persons, old and young, male and female, with all their traps and accoutrements, from the State of New Hampshire, on their way to a new and unseen home in Oregon.

What Caesar and I first did was to discuss the pork and beans, and how we did it need not be described; and other matters discussed in the course of the evening must be brief, if noticed at all in this place.

Thirty-six days before, this party had started from Fort Leavenworth, on the Missouri river, in eight wagons and two carts, drawn by oxen, and using no horses. Their wagons, which supported hoops covered with sail-cloth, were all made new and of great strength, expressly for the purpose. Their oxen were shod like horses, to preserve their feet, and grain was transported for their food, to be used in places where the grass should give out.

In rising from the prairies on to the arid plains of the mountain regions, the wood of their wagon-wheels shrunk, and the tires were loosened; and without smithing utensils their misfortunes became irreparable, and all but fatal to their existence. Wheels that went to pieces were left by the way side; wheels were withed and mended as well as ingenuity could devise, and changed from axle to axle until wagons were left, and at length oxen after oxen, as they died, or fell and gave out from fatigue which they could no longer endure. And when we met them, but three of their wagons remained, and less than half of their oxen were living.

Substantial food they had transported enough of; and their little children, as well as the rest of the party, were in good health; and all, yet in unbroken spirits, approaching, with a prospect, their new homes.

They had met that day a half-caste interpreter from Fort Hall, to which they had been steering, from whom they learned that the trading post was yet twenty miles in advance, which showed me how far Caesar and I had mistaken our course in entering the valley.

These people told me that, since they entered Sweet River Valley in the mountains, they had passed over one hundred and fifty carcasses of oxen lying by the wayside; some partly devoured by wolves and bears, and others not in the least decayed, though they had been dead for weeks and, perhaps, months. Such was the unaccountable and almost incredible pilgrimage, in those days, from the States to the "promised land" on the Columbian coast.

This party, where we found them, had left the travelled road for several miles to get grass for their cattle, and they assured me that, for fifty miles which they had last passed, there was not a blade of grass left for poor oxen or horses to live upon; and, by the interpreter they had met, they were informed that, such had been the crowd of emigrants over the mountains, that, for the distance of ten miles around Fort Hall, every particle of grass had been exhausted, and the people in the fort, as well as their horses, were in a state of almost absolute starvation, and had notified all emigrants and travellers to keep at a distance from them, where they and their animals might possibly find something to subsist upon.

This little caravan started the next morning on their route, in good spirits, leaving Fort Hall on their right, and steering for Fort Boissey, another trading house, one hundred and forty miles further west, towards their destined home.

Caesar and I "saddled up," and, to their great delight, started in company with them, our destination being the same. We were soon on the emigrants' road, and both they and we in absolute apprehensions of losing our animals conveying us, the poor creatures getting but here and there a bite of short grass that had been twenty times bitten by other animals before them.

The stench exhaling from the carcasses of oxen and horses that we passed on the wayside became sickening and almost unendurable. I did not count, but, I believe, that, in the two days, we passed more than fifty; and, in one of these instances, two of these poor creatures lay dead in the yoke together! Such was the lamentable fate of these poor and faithful beasts; after dragging man and his effects over the vast prairies and arid mountains, a distance of 1400 miles, and not even getting their food for it.

On the second day, the interpreter of whom I have spoken overtook us, galloping on a very fine horse - a half-caste Snake (or Shoshonee) Indian - a rakish looking young man, speaking French, English, and several Indian languages; dressed out in all the flaming colours that broadcloths and ribbons could give him, and carrying in his hand a first-rate rifle.

I at once suspected, and soon learned from him, that his business was that of galloping about amongst the lost, the straggling, and suffering parties that were traversing the country at that time, guiding them and interpreting for them, and depending upon their generosity for compensation.

Learning from him that one day's ride would bring us to the great, or "smoky" falls of the Snake River, the vicinity of which he told me was his native place, and with the whole localities of which he was familiar; I made an arrangement with him to conduct me there the next day, which he did, we having procured several days' provisions of the little, and as yet, stouthearted colony; and taken leave of them, at all events, for a few days.

They travelled so slow that we could easily calculate on spending a day or two about the falls, and overtake them before they reached the settlements. Our ride to the falls took us the most of two days, instead of "one," over a sandy and barren waste; but, with a guide who knew the way and the modes of the country, we felt secure, and rode it with tolerable ease.

The great, or "smoking," falls of the Snake River may well be classed amongst the greatest natural curiosities of the world. Not that they resemble, in character or magnitude, the *chûte* of Niagara; but, from a character peculiarly their own, of an awful grandeur which strikes the beholder in quite a different way.

For a hundred or two miles around, in different directions, the country is chiefly as barren a waste as the deserts of Arabia. The earth is everywhere almost entirely destitute of vegetation, and even of birds and insects, and covered with a light and moving sand or dust, composed of pulverized pumice and volcanic ashes.

In the midst of this vast plain of desolation we discovered, at many miles distance - not a pyramid of spray rising, forming and piling away a mass of clouds in the heavens, as we see above the fall of Niagara - but a chain, of several miles in length, of jets of spray, rising apparently out of the level ground, not unlike the smoke of the camp-fires of an army of men; and, approaching it, we can scarcely realize its origin until we are quite upon the brink, and the awful abyss, with all its grandeur, is beneath us; and, even then, it is but here and there that we can approach near enough on the sand-covered brink, with no tree or rock to cling to, to catch more than a partial view of the scene before us.

Instead of looking upwards, as we usually do, to see a waterfall, or of seeing it leaping off from the rock on which we are standing, all is here below us, at the bottom of an awful chasm, and the very surface of each successive fall is several hundred feet below us.

The term "Great Fall," and which has been known for more than half a century, is applied to a succession of leaps which the river makes within the space of three or four miles, dashing and foaming from side to side, in a zig-zag channel cut in the solid rock, varying from six hundred to eight hundred feet in width, with precipitous - and, much of the way, perpendicular - walls of basaltic rocks on either side, from one hundred and fifty to two hundred feet in height, and with here and there an avalanche or graded way, where, with great fatigue, and with somewhat of danger, we can descend to the bottom of the chasm, and, at the water's edge, behold with wonder and enchantment the spirit of these wild scenes.

Owing to the zig-zag shape of the channel, the views from these points are exceedingly limited; but the frantic rage (or play, for it seems to partake of both) of the leaping, bounding, and foaming torrent, dashing alternately from wall to wall, with the overhanging rocks on either side, furnish for the artist's pencil scenes of spirit and wildness which I never have been able to see anywhere else, and which no imagination could create.

Comparatively but a small portion of the cataract can be viewed from below, owing to the few chances there are of descending to the river's bed; and where we descend we are obliged to retrace our steps, as we can neither follow the shore nor cross the stream.

From the top of the wall, with great fatigue, and with the guidance of our good cicerone, I was enabled to see the whole extent of this wonderful scene. Owing to the depth of the chasm, when looking down from the top of the wall, the water seemed to be running nearly on a level, though its tremendous leaps and bounds, as well as the corresponding decline of the brink of the opposite wall, gave us something like an estimate of descent in the various *chûtes*.

The trappean bed through which this wonderful gorge is cut slopes to the west, and as the heights of the walls on either side are generally about the same, the gradual descent of the summit surface, for the distance of four miles, would indicate a near estimate of the descent of the river in that distance; and judging as well as I could from these premises, without the use of instruments, I was led to believe that the whole descent in four miles was something like three or four hundred feet.

I have seen some statements, recently made public, of travellers who reported the great perpendicular fall of Snake River to be 198 feet; "thirty-five feet higher than the fall of Niagara, and the volume of water quite equal to that of Niagara River." This statement is certainly quite Quixotic, and demands contradiction, if it were only for the benefit of school-boys' education.

The Snake River has its extreme source but about 150 miles above these falls, and has no large tributaries above the falls to swell it; therefore the statement that this volume of water is equal to that of the Niagara is necessarily incorrect. There is one point of view from which, looking up the stream, four or five successive leaps are seen in the distance, so ranged one above the other as to appear at the first glance to be one entire fall of great height; but from other points these are seen to be separated by intervening distances of a quarter or half a mile.

In all the cataracts which compose what is called the great or "smoking" fall on the Snake River, however terrific and picturesque they are, there is not amongst them, I should think, a perpendicular leap of more than forty feet. And the Columbia River at the Dalles, 400 miles below, after uniting the Snake and Salmon Rivers with the north fork of the Columbia, contains, from the nearest estimate I could make, but about one-fifth of the volume of water that passes over the fall of Niagara; and the Snake River, at the great (or smoking) falls, probably not more than one-twelfth or one-fifteenth part.

Few travellers who visit the fall of Niagara are aware of its real magnitude; no subject on earth more completely deceives the human eye. In 1830, I spent six months at the falls, making a survey and estimates for a model; and even then I was in ignorance of its real magnitude until I went to Black Rock Ferry, twenty-five miles above, where I ascertained by measurement the width of the river to be seven-eighths of a mile, and its average depth eighteen feet, and its surface movement four and a half miles per hour; which, as the river at that place glides over the smooth surface of a level rock, would give a mesne movement of four miles per hour. Such a moving mass of water, at the rate of a man under a fast walk, is easily contemplated; and with pen, ink, and paper, one can soon bring into cubic feet and avoirdupois weight, the quantity of water per minute, per hour (and per annum, if figures can define it), which pours through the rapids at Niagara, and leaps down a precipice of 163 feet.

Such is the might, and such the magnitude of Niagara, which, amongst waterfalls (like this little book amongst Indian books), still will stand without a rival on the globe!

After having examined all the features of the great falls, and made my sketches, we laid our course for Fort Boissey, following the course of the river for many miles, which still ran through a deep and rocky *cañon,* and from the summits of its banks we had often views of its deep-bedded and foaming waters, still dashing amongst rocks and down precipices, with a continuous wall on either side, of several hundred feet in height.

Near a ford which we were to make, we met an encampment of Shoshonee (or Snake) Indians, about thirty in number, and being all men, and without women, I supposed them to be a war party; but our guide said no that they had no enemies near them to fight, and had been down to Fort Boissey to trade. He knew them all - was amongst his relatives, and introduced us without any difficulty.

I had previously seen but a specimen or two of this tribe, and when meeting face to face this fine and elegant *troupe* of young men, I said to myself, "These are Crows!" The impression was instant and complete. I then said to our interpreter that these people resembled the Crows, whom I had just been amongst. "Well they may," said he. "The Crows are our friends and relations, and we know them all." I said, "then you are Toltecs." This I could not make him understand, as he never had heard of Mexico or Yucatan; but as the Snake Indians occupy a great portion of the mountains lying between the Crows and Mexico, it made a strong impression on my retina, as regards the origin of the Toltec and Aztec tribes, which history says poured down from the mountains of the North-West into Mexico and Yucatan.

These handsome young men had been playing a desperate game of ball at Fort Boissey, and having their ball-sticks and balls with them, were proud to show us what they could do with them. The ground was not good, but from the beautiful catches and throws which they made, I consider them quite a match for the Sioux or the Choctaws, and their rackets are formed much in the same way.

We spent a day very pleasantly with them, Caesar showing the pictures, and I painting three of the young men, their names *Yau-nau-shaw-pix, Na-wen-saw-pic* (he who runs up hill), *On-da-wout* (smooth bark).

All objected to being painted until the portrait of the Crow chief, *Ba-da-ah-chon-du,* was shown them; they all recognized him, and the gallant little fellow, "*Yau-nau-shaw-pix*," then sprang upon his feet, and throwing a beautiful Crow robe over his shoulder exclaimed, "There! you may paint *me* - I am not afraid."

The rest then all agreed to be painted, but I selected the three named above, and got the rest to wait until I should come again.

We parted, but not without regret, from our friends the Snakes (not *Rattle*-snakes), who went on their way to their village, near the base of the mountains, and commenced our winding and dangerous descent of some hundreds of feet, to the river shore, where we were to make the ford. There was no other place for a great many miles, where it was possible to descend to the bed of the river, or to ford it if we could get to it.

I had engaged our gay and dashing chevalier to lead us safely across the river, and to put us fairly in the track, for the frontier settlements, instead of Fort Boissey, which I felt a confidence in reaching from that place, without a guide, there being a well-beaten road to follow.

Down at the bottom of the terrible gulf, the river, with its transparent waters, was smoothly, but rapidly gliding along before us. The next thing was to cross it, and the thing next to that, to reach the opposite shore above, a huge point of perpendicular rocks projecting into the stream, and below which our interpreter said there was no chance of getting out.

The river here was some eighty or a hundred yards in width, with a pebbly bottom; and from the various contortions of the surface of the water, evidently of unequal bottom, and full of bars. Our guide explained to us, as well as he could, the circuitous route we were to take, after we should get into the stream, not to fall into the troughs and currents; and to show us the course, dashed in and led the way.

We stood and watched him closely, and seeing the water nowhere higher than his stirrups, our apprehensions were all at an end. He mounted about half way up the opposite cliff, and dismounting from his horse, sat overlooking our movements. We had but one fear, and that was for our pack-mule, which was a little creature; and Caesar, a tremendous tall fellow, said, "Massa Catlin, I radder wade, and den I take 'Nelly' moa safe."

"Well," said I, "Caesar, do so - give me the portfolio (which I slung on my own back), and I will lead your mule when I see you and Nelly safe over."

He handed me his pantaloons, and was on his way, his rifle in his left hand and his donkey in the other, whilst I was sitting on my horse and watching the result. When about the middle of the river, I observed they were at a halt; the mule was pulling one way and he the other. Instead of the lasso around its neck, he was leading it by a halter with a rawhide headstall, somewhat in the shape of a bridle. After mutual and stubborn pulling in this way for a minute or so, I saw Caesar, who had been standing up to his navel in the water, fall suddenly back, and quite under the surface of the water! The bridle had slipped from the animal's head, and they at once took different directions.

Caesar, it seems, falling backwards, was thrown from the shoal water into a deeper channel, where the current was stronger, and off from his feet, he was rapidly drifting away, his head and his hands now and then above the water!

I instantly threw my portfolio and my rifle to the ground, and dropping the rein of the mule I was holding, I plied my spurless heels with all the muscle that was in me, to the sides of my slow and stubborn "Rozenante" and thought, "Oh (not my 'kingdom,' but) my 'collection,' for a horse! for *'Charley'* for my *'Ancient Charley!'*" But I believe my convulsive kicks and blows frightened my poor beast into untried leaps and bounds, which soon passed me over the bar of shoal water into swimming depth, where Caesar, ahead of me, and not able to swim, was paddling with his hands, and keeping his head, most of the time, above the water.

He saw me coming, and I hailed him - "Hold on, my brave fellow - you are safe."

"Well, de Lord o' massie!" I heard him exclaim.

My horse was all below the water but its head and tail, and I was down to my armpits. There was but *one* way - and as I got near to him I said - "Now mind! - as I pass by you, don't touch me, but seize my horse by the tail, and hold on!"

I passed him, and looking back over my right shoulder and seeing nothing of him, I instantly exclaimed, "Oh, mercy! he's lost!" - when added to that, without a period or a comma -

"Dat ar berry good, now I guess I go ashoa!" And looking over my left shoulder, with an astonishment that nearly threw me from my saddle, I saw he had both hands clenched to the tail of his own riding mule, which, it seems, had plunged in when I threw down its bridle, and without my observing it, had swam by my side, and a little back of me, to the rescue of poor Caesar, who it was now pulling to the shore! I reined my horse towards the shore, and Caesar, holding on, was gliding along by the side of me -

"Well, Massa Catlin, dis ar beat all; I no feas now!"

Our horses' feet were now getting hold on the bottom, and at that moment came down the shore at full gallop, and dashing through the water, our faithful guide, who, thoughtless of any accident, had placed himself too far from us sooner to lend a helping hand.

We were all upon the beach, and safe, and our little pack-mule, with all our baggage soaked, had swam to the same shore from which it started, but half a mile below, and was standing in a nook of rocks, from which it did not know how to escape.

Our demi-"Snake" dashed into the river to recover it, and I hailed him - pointing to my rifle and portfolio, left on the beach. He soon had them strapped on his back, and the donkey in his hand; and, with little difficulty and without fear or danger, was soon with us.

"Now," said I, "Caesar, we are all saved, and there is but one thing that I see missing, that is the old minié."

Caesar, whatever might have been his education, or want of education, was a very moral and a religious man - a Catholic; and in all my travels with him, under the hundreds of instantaneous excitements and vexations which we had met together, I never heard him use a profane or an indecent word; but his sudden exclamations were, "De Lord o' massie! Oh, de goodness me! My soul alive!" &c; and on this occasion, such was his attachment to the minié rifle, "Well, as I am a libbin being, I guess, Massa Catlin, dat ar gun is neber seen no moa! I no recollection; but wen I slip in de deep water, I guess de minny has slip from my hands widout my know it; I berry sorry."

The fact luckily was, that the eyes of our guide had been upon it when it slipped from Caesar's hand, and, marking the place where it sank, he was now wading his horse to the spot, and with his eagle eye was scanning the bottom through the clear water, and, after wading and then swimming awhile, he gave a piercing yell and a wave of his hand, signifying that he had discovered it. He instantly rose, with his feet upon his horse's back, and making a plunge headforemost, brought it up; and then, not swimming for his horse, made his horse swim *to him,* for he had a long lasso of raw hide of ten yards in length, fastened around its neck, and its other end in his hand.

"Well, now, dat ar de mose wonderful man I eber saw yet! I neber see de like afoa!"

There is no sunshine in the deep and gloomy *cañon* of this part of the river; and rising the avalanching cliff, and fairly on its top and in the sun, our soaking packs were spread out to dry. We all took a lunch and a sleep, and our animals found a little grass to regale upon.

Our guide gave us instructions for the ride that Caesar and I were to make alone; and, putting into his bullet-pouch what he acknowledged as a liberal compensation for his services, he galloped off, intending to overtake his party of Snake warriors during the day.

In our course, after riding a mile or two, I halted, and said to Caesar, "Have you got your rifle dry and in order?"

"Yes, massa; and loaded."

"Then," said I, pointing to a bunch of wild sage at a little distance, "go and fetch that rabbit; it is a very large one, and has set down behind those weeds. Be careful, and don't touch anything but its head."

"Yes, Massa; you hold de mule."

This rabbit, the first fresh meat we had had for a long time, came in admirably well with our salt pork, and was the first creature of the kind that we had seen since we left the coast of the Pacific.

Six or eight days of hard work, and fording the Snake River at two different places on our way - (but why should I stop to narrate more particularly here?) - brought us to the border settlements near Fort Walla Walla. I had then a horse and two mules to dispose of - an affair that, as well as buying, I have always approached with a displeasure; for, until now, in all my travels, when I have wanted to buy horses, I have been "a little too late; there were a plenty here for sale a few days since, but the last of them have been bought up and taken away." And, when wishing to sell, "They would have brought you a good price a little back, sir; but so many have been brought in lately, that they are a mere drug now. You may be able to *give* them away, but I am not sure that you will even get a thankie for that."

However, in this instance, I was not long in looking up Thompson, the man of whom I bought the animals for my campaign to the Salmon River Valley. I said to him, "What will you give? they are all in tolerable trim, and as valuable as when I bought them." I expected him to name about half the price I had given him for them, and I was quite ready to have taken it.

"Well, I know the animals, and I don't care to give you the same that you gin me for them."

"Agreed," said I; and, having the money in his pocket, the affair was soon ended. I said, "Thompson, you are a very prompt dealer, and I like to deal with such men."

"Well," said he, "I'm glad you are satisfied, sir. You see, sir, there's just now sich a crowden into the diggins, that they've taken up the last crittur; and, notwithstandin' that, horses is about at a stand still, but mules has riz."

He got about double the price for his "critturs" an hour afterwards. They went to the "diggings," and Caesar and I steamed from Portland to California.

Chapter Five - California

The reader must not think that because we were again in California, we were at *home,* and our Indian peregrinations finished. In California we were on the wrong side of the mountains; and, as I hinted in a former chapter, that though a straggling Apachee was once in a while seen there, better specimens of that interesting tribe would probably be seen on our return.

The Apachee Indians, at this time probably the most powerful and most hostile tribe in America, hunt over and claim a vast extent of country within the Mexican lines, through the province of New Mexico, and extending northward nearly to the Great Salt Lake, and westward quite to the Pacific Ocean, embracing the silver mines of Sonora, and, until quite lately, the gold mines of California. At this last point continued struggles, with much bloodshed, have resulted from the claims of white people to the gold mines on the Sacramento River, and in and east of the Sierra Nevada. These Indians, met by the California miners, are known by various names, and so the Indians from San Francisco to St. Diego, and the peninsula of Lower California, though, they are but bands of the great family of Apachees, speaking dialects of the Apachee language.

The aggregate of this great tribe, when counted altogether, is something like 30,000; and the traveller who only meets a few of their border bands, or the gold-digger who sees only those bands on whose rights he is trespassing, gets but a partial knowledge of their real numbers, or of their actual strength.

I learned from one of their chiefs, the "Spanish Spur," that they could muster 8000 men, well mounted, and equipped in the same manner as a war party of 300, which I saw him review. This gallant fellow had gained his laurels in his battles with the Mexican troops on the Mexican frontier; and his name, from a pair of huge spurs which he often wore as trophies, taken from the heels of a Spanish officer whom he had killed in single combat.

The greater portion of this tribe are strictly migratory, changing the sites of their villages several times in the course of the year. And to reach the village of this chief's band, at present some thirty miles north of the Ghila, the voyageur should cross the Rocky Mountains from Santa Fe, taking the "Pony Express" route, or start, as Caesar and I did, from Santa Diego, on the Pacific Coast, with a strong mule under him, and a light mule to carry his packs, and ride to La Paz, on the Rio Colorado, and thence to the great village of the *Ghila Apachees* - north bank of the Ghila, some sixty or eighty miles from La Paz, and thence cross the mountains to Santa Fé.

The Apachees, like the Snakes, are a part of the Great Crow or Toltec family. As with the Snakes, from a wandering specimen or two I was not struck; but looking about me in the centre of the tribe, I was instantly impressed with the conviction of the relationship, and unity of type which I was regularly tracing from the Belantsea (or Crow) to the mountains of Mexico.

Like the Crows, their tradition is, that their tribe is the father of all the existing races - that seven persons only were saved from the Deluge by ascending a high mountain, and that these seven multiplied and filled again the valleys with populations; and that those who built their villages in the valleys were very foolish, for there came a great rain, which filled the valleys with water, and they were again swept off."

The Apachees in Mexico, being mostly in the vicinity of the Catholic missions, have made some progress in civilization, and are clad in pontchos, in leggings and tuniques of cotton-stuffs or of bark, and broad-brimmed hats of grass, of Spanish manufacture. In the province of New Mexico, and the vicinity of the Ghila, and the mountains of the North-East, they are dressed in skins, when dressed at all, and in their costumes and weapons bear a strong resemblance to the Comanches.

Their manufacture of flint arrow and spear heads, as well as their bows of bone and sinew, are equal, if not superior, to the manufactures of any of the tribes existing; and their use of the bow from their horses' backs whilst running at full speed, may vie with the archery of the Sioux or Shyennes, or any of the tribes east of the Rocky Mountains.

Like most of the tribes west of, and in the Rocky Mountains, they manufacture the blades of their spears and points for their arrows, of flints, and also of obsidian, which is scattered over those volcanic regions west of the mountains; and, like the other tribes, they guard as a profound secret the mode by which the flints and obsidian are broken into the shapes they require.

Their mode is very simple, and evidently the only mode by which those peculiar shapes and delicacy of fracture can possibly be produced; for civilized artizans have tried in various parts of the world, and with the best of tools, without success in copying them.

Every tribe has its *factory,* in which these arrow heads are made, and in those, only certain adepts are able or allowed to make them, for the use of the tribe. Erratic boulders of flint are collected (and sometimes brought an immense distance), and broken with a sort of sledge-hammer made of a rounded pebble of horn-stone, set in a twisted withe, holding the stone, and forming a handle.

The flint, at the indiscriminate blows of the sledge, is broken into a hundred pieces, and such flakes selected as, from the angles of their fracture and thickness, will answer as the basis of an arrow head; and in the hands of the artizan they are shaped into the beautiful forms and proportions which they desire, and which are to be seen in most of our museums.

The master workman, seated on the ground, lays one of these flakes on the palm of his left hand, holding it firmly down with two or more fingers of the same hand, and with his right hand, between the thumb and two fore-fingers, places his chisel (or punch) on the point that is to be broken off; and a co-operator (a striker) sitting in front of him, with a mallet of very hard wood, strikes the chisel (or punch) on the upper end, flaking the flint off on the under side, below each projecting point that is struck. The flint is then turned and chipped in the same manner from the opposite site; and so turned and chipped until the required shape and dimensions are obtained, all the fractures being made on the palm of the hand.

In selecting a flake for the arrow-head, a nice judgment must be used, or the attempt will fail: a flake with two opposite parallel, or nearly parallel, planes is found, and of the thickness required for the centre of the arrow-point. The first chipping reaches near to the centre of these planes, but without quite breaking it away, and each chipping is shorter and shorter, until the shape and the edge of the arrow head are formed.

The yielding elasticity of the palm of the hand enables the chip to come off without breaking the body of the flint, which would be the case, if they were broken on a hard substance. These people have no metallic instruments to work with, and the instrument (punch) which they use I was told was a piece of bone; but on examining it, I found it to be a substance much harder, made of the tooth (incisor) of the sperm-whale, or sea lion, which are often stranded on the coast of the Pacific. This punch is about six or seven inches in length, and one inch in diameter, with one rounded side and two plane sides; therefore presenting one acute and two obtuse angles, to suit the points to be broken.

This operation is very curious, both the holder and the striker singing, and the strokes of the mallet given exactly in time with the music, and with a sharp and *rebounding* blow, in which, the Indians tell us, is the great *medicine* (or mystery) of the operation.

The bows also of this tribe, as well as the arrow heads, are made with great skill, either of wood, and covered on the back with sinew or of bone, said to be brought from the sea-coast, and probably from the sperm-whale. These weapons, much like those of the Sioux and Comanches, for use on horseback, are short, for convenience of handling, and of great power, generally of two feet and a half in length, and their mode of using them in war and the chase is not surpassed by any Indians on the continent.

In Plate No. 14 are copies of three of my portraits made in their great village (*a*), the chief, *"Spanish Spur,"* wrapped in a beautiful buffalo-robe, with his battles painted on it; (*b*). *Nah-quot-se-o* ("the Surrounder"); (*c*). N*ic-war-ra* ("the Horsecatcher"), two distinguished warriors, in war costume and war-paint, armed, and ready for battle.

We remained several days in this village, and found abundance of curious customs and things for our amusement; and on the day before we left we had the luck to witness an excitement of curious interest, and which might, with propriety, be called "Tir-national."

Much like the Sioux and Comanches, this tribe are all mounted, and generally on good and fleet horses, and with their simple bows and arrows, from their horses' backs, while at full speed, they slay their animals for food, and contend with their enemies in mortal combat. With their short bows, which have been described, as they have but a few yards to throw their arrows (the rapidity of their horses overcoming space), their excellency in archery depends upon the rapidity with which they can get their arrows upon the string and off, and the accuracy with which they can throw them whilst their horses are at full speed. Their practice at this is often and very exciting, and certainly more picturesque than rifle-shooting of volunteers in the educated world.

For this day's sport, which is repeated many times in the year, a ground is chosen on the prairie, level and good for running, and in a semi circle are made ten successive circular targets in the ground by cutting away the turf, and making a sort of "bull's-eye" in the centre, covered with pipe-clay, which is white. Prizes are shot for, and judges are appointed to award them. Each warrior, mounted, in his war costume and war paint, and shoulders naked, and shield upon his back, takes ten arrows in his left hand with his bow, as if going into battle, and galloping their horses around in a circle of a mile or so, under full whip, to get them at the highest speed, thus pass in succession the ten targets, and give their arrows as they pass (Plate No. 15).

The rapidity with which their arrows are placed upon the string and sent is a mystery to the bystander, and must be seen to be believed. No repeating arms ever yet constructed are so rapid, nor any arm, at that little distance, more fatal. Each arrow, as it flies, goes with a yelp, and each bow is bent with a "wuhgh!" which seems to strain its utmost sinew, and every muscle of the archer.

This round and its scoring done, a little rest, and the same strife repeated. And after the tenth round, when each warrior's arrows have been claimed by his private mark in their feather, and the scoring done, the stakes and honours (not medals) are awarded, and a feast is given to the contending archers. I have seen "tirs-national" and "tirs-*inter*national," but amongst them all, nothing so picturesque and beautiful as this.

Taking leave of the great Apachee village, our little party (now consisting of two Santa Fé traders acquainted with the route two brothers Gleeson, of Texas, Caesar, and myself) laid its course for the "Santa Fé Pass," in the Rocky Mountains, unknown at that time as the "Pony Express" route, being, twelve years ago, but known to Kitt Carson and other guides in the habit of conducting parties through those dark and dreary solitudes.

The first mountain passed, in a beautiful valley we were in another Apachee village; and *another* mountain passed, we found another village of Apachees; and fifteen days of riding, of walking and leading, and prying and lifting on sides of hills, on avalanches of snow and mud, and through ravines, and in the beds of roaring and dashing torrents, with overhanging rocks, and gloomy hem locks and pines, we crept out of, and began descending, the eastern slopes of the Rocky Mountains, with the Spanish town of Santa Fé a great way ahead of us, and in the valley near it, the Rio del Norte (if we should ever get to it), an easy and safe highway to the Gulf of Mexico.

Descending from the base of the mountains into the plains, and rising out of a deep ravine, which we had followed for some miles, we came instantly, and without a moment's warning, on to a group of human beings, lying mostly stretched upon the grass, in a sunny place, without fire, and apparently seeking the warmth of the sun. Nothing could surpass the expressions of astonishment and fear exhibited on their faces when they arose, and seeing the inutility of trying to escape, they were, with uplifted hands, imploring for mercy, as we were all mounted and armed, and white men, their enemies.

The little party, about twenty, were all women and children but two, who were old men, and rheumatic, and were almost unable to walk. From our signs they soon saw that we did not wish to harm them; and riding up to them, we saw that they had not a weapon of any sort with them, and, from their haggard looks and signs, that they were in a state of starvation. We dismounted, and one of our Santa Fé companions, who understood something of the Apachee language, learned from them that they were the wives and children of a little village of Apachees that had been a few days before destroyed, and all their warriors killed, by a large army of white soldiers, after many terrible battles - that they had fled so far, and had nothing to live upon but roots from the ground, and no one to hunt for them that the whole country to the north and the east was full of white soldiers, and that the whole Indian race were being killed off!

This was the first knowledge we had of a border war that it seems was then raging between the United States dragoons and volunteers, and the Apachees, united with the Yutahs, their allies; and from which we drew the instant inference of the danger we were facing in moving further in the direction of Santa Fé!

We had no alternative but to leave those poor and helpless and pitiable objects, with their little children, as we found them, dividing with them our provisions, which were then running low, and laying our plans to save ourselves in the best way we could. I gave to one of the old men part of a box of lucifer matches I had, and showed him how to make fire with them, to warm their children by, for, from the snowy atmosphere from the mountains, the weather was very cold there; he thanked me as he took them, but said, "to make a smoke would be our certain destruction!" They all came up and shook hands with us, with the pitiful "Ya, ya," as we were mounting our horses; and with tears in our eyes, I believe all felt as I exclaimed, "Would to God that we could save those poor creatures!"

Our trail leading to the north-east, right into the hostile ground, was now a dangerous one, and I said to our Santa Fé companions, "Is it possible that these are Apachee Indians, and that a nation of Apachees is living on the *east side* of the mountains?" "Most assuredly, sir," said the Santa Fé gentlemen, - "the *Jiccarilla Band,* and half a dozen other bands; they are everywhere, and the greatest set of thieves and rogues in the world."

Our course was towards Santa Fé, but we rode in trembling and doubt; and a couple of hours after we left the group of women and children, whilst passing through a narrow and rocky defile, two dashing and naked Indians on high-mettled horses plunged into our view and in our path, some forty or fifty rods ahead of us. They halted for a moment, and evidently were alarmed, seeing us all with our rifles in our hands. There was no escape, except by retreat, which they seemed unwilling to attempt. We all agreed to move on without changing our course or halting; and they, no doubt discovering from our costumes and our pack-mules that we were a party of travellers, and not soldiers, advanced slowly, lowering their rifles, and we did the same, and made the signs of friendship at the same time.

We met and shook hands, and the foaming state of their horses showed us at once that they were riding on an express, the object of which we suspected, and our Santa Fé companions soon drew the same from them, and, also, that the whole country to the north-east was in a state of the most bloody warfare, that the country was filled with soldiers, and that several hundreds of the Jiccarilla Apachees and Yutahs had already been killed, and their villages burned, and that they two, one an Apachee and the other a Yutah, were on an express to the great Apachee villages west of the mountains, to call for reinforcements. Their halt with us was very short, and they rode off, suggesting to us very distinctly that the course we were pursuing was in a very dangerous direction. On emerging from this mountain defile, we struck upon a strong trail leading to the south-east, which was known to lead to St. Diego, a small village on the bank of the Del Norte.

Here, from the intelligence obtained from the two unexpected interviews we had just had, a sort of council of war was held, in which it was decided that the two Santa Fé traders and the elder Gleeson would continue on their route to Santa Fé, and run all the risks of meeting the Apachee and Yutah war parties; and that Caesar and I, who had no particular desire to see Santa Fe, should take the trail leading to St. Diego, and with us the younger Gleeson, who, like ourselves, was destined for Matamoras, at the mouth of the Rio del Norte. [1]

Our tracks here diverged; the one leading to Santa Fé tending to the northeast, and ours to the south-east. Ours was but an Indian trail, and difficult to follow, and was still over mountains, through valleys, and across rivers and swamps; and yet we kept it, not learning from any landmark, or from any human being, whether one day or one week would bring us to the bank of the Rio Grande, and knowing only by my faithful and never-failing little pocket-compass that we were advancing in the right direction.

Impressions are daily and hourly made in rides through such vast and dreary solitudes as these, that are never effaced from memory; and one, at the end of our first day's march, that was curious enough for narration. On a little plateau of a few rods in breadth, covered with grass, and near the bank of a small stream, with a tremendous and dreary forest of rocks and pines behind us, we had bivouacked at sundown, and for the night.

Gleeson had taken the lassos off the animals, and gone down a little descent, nearer the stream, where the grass was more abundant and fresher for the horses. Caesar had collected dried wood and made a rousing fire, and was boiling the pot, whilst I, at a distance of ten or fifteen rods from him, seated on the bank of the stream, and with my back towards him, was making a sketch of the picturesque landscape before me. "My soul *alive!* wat you want dar?" suddenly exclaimed Caesar; and turning round, I saw him on one hand and one knee, by his fire, swinging around and over his head a flaming firebrand; and in the direction where he was aiming it, and but a few rods from him, two grizzly bears of the largest kind, one seated, and the other in advance, and galloping upon him!

The firebrand fell a few feet before it, when the beast sprang upon it with both paws, and seized it in its mouth! He dropped it, and wheeling about, and crying in the most piteous manner, retreated, wiping his nose and his paws upon the grass.

The female, with the curiosity (perhaps) natural to her sex, must have a smell of it too, and was advancing for the purpose. An instant snuff (and I think a *taste*) was enough for her too, and they both galloped off together, whining in the most doleful manner as they disappeared amongst the rocks!

Gleeson knew nothing of the affair until he heard our relation of it; and all of us, without our weapons in hand, were spared the necessity of asking mercy of those unmerciful beasts, only by the whirling of a firebrand which Caesar happened to have in his hand at the moment, instead of vainly attempting to run for his rifle!

Delivered thus from the jaws of those monstrous animals, which had gone off evidently with a distaste for us, we began collecting wood for the night, each of us carrying a firebrand in his hand, as a precaution; and, between two rousing fires, and our horses close picketed to our heads, and one of the three always on sentry, we slept tolerably well.

After several days from this, and continuing our course over hills and valleys, and, in the latter part of the way, having lost the trail, we at length approached a conical hill of considerable height, and with the appearance of a low, level country beyond it, which we had reason to believe was, at last, the valley of the Rio Grande del Norte, and that we must necessarily be nearing the settlements on its borders.

It was agreed that Gleeson should turn it on the right, and that Caesar and I would flank it on the left; and that, as our horses were shod, and a sandy plain with thin grass was around it, we could not cross each other's tracks without recognizing them; and, in this way, with a certainty of joining company again somewhere beyond the mound, one or the other of us would probably stumble upon some trail leading to the settlements.

Caesar and I, after a few miles, came upon a well-beaten track of shod horses, showing us beyond doubt that we were near the settlement; and, in a little time, following it, we turned a small hillock and came upon a settler's hut - a well-built log house - and its smoking chimney showed us that it was occupied. We rode up in front of it, and a nice and tidy middle-aged woman, with two little children, came to the door.

I addressed her in Spanish, inquiring how far we had yet to ride to reach the Mission of St. Diego, or any other town on the Rio del Norte. She replied, in English, that she did not understand Spanish. I then asked her in English, when she promptly answered that we could not get to the river that night.

"Then," said I, "good woman, can we get lodging here to-night, and something to eat; for our provisions are entirely out?"

"Well, sir," said she, "I am very much ashamed; we have been here but a very short time, and we hain't got things a goin' very well yet; but you shall be welcome to the best we have got, if you can put up with it."

"Don't have any fears, madam," said I; "we are not very particular, and I know what allowance to make. We don't require beds; we have each a good buffalo robe, and all we will ask will be a part of the floor to spread them on where the planks are not too hard."

"Well, I'm sorry to say, sir, we hain't got our floor laid yet. We've nothin' but some birch bark for floors now, but I think you will find 'em dry."

"That's enough, madam; the principal thing we want is shelter."

We dismounted, and Caesar picketing the horses, - for there was abundance of good grass I then sat down in conversation with the good-natured woman.

"I can give you a steak," said she, "and panbaked bread, and a cup of coffee, but we have no sweetening for it but molasses."

"Never mind," said I; "that's quite enough - we don't wish to fare better."

From a few minutes' conversation, I learned that she was a native of Ohio; that she was married in Texas, and, a year or two previous, had, with her husband, moved to Santa Fé; and, not satisfied with Santa Fé life, they had squatted on the fine little prairie of rich land on which they were living, which cost them nothing; and that they had no neighbours nearer than three miles.

Caesar and I had supped on the steak and coffee promised us, and we had enjoyed it very much; and night had approached. "But Gleeson, where is he? he has not arrived, he has not struck our trail! May-be a grizzly bear has chewed him up, or that some of those Navaho Indians have taken his scalp in order to get his horse. We have got to go back in the morning and look him up."

The morning seemed to come very quick; and, having taken a steak and our coffee the same as the evening before, Caesar led up our animals, and, as we were saddling them, Gleeson turned the little hillock and rode up.

His circuit the day before had been so much longer than ours, and having been impeded by a difficult stream to cross, he had struck our trail too late in the day to overtake us, and had slept in his saddle all night, without anything to eat. I presented him to our kind landlady, and told him I believed he could get a steak for his breakfast. But the poor woman, who seemed embarrassed at this, replied that she was sorry she could not give him a steak; "for," said she, "I cooked the last I had for your breakfast. We can't get any meat here, gentlemen, except what my husband kills with his gun. All game is very scarce now, and he has had very bad luck lately; he was out all the day before yesterday and got nothing; and yester day he went out again, and hasn't got back yet; and, to tell the plain truth, we have had no meat but that *painter* for the last two weeks."

"Painter!" said I, "what painter?"

"Well, *dear* me! now, I'm afraid I forgot to tell you that them steaks was *painter's* meat. I should have mentioned it; and if I forgot it, I hope you will excuse me."

Gleeson, who was standing by, and starving, relieved the poor woman in a measure from her embarrassment by exclaiming, "Why, my good woman, I am nearly starved to death; I could eat anything! Have you not got the *tail* of the panther left? I could make a breakfast on that, without any ceremony."

"Well, no, sir; I am sorry also to say that the animal was very fat, and we roasted the tail the first night when it was brought in."

I helped the kind woman as well as I could, by assuring her that the steaks which we had eaten were very good, and that I should be glad if I could get another like them for my supper. And sympathetic Caesar, who had been listening, put in, "Well, I guess, missus, no harm is done, anyhow."

Gleeson took a turn at the pan-baked bread and coffee, after which we took leave of the good and hospitable woman, by leaving with her what Caesar called "a silber dolla," though she positively refused to make any charge for what we had eaten.

We reached the Rio Grande del Norte, sold our jaded animals - in my accustomed way - for less than half the price we had paid for them, took a "dug-out" [2] and paddles, and began drifting towards Matamoras, then eight hundred miles ahead of us.

This, being in the spring of 1855, was five years before the civil war in the United States, and seven years before the French invasion of Mexico; so that all was peace and goodwill on the banks of that noble and beautiful river, of which I may say something more near the end of this book, if there should be space enough for it. From Matamoras, a sailing vessel took Caesar and I to Sisal, in Yucatan; and, after a very short visit to Uxmal, and some points of interest on the coasts of Campeachy, I started for Liverpool.

Discoveries I had made, not amongst *Indians,* but amongst *rocks,* decided me to make a visit to my friend and correspondent, the Baron de Humboldt; and, in July of 1855, I started for Berlin. I was received with great kindness by that great philosopher, and by him was presented to the King and Queen of Prussia, at "Sans Souci."

The Baron de Humboldt approved, without exceptions, the theory I had come to advance with regard to the rocks of America, and which interesting subject was then determining me to make a second voyage to South America and the West India Islands.

Of my interviews with him, and the objects I had in view in visiting the greater and lesser Antilles, more will be said in a future chapter of this book. Enough at present. With letters from him to his old travelling companion, "Bonpland," then living in Uruguay, and others, I sailed for Cuba; and, having visited most of the lesser Antilles, steamed for Rio de Janeiro; and, with Patagonia and Terra del Fuego ahead of me, there were rocks and Indians enough yet in advance for long and patient investigations.

[1] After reaching the frontier settlements I learned that a most relentless and bloody war had been waged for several months past between the United States forces and the Apachee and Yutah Indians; that Lieutenant St. Vrain and Colonel Fontleroy, with large forces, had destroyed a great many of the Apachees, and that our position had been one of great danger.
[2] A pirogue.

Chapter Six - Rio de Janeiro

Ascriptions of long voyages, in a short book, must necessarily be discursive and disjointed; and with jumps like those of kangaroos, they must *leap,* not *creep,* from. points to points, that voyage incidents and the end of the book may terminate together.

Under this necessity, from the beginning of the first volume, I have had the somewhat painful task of inviting the reader to *imagine* the intervening incidents, which the want of space has often prevented me from narrating. In this dilemma we now are. After a long and interesting voyage - or series of voyages - we are at Rio de Janeiro, in Brazil; a beautiful city, with its overtowering escarpments of black and frowning rocks behind it, and the marvellous bay of Botafogo, like a beautiful apron, in front of it. Its foaming and dashing cascade of the Corcovado is a fixture, and, like the rest, an ornament eternal. But what are more beautiful - or, at all events, more exciting and interesting are its grand, and mighty, and impenetrable forests, and rivers, and swamps, and mosquitos, and fireflies, and butterflies, and alligators, and tigers, and monkeys, and parrots, and Indians, that lie west and south of it.

Rio, I have said, is a beautiful city; its rocky walls are grand, its Botafogo charming, its Plaza amusing, and its museum; its inhabitants are gay and rich, and its ladies are beautiful; its civilization is of a high and noble cast. But what of all this? why should we stop here? The Bay of Botafogo, and these dark and frowning escarpments of rocks, and the glistening cascade of the Corcovado will be the same a thousand years hence; the Plaza will be better built, its inhabitants will be more rich, its civilization will be higher; and its ladies, not more beautiful, but there will be more of them. Then why detain us now? We travel to see the *perishable,* not the *eternal.*

These grand and sublime forests which we are to enter will soon fall by the axe; these beautiful, crouching, creeping, spotted, and glistening tigers, and the muddy alligators, will soon be seen, with glass eyes, in our museums; these thousands of leaping, vaulting, and peeping monkeys, and chattering parrots and parroquets, and gilded butterflies, and anacondas will be there also; and all those endless clusters and bouquets of wild flowers, and everything else of Nature's blossoming and breathing works, including the wild and frolicsome Indian, who now exultingly smiles as he draws his long and unerring bow amidst the jungle, or paddles his light canoe, are soon to be metamorphosed - to be spoiled, if not obliterated, by the ruthless march of civilization.

Why, then, stop to see the imperishable and the progressive, which can be seen a hundred years hence as well as now? We are of a different caste and a different taste. We travel to see the perish able and the perishing; and let us see them before they fall; let us hie away then to Buenos Ayres. There are no Indians, no tigers, no alligators, no anacondas, here. The steamer leaves tomorrow for Buenos Ayres. I'll take this little book along, and my pencils. The

Uruguay, with its clear and blue waters comes in there, and on it, in their light canoes, the tall and handsome *Payaguas,* the *Tobos,* the *Linguas,* and the *Bocolis,* and the *Botocudas.*

The mighty Paraguay comes rolling along there also, with the waters of the long Parana, both rising in the mountains in the centre of the empire; and, in their course of 1800 miles, afford a highway and food for more than fifty tribes of Indians, and their waters and their shores, localities for 50,000 tigers, 150,000 alligators, 1,000,000 of monkeys, 5,000,000 of parrots, tens of thousands of anacondas and rattle snakes, and, now and then, a boa-constrictor.

What a delightful field have we then before us at Buenos Ayres! And yet, not far off, to the south, the *Aucas,* the *Puelches,* the *Auracanos,* the *Patagons* and *Fuegians*. Oh, how inviting and how exciting! I cannot crowd them all into this little book, I am sure of it; but I will abridge when I can, and go on while the paper lasts.

Caesar left me a year ago, at Sisal, and I am lost. The vessel that took us from Matamoras was going from Sisal to Para, and there he was impatient to unfold to *"Sally Bool,"* a beautiful mulatto girl, who sells oranges at the head of the quay, the wonders of his voyages. Our parting was sorrowful, as my young readers can easily imagine - he going to see his old sweetheart, "Sally Bool!' and I going to my old friend, the Baron de Humboldt. We shook hands three times, and, at the end of the last shake, he exclaimed, "Oh, de Lord preserb you, good Massa Catlin!" I never will forget it.

My friend Thomas, in whose house J was made welcome whilst in Buenos Ayres, recommended to me a faithful servant man - Jose Alzar (pronounced Althar) - whom he had employed for several years, and whose native place was Corrientes, some hundreds of miles up the Paraguay, and at the mouth of the Rio Parana. His knowledge of the country, and of several of the Indian tribes, and of their languages, was just the thing for me; and, with Jose Alzar, I was again soon ready, by steamer and canoes, and without horses, for Indian peregrinations.

I put into Alzar's hands the now famous minié rifle, first carried on the Essequibo and the Trombutas, as has been described, by my worthy companion Smyth, and afterwards by Caesar, for more than ten thousand miles. I reduced the number of cartoon portraits, in the portfolio, to about a dozen, and, strapping it on to his back, we started on a steamer for Corrientes.

Of Corrientes, which is a large and flourishing town on the right bank of the river, I have little other recollection than that of seeing from the deck of the steamer, before we landed, several groups of tents of Indians lining the shore of the river, above and below the town.

I recollect landing and taking my luggage to an hotel; but my subsequent and stronger impressions were got in the wigwams, to which I was a quick and constant visitor.

One can easily imagine the facilities and the confidence rendered me by my new *employee,* who was now in his native town, and with the Indians of his personal acquaintance around him. Three families of the Payaguas tribe were there, and several tents of the Botocudos, who had made long voyages in their canoes, and were soon to return to their native countries.

The Payaguas, the representatives of a tribe nearly extinct, and whose modes were purely primitive, were chiefly naked - both men and women wearing but a "fig-leaf" the width of the palm of one's hand, made of cotton-cloth or of bark - made a new impression upon me, of native man in physiological development and dignity. Not even the Osages or the Shyennes of North America were equal in stature to them, nor man whom I ever saw in any society. Six feet and nine inches, six feet and seven inches, and six feet and six inches, were the measurements of the three men of the party, and six feet the measure of a boy of sixteen years.

My interpreter, who had seen the whole of the tribe, assured me that these were about an average of the tribe; and these men told me there were many others taller than themselves. And until I shall see the Patagons, I shall believe them the tallest race in America. They are canoe Indians, and, like all of that class, from the constant use of their brachial and pectoral muscles, are broad and muscular in the chest and shoulders, but, in proportion, slight in their legs, from their habitual squatted positions and little use of their nether limbs.

The *Payaguas* live on the right bank of the Paraguay, and have, on the opposite bank, the *Chacos*, a race of horsemen, who have extensive prairies for the chase, and consequently, like the prairie Indians of North America, exhibit a different symmetry in proportions. These two tribes, though always at war with each other, and inveterate enemies, have been unable mutually to inflict more than partial injuries on each other the canoe-men too wise to be caught upon the prairies, and the horsemen unable to contend upon the water.

The Payaguas live chiefly in one long cabin or tent (*tolderia*), in the form of a shed, standing on the bank of the river, of some thirty or forty rods in length, built of upright posts at equal distances, set in the ground and covered with a curious and beautiful thatching of palm leaves - a roof merely, and no walls, with a curtain of palm leaves or of rush mats forming a hanging partition between the different families. A community excessively droll, and too closely associated to be otherwise than social and peaceably disposed.

They live principally on fish and turtle, with which the river abounds, which are easily taken, and, at all seasons of the year, without the slightest danger of default.

The Botocudos, who come from near the sources of the Uruguay, are quite a different race in appearance and in language; the remnants of a warlike and numerous tribe, recently reduced to a few hundreds by those universal pests of the American Indians - rum, and whiskey, and the small-pox. Of ordinary stature, they are a better proportioned race than the Payaguas, and with an approach to civilization, are in a measure clad, with tuniques and ceintures of cotton-cloth, which they barter for with the border traders.

Both the Botocudos and Payaguas wear the block of wood in the under-lip as an ornament, like the Nayas Indians of Queen Charlotte's, in North America, and already spoken of. How surprising this fact! that, on the north-west coast of North America and on the south-east coast of South America, almost the exact antipodes of each other, the same peculiar and unaccountable custom should be practised by Indian tribes, in whose languages there are not two words resembling, and who have no knowledge of each other. Such striking facts should be preserved and not lost, as they may yet have a deserved influence in determining ultimately the migration and distribution of races. In plate No. 16 I have given copies of three of my portraits of Botocudos, illustrating the singular customs above described.

Who can imagine, who can understand, but myself, the astonishment and also the amusement which my portfolio produced amongst these poor people, when I showed them a couple of portraits of the Nayas Indians, with the block of wood in their under-lips, whom, as I told them, I had recently visited, and who were at least three hundred days' march (their only mode of computing long distances) from them, and also on the exact opposite side of the earth, which was round - a new idea to them?

What a pity poor Caesar lost this! By the portraits which I showed them, I explained also that the custom of slitting and elongating the ears, and wearing in them oval blocks of wood, was precisely the same, when the chief of the party pronounced them "brothers," and a facetious old *medicine-man,* with his head painted white, disposed to be witty, observed that he thought "the Nayas Indians were very *distant* relations."

By going to my hotel and opening my luggage, I was able to return in a little time to these astonished people, with three of the blocks which I had brought from the Nayas tribe, and which were polished by long use. At the sight of these, which they could take in their hands, they seemed to draw more practical proof, and all the men set up a terrific howl, started by the medicine-man, whilst the women covered their mouths with both hands. This, my interpreter told me, was their mode of recording a truth, an *established, proved* fact, which no one was allowed afterwards to deny. A *recorded fact.*

I explained to them the slight difference in the shape of the blocks those of the Nayas, as seen in plate No. 10, being of an oval form, and concave on the upper and lower sides, and grooved around the rim, whilst those of the Payaguas and Botocudos were round, and both surfaces and the rim perfectly plane.

The chief replied to this, that he could recollect perfectly well when the Payaguas shaped their blocks in the same manner as the Nayas; but, for the greater facility of slipping them in and out, and also to save the labour of excavating them, for which their tools were very bad, they changed their shapes to what they now are. On inquiring what their object was in wearing such things in the lip and in the ear, I met at once some difficulty, which seemed to be raised by the fidgety old *medicine-man*. He seemed to meet the inquiry with some suspicion, or to treat it, at least, as he suggested, as a thing which I ought to have learned from my friends, the *Nayas,* "on the other side of the world," - a queer thing running still in his head; and, as I learned through the interpreter, had fed him to doubt, in some measure, my strict sanity.

The chief, however, took a different view of the affair, and gave me in a very few words, as well as he could, an answer to my inquiries. He said, in the first place, he believed the reason why the custom was practised was that their ancestors had practised it before them; that he had always thought it a very foolish practice, and, as it was chiefly confined to the women, it was not likely to do any harm; that the women seemed to think it improved their appearance, and that, in such things, the men generally let the women have their own way.

He said, there was now and then a man to be seen with the block in his lip, but that in such cases it only got him the name of an "old woman." The men of his tribe, he said, all have the under-lip pierced, so as to wear ornaments of various kinds. "This we can't avoid," said he, "for it is done by our mothers, when we are infants and under their sole control; and there are many men in our tribe whose ears and lips have been thus cut, and who never have worn an ornament of any kind in them, and I think it is much the best way."

In speaking of this strange custom amongst the Nayas Indians of British Columbia, I described the manner in which the orifice in the lip was produced, as well as the mode of slitting and elongating their ears, by wearing weights in them, and the mode seems to be precisely the same here.

After having expressed my surprise at finding two peoples, on opposite sides of the globe, practising alike this unaccountable custom, it is not less surprising that the Rev. Dr. Livingstone should have found a native tribe in the centre of Africa wearing blocks exactly similar in shape and dimensions in the *upper-lip,* and called by the natives, Pé-lé-lé (pronounced *Pay-lay-lay*).

From his description, the blocks are from one-and-a-half to two inches in diameter, and the mode of perforating the lip in childhood, and increasing the size of the blocks as the wearer advances in age, are the same as I have described above; and he adds, that the only object for which they are worn, as far as he could learn, was that of ornament.

Now if, in my eccentric peregrinations, I should stumble on to a tribe, or meet an individual Indian lady, ingenious enough to have united the two - wearing a block both in the upper and the under lip - what a beautiful and useful improvement it would be, and what a wonderful addition to the honourable discoveries of my roving life - *a double Pay-lay-lay!* The very thought of its being a possibility ahead of me, stimulates me, and Alzar and I will move on.

A sort of barge, not unlike the keel-boats of the Missouri, propelled by eight oars, and freighted, not unlike the crafts of that river, with stuffs, and hardware, &c, (and, no doubt, in the bottom of the hold, with rum and whiskey), was starting for the upper waters of the Parana; and Alzar agreeing to handle an oar, and myself to lend a hand in rapid water, got us an agreeable and amusing passage to the mouth of the Iguazu River - a distance of 500 miles - from which point we designed to cross the country to the upper waters of the Uruguay, and descend that river to Buenos Ayres, visiting many tribes of Indians on its banks, and killing some of the black tigers that fatten on the peccaries and soft-shelled turtles that abound along its shores.

Alzar, with these boatmen, was at home; and his acquaintance with them and their modes of life made the boat, though a rough one, an agreeable home for me.

I had promised him, at the end of our campaign, in addition to his monthly wages, to leave him, as a present, the minié rifle; and one can imagine better than I can describe it, the infinite pleasure he was taking in cleaning, polishing, and handling it, and "heaving his lead ashore," as Smyth used to do on the banks of the Trombutas and Essequibo. Alligators, peccaries, swans, wild geese, and ducks, were constantly marks for him; and his long and deadly shots were not only amusement, but astonishment for his comrades, who never before had seen a minié rifle, or even dreamed of its long range and accuracy.

The high and perpendicular walls of red sand stone, and overtowering forests of lofty trees, alternating from one side to the other, and fronted by islands and the opposite shore, covered with forests of orange and wild peach trees, bending down with their yellow and red fruit, and interspersed and interwoven with the deep green of rhododendrons and the massive purple of thorn blossoms, presented a picture as new to me, as if the river and mountain scenes of my former voyages I had passed blind folded.

"Sam," - a name not made known even to Alzar as yet - "Sam Colt," a six-shot carabine, made expressly for me by my old friend, Colonel Colt, and which has answered to the nick-name of "Sam" in my former travels, had been so far under cover; but the constant flapping of wings about and over us, and the total nothingness else for me to do, brought it out, and a new excitement and a new astonishment amongst the boatmen, who had barely heard the word "*revolver*" pronounced, but never in those days had had the chance of seeing one.

But why should I spend time and space here, with the thousands of incidents that took place on this beautiful river? We have a long journey before us, Indians in abundance, and, perhaps, a double *Pay-lay-lay;* and, getting towards the end of my little book, I may have yet to strike, out the fifty last pages that have been written. One thing, however; by the way, rowing against the stream, we saw few tigers - not even their heads - for, at the grunting of our boatmen and the noise of their oars, they lowered themselves in the weeds, and peccaries stood in the shade as we passed; but the wildfowl, unused to the sound of a gun, sufficient for our larder, I daily seduced with "Sam," from my comfortable seat - a keg - which made me a sort of "figure-head" in the bow of the boat.

Rapids became frequent, and laborious, and tedious, and were said to be more so ahead of us, and the sun insupportably hot; and, before our 500 miles were finished, we were at Candeloria, a small town on the east bank of the river, where our trading companions had business to do, and an encampment of Botocudos promised work for me, and Alzar and I halted. After a couple of days, our trading companions continued on their course, and we got conveyed across the "*Entre Rios*" mountain to the small village and mission of Conception, on the upper waters of Uruguay.

Alzar renewed old acquaintances there, and with the "old minié" in his hands and the portfolio of Indian portraits on his back, and the tact and facetiae of a son of a Portugese father and a Creole mother, one can easily imagine rapidly gaining new ones, and raising a sort of *furor* in the peaceable and silent little village into which we had entered.

No Indians were there, and after sleeping two days ahead, whilst Alzar was stipulating for a "dug-out" canoe, and laying in salt meat, coffee, sugar, salt, &c, for our voyage down the river, I stepped with him into our lazy, ugly, but solid and steady little craft, in which he had seated a stout and first-rate paddler of his old acquaintance, who was wanting to go to Buenos Ayres, and was willing and glad of the chance if he could be allowed to "work his passage."

To this lucky occurrence there was no objection; and with three good paddles and three good paddlers (not peddlers) from *Conception* - a very good starting point? - we started off.

To go down stream in a solid and dry canoe, in such a climate, and on so clear and beautiful a river, with hard biscuits enough, and coffee, and sugar, and salt, and a few pounds of salt pork for cooking, and plenty of powder and ball and fishing-tackle, is one of the delightful things of this world. To paddle or to sleep, as we choose, we still go on, and the stillness with which we can travel brings us within pistol-shot, if we wish it, of the staging tigers, whose heads are above the grass and weeds on the bank.

As Smyth and I had been tiger-shooters on the Trombutas, so Alzar and I, with the same weapons, were tiger-slayers on the shores of the Uruguay. And why not? It costs nothing, no apprenticeship is necessary; no courage, or rashness, or recklessness is called into question; no great skill in shooting is requisite, for they hold their heads perfectly still - there is a beautiful mark in the centre of their foreheads, the right spot exactly, where the black lines radiate - the smooth current does not in the least interfere with our range, and brings us within fifty paces if we desire it.

The whole cost, therefore, is the price of a conique ball and a charge of powder. And for these, if the animal be fat, which is generally the case, the tail itself pays a hundred times over, and leaves us the skin, which is worth twenty dollars.

"A tiger's tail, ha! you eat a tiger's tail?"

Yes, to be sure, a tiger's tail - but it cannot be cooked in a kitchen - it would be useless to try it. It must be bandaged in the leaves of the wild cabbage (or *wapsipinnican*), and roasted under the embers of a camp fire, on the ground. Nothing that ever was cooked exceeds it in deliciousness of flavour, and pleasure of digestion. These often weigh some six or eight pounds, and an evidence that they are, by the Indians, considered the choicest of food, is, that, in my South American travels, I have met at least a dozen Indians of the highest rank, surnamed the *"Tiger's Tail,"* from some peculiar excellence; and I have myself twice received this high and flattering distinction from those poor people who have hearts, but no decorations, to give.

Like the Rio Trombutas, the banks of this beautiful river are chiefly covered with dense and magnificent forests, abounding in monkeys and parrots, and peccaries and tigers, and the bed of the stream, from their emptied shells on the beach, would seem to be paved with soft-shelled turtles. Fish of many kinds, and of delicious flavour, and for the names of which I was obliged to appeal to Alzar, were constantly raised by our trolling lines. And ducks and geese - and swans and pelicans if we wanted them - were constantly at our service, and an easy prey; and the islands of the lower half of the river, like those of the Parana, covered with oranges and wild peaches of delicious flavour.

We generally slept on islands, for on them tigers more seldom walk, and rattlesnakes generally fail to reach them; but on these, as on the main shore, like the islands and shores of the Missouri and the Amazon, those invulnerable and unconquerable pests, as universal and as omnipresent in that country as the air itself, the relentless mosquitos, were always at war with us as soon as the sun was down.

On the shore at that time it was necessary to be, to boil the pot and cook our food, but that done, and each one armed with a bunch of bushes, our provisions and culinary articles were taken into our canoe, and pushing into the stream, and whipping off, the flying, whirling cloud was soon ashore; and casting anchor, we had till ten o'clock, or thereabouts, a quiet and delightful time to get our first nap in our canoe. At that hour, by some police that those creatures have, and which I never could exactly understand, hungry or not hungry, they are all housed until near sun-down of the next day.

So at ten o'clock, or a little after, we always went quietly to the shore and slept - "where?" Not in hammocks, but in our strong and dry canoe, ready, at a moment's warning, if danger was at hand, to push off upon the boiling current. And if it rained, by an unrolled mat, constructed of palm-leaves by Alzar and his passenger, as we floated along, covering the canoe from stem to stern, we were perfectly protected from the entrance of a drop of water. The heaviest thunder-showers pelted us, and poured on to us, but in vain; but against mosquitos our roof was no proof, for where air comes, in South America, there *will* come (during their daytime) mosquitos also.

And how strange! What a mysterious order of nature! The billions on billions of millions of these sanguiniverous insects created to exist but a few weeks of time, with a taste for blood, and a proboscis for boring, and for drawing it through the thickest of hides, and, probably, not one in a hundred millions ever tastes the food they were made to procure and enjoy; and from which, if they are allowed to be gorged by it, they are known to die in a few minutes.

How strange also, that the beautiful provision of nature, given them for penetrating the skin, and drawing the food which nature has indicated for them, should inflict such insupportable pain as completely to defeat their efforts to procure it! No animals of the country allow a mosquito to bite; and man, at the few points where he is exposed, though he often feels the sting, allows the insect no time to draw his blood.

Is it then that here is an order of nature frustrated, or was it the intention of nature that the proboscis of these murderous creatures should have been used for a different purpose, and that the cruel and sanguinary use they are making of them is but a wicked perversion of an instrument intended for a different object?

How strange, also, that the proboscis of this insect, which will go through the thickest clothing and the skin of a white man, and even at times through his buckskin leggings, has little or no effect upon the naked Indian, not that it lacks the power, or that the blood is not as easily' drawn, for the Indian's skin is as soft and as thin as that of a white man.

There have been various theories advanced on this subject. Some have supposed some peculiar quality in the Indian's blood make it unpalatable to the mosquitos. And others have thought that the Indians had some oil or drug which they rubbed over their bodies and limbs as a protection; but it is more probable that the constant smoke they live in, and which mosquitos always avoid, forms a surface on the skin repugnant to the olfactory nerves of the insect.

The Indians of South America, and particularly those of the Amazon, sleep under sheds, in the open air, and entirely naked, unmolested by mosquitos, where a white man, bound with cords, and naked, could not possibly exist one hour; not loss of blood, but inflammation, would be the death of him. And if the whole human (civilized) race of the globe were spread over the valley of the Amazon and its tributaries, and exposed in the same way, one day, from sundown to ten o'clock at night, would end the whole of them.

But enough of tigers and mosquitos. I fear I shall have to strike them all out of my little book before I get through, for want of space. We are travelling with the Indians. However, I will venture to insert here the following recipe which I wrote out to please Alzar; and after that we will proceed on our course.

How to make Mosquito Soup

"RECIPE. - Descending the Missouri or Arkansas rivers in North America, or the Corontyns or Uruguay in South America, run your canoe ashore in a thick bottom, just at sundown, having filled your tin kettle about half full of river water, which is very pure and wholesome. Before landing, however, throw a couple of spoonfuls of salt (or, what is better, if you have it, half a pound of salt pork) and one of black pepper into your kettle, and a dozen or so of the small prairie onions (*cop-o-blos*) a sort of wild onion about the size of a rifle-bullet, and which no travellers in those regions should fail to gather and carry along, as important aids in cooking. In fact, a wild turkey or goose cannot be well roasted without them, as your *stuffing* otherwise will be a complete failure.

"All these things be sure to arrange before you land, as it might be difficult to arrange them on shore. Also, before being put on shore, if you be the cook, you should draw a pair of Indian buck skin leggings over your pantaloons, tying them very tight around the ankles. Leave your hat or cap behind, covering the head with a large silk hand kerchief or shawl, passing under the chin, and covering the face as high as the bridge of the nose, and tie it firmly in the back of the neck: then, with a bunch of willow boughs in your left hand to protect your eyes (keeping it constantly in motion), whilst your right hand is free to work with, a thick pair of buckskin gloves or mittens on your hands, and your pantaloons' pockets turned inside out, your person is tolerably secure from all approach, and you may venture to step ashore; but keeping your body and limbs constantly more or less in motion, which will defeat the aim of such proboscis as may occasionally have found their way through the imperfect seams or otherwise vulnerable parts of your dress.

"In these heavy wooded bottoms there is always a plenty of dried mulberry limbs and trees, which gather as quick as possible; they burn free, with a light flame and little or no smoke to frighten the mosquitos away. Set your kettle exactly in the middle of the fire, so that the flame will rise equally all around it, and some twelve or fourteen inches above its rim, which is abundantly high.

"The rest of the party, having left you ashore, should then lose no time in paddling into the stream, each one with a bunch of willow-boughs whipping ashore all the insects that are attempting to follow the canoe, and leaving you, the cook, alone to 'walk the kettle,' as one alone concentrates the flying cloud better than several.

"The cloud beginning to gather in promising quantities around you, you may commence walking at a regular pace, with short steps, around the fire and boiling kettle; the swarm will follow in your wake, and, to shorten the distance, they will constantly be flying over the fire, when, their wings being singed, they fall into the kettle; and whilst keeping your eyes clear with the willow-boughs in your left hand, if you aim your blows right, a great many may be thus knocked into the kettle that perhaps are too wary to get their wings burned.

"There is no limited time for this operation, nor any end to the arriving multitudes; but you must be guided entirely by the apparent quantity, by lifting off the kettle occasionally, when the boiling ceases, and their carcasses rise in a large clotted mass on the surface, which with a large wooden spoon you should throw off, as the *fat* is all extracted from them, and their bodies should give way to a fresh supply, in order to obtain the requisite richness of the soup.

"If you observe occasionally a gallinipper or a mosquito hawk falling in, which is very apt to be the case, where they are so confusedly grouped together, all the better, for they are always gorged with a fresh supply of these insects; and if in the desperate struggle any part of your dress should have given way, and the mosquitos should have succeeded through the breach in getting a few ounces of your blood, no matter - never mind it; it will add to the richness of the soup.

"The boiling operation being finished, and the canoe called ashore, the kettle should be handled as quickly as possible, and taken on board; all hands, as they are armed each with a bunch of willow-boughs, will be able to whip the following swarms ashore as the canoe enters the current, over which they never venture to fly more than a few rods.

"Then, landing on some barren sand-bar which has no vegetation, and consequently is uninhabited by these torments, a comfortable night's rest may be enjoyed; and the soup, when it is sufficiently cooled, and the again collected mass of their light and emptied carcasses floating on the surface are again skimmed off with the spoon, and some hard biscuits crumbed in, your kettle of 'Mosquito Soup' is ready for use. [1]

"GEO. CATLIN, Rio Uruguay."

From Conception, where we started, to the little town of Santa Cruz, 200 miles, and from that to San Pedro, on the west bank of the river, 200 miles further down, here and in the neighbourhood were Indians a plenty. But *one* incident more - *a tiger story*. It never again can be told, and should be history. I can tell it in a few words, and then we will go on with the Indians.

On the Missouri, with Bátiste and Bogard to paddle, I always steered; but on the Uruguay, the steering-paddle was in the hands of Alzar, and I sat about the middle of the canoe, whilst our passenger "working his passage" was near the bow, with his propeller always at work, like a machine.

Some thirty or forty miles below the town of Santa Cruz, and whilst we were passing great quantities of turtle-shells, and half-devoured carcasses of turtles lying on the sandy beach, signs incontrovertible of tigers, I had charged Alzar to keep a bright look-out, and to let me know if any game was discovered, and I had fallen asleep. In the midst of this (I forget what I was dreaming about), Alzar whispered in my ear, -

"Señor, there's a beautiful tiger ahead - stands out whole neck and head above the grass!"

Before getting my eyes fairly open, "Slip back," said I, "to your seat, inch by inch, and keep your paddle down, and both hands close to the water's edge, and steer the canoe a little in; we are rather too far from the shore."

Before he retreated he had given me, with his forefinger, the direction, and I was beginning to see the staring, glaring round head of the villain above the grass on the top of the bank.

But why, by the way, should I say "villain?" These poor creatures slay only for food; we kill for amusement, not for food, not for the carcass - and for the *tail,* we sometimes don't even take that. But a "Tiger a-head!" is a poor place for moralizing or sympathizing. "Sam" was in both hands, and, of course, near my cheek! The smoke cleared away, I could see nothing; but both of the men exclaimed - "Dead shot, dead shot! Señor."

I told Alzar to steer the canoe in, and put me ashore. He landed me a few rods below where the animal had sat, and advancing along the edge of the stream until I got opposite to the place, I directed him to keep the canoe a little out from the shore, and in front of me, and his rifle up and ready in case of any necessity.

Though my men had seen the animal fall, I took this precaution, as I was about to ascend the bank of some thirty or forty feet, and covered with tall grass and weeds, under a sort of conviction, from the rather slow fire of my rifle, that I had missed, or only grazed the creature's head, and that it might be lying in the weeds, and ready to make a spring upon me; or, if the animal were dead, as my men believed, its mate might be lying by its side, and ready to do the same thing for me.

I had five shots left in the cylinders, however, and ready at the instant, and was ready to run all risks of rising the bank alone, imprudent as it was. The bank was something like thirty feet higher than the river, and from the water's edge rose at an angle of thirty degrees, and was covered with grass and weeds as high nearly as my head. I ascended very slowly, and with my rifle raised; and when near the brink, I was no doubt soonest discovered, being in motion. And, as if shot from a cannon, the beast struck me, its breast meeting the muzzle of my rifle, which was thrown over my shoulder, and quite into the river - and myself, backwards and headlong to the water's edge! It was a blow and a rebound; and the animal, at one leap, was out of sight!

I was paralyzed by the shock, and in that condition was taken into the canoe; and might as well have been taken and lugged into the thicket, the helpless prey of my adversary. When consciousness came, beyond the shock, I knew nothing of what had transpired except what my men related to me, nor had I then the slightest recollection of having seen the animal, in its flight, coming upon me, probably from the quantity of weeds between us hiding it from my view.

We got into the stream and floated off, all hands (judiciously, no doubt) agreeing to a drawn battle, rather than risk anything further to gratify curiosity.

The animal that I fired at might have fallen dead, as my men still declared, and its mate, lying by, might have sprung upon me; or I might, as I think, from the dampness of my powder, have grazed its head, and brought it, in the manner described, upon me; but, whichever might have been the case, we were quite willing to leave it to tigers to decide.

Whilst exulting in my lucky escape, I began to feel pain in my left arm between the wrist and the elbow, and blood beginning to issue freely from it, I was convinced that the animal, though instantly as it had rebounded, had had a grab at my arm; and getting at it, the incisions of two of its teeth were visible on the upper, and one on the opposite side. And, as proof that the creature intended to have taken me along with him, one paw had gone over my left shoulder, and, failing to take me along, had opened my cotton paletôt for a considerable distance, and left the furrows of two of its nails in the flesh. My wounds, therefore, like those of a woman's fight, were but scratches, and easily dressed, and were quickly forgotten, though the marks of them still remain.

At San Pedro I said we should find Indians, and in it and its near vicinity we found a plenty of them. The *Tobos,* the *Lenguas,* and the *Bocolies* - small tribes, the survivors from rum, and whiskey, and smallpox, by which the greater portion of those once numerous and warlike people have been swept away.

Of these the *Lenguas* and *Tobos,* which seem to be an amalgam of two tribes, is the most numerous and the most interesting. Their village (*tolderia*) is all in one long shed, standing on the bank of the river, and forty rods in length, and built much like the *tolderia* of the Payaguas, which has been described; and resembling also the sheds of the Connibos and Sepibos, on the Rio Yucayali, in Peru, and already described in the first volume of this work. The *people,* also, in their personal appearance and customs, resemble the Connibos enough to be their brothers; and yet they resemble the Botocudos, of which people they are no doubt a part. Like the Botocudos, they wear the block of wood in the lip, and slit and elongate the rims of their ears.

This extraordinary and curious custom, of which I have spoken in former chapters, I had opportunities of more closely examining in this tribe, and which examinations will justify a few further remarks in this place. The greater portion of the tribe have long since abandoned so useless and so ridiculous a custom, and others still study eccentricity by keeping it up.

In several instances I was permitted to examine closely the orifice in the lip, when the block was not in, and, to my surprise, in each instance, such is the elasticity and contraction of the lip, that from the moment a round block of wood, of two inches in diameter, was taken out, the lip contracts to its natural shape and proportions, and the orifice is so perfectly closed that not even the saliva from the mouth escapes through it; and to the passing spectator the mark of it is scarcely visible in the face.

From one of their medicine men, whose portrait I was painting, with the block in his lip, I got many curious particulars relating to the custom, and amongst others, he put his finger on several holes in his cheeks, from which he told me he suspended strings of beads, and feathers, and other ornaments, on certain occasions, in their dances, masquerades, &c. And I pointed to one that I discovered in his *upper* lip -

"Yes," said he, pulling down the lip and running his thumb through it, "and I have sometimes worn the block in it."

I had just before bartered for a couple of these blocks, which I had at the moment in my pocket; and handing him one of them, he knew my object, and in an instant it was adjusted in his upper lip! Here it was that I "stumbled on a *double pay-lay-lay*." It made a great laugh amongst the Indian bystanders, which showed that it was an eccentricity of the moment, and not a custom. The droll old doctor found, however, that he could talk better with the two than he could with the one only, and the clacking and clattering sounds of his wooden lips, and the curious grimaces of his face, produced a short spell of excessive laughter and amusement.

Besides this singular mode of *ornamentation,* and the modes of *deformation* already spoken of, practised by the Flatheads and Peruvians, there are yet many others not less. curious, which I have witnessed, and of which the world are as yet not generally aware. And of these, none more curious and extraordinary than those practised by the numerous tribes on the upper Amazon and its tributaries, whom Caesar and I visited several years before, and of whom I spoke, very briefly, in the first volume of this work.

Of all the tribes on the Continent of America, those of the Amazon and its affluents are the most nude - the most ill-shaped - the least ornamented - the least warlike, and the least hostile.

The equatorial climate in which they live, almost absolutely denying the use of clothing of any sort, and their fisherman's modes of life, living almost constantly in their dirty and wet canoes, destructive to costumes of all sorts, presents thousands of those people in a state of nudity almost as absolute as when they were born, and, of course, in a state of nature too literal for the artist's pencils, the males only wearing a "fig leaf" of cotton or of bark, the size of one's hand.

The traveller, when he enters their humble wigwams, where he is welcome, feels embarrassed at their nakedness, but not so those poor people, who practise modesty without cloaks, and whose artless and unstudied propriety teach civilized man things that in the abundance of his conceptions he never thought of before.

Ill-looking, as many of the Amazon tribes are compared with the other American races, there are still tribes amongst them that remind the traveller of the Winnebagoes, the Menomonies, and other Canoe Indians of North America, and are quite their equals.

On the Amazon and its tributaries, from the mouth of the Rio Negro to Nauta, which constitutes but a half of that river, there are more than one hundred tribes speaking different or dialectic languages; and though ugly enough from Nature's hands, they have been caricatured in a manner that reflects little credit to Art, and stigmatised as *Cannibals,* in language as little worthy of historians.

The whole country, a distance of 800 miles, if it were possible to traverse its vast forests and swamps on both sides of the river, might be travelled in security by a man with his wife and his children, and unarmed, without harm from the Indians; and amongst them he would find helping hands when ever difficulties were in his way. These people are friendly to the whites, because there are no buffaloes nor beavers in their country to excite white man's cupidity - because they have nothing with which to buy rum and whiskey, and because their lands are so vast, and covered with such unmoveable forests of timber that white men do not want them; and hostility amongst themselves is little known - the tribes are too small to wage desolating warfare - they have no defined boundaries to protect, or hunting grounds to defend. They cannot hunt; the denseness of their forests forbids it; and living by fishing, the rivers which they fish upon admit of no boundaries, and are alike free to all; and the movements of their canoes, propelled only by the muscles of the warrior's arms, are less inspiring to deeds of war than the movements of the horse, which often lead the crazed warrior into rash and mortal combat.

Like most canoe Indians, the peculiar, modes of their lives, sitting in their wet canoes or wading in the water, forbid their dressing their feet and their legs, and, unlike the Indians who ride on the prairies or travel on foot amongst the rocks, they are gene rally barefooted; and the labour of propelling their canoes without the use of their nether limbs, gives them physiological disproportions - an over-development of the muscles of the arms and chest, and a narrowness in the hips, and a lankness and deficiency in the legs.

The horsemen on the prairies, on the other hand, who always exercise astride of their horses' backs, and using their arms only for their light bows and the bridle, beget a lack of symmetry almost equally striking; an over-breadth in the hips, - expansion and curvature of the upper legs, and comparative lightness and slightness in the arms and chest

The fisherman is beautiful as he glides along in his canoe; but placed upon his naked feet, he cringes and looks to the ground before his steps, and loses the dignity and grace of the mocasined man, who fearlessly and solidly sets his foot, and uses his eyes for the distance.

These circumstantial departures from the natural symmetry of man and his movements, are plainly exhibited amongst all the horse and canoe tribes of America; but there is another, the Mountain Indians, who have neither horses to ride nor canoes to paddle, who have no fish to catch and no buffaloes to chase, who draw their sinewy bows whose steps and leaps, upwards and downwards, and climbing, amongst the rocks, exercise alike, all the muscles of the body, and the limbs, where perfect symmetry of form alone can be found.

The numerous tribes on the *haute* Amazon - about the mouth of Rio Negro, and from that to Nauta, and upon the shores of the Yucayali, of whom I have spoken as canoe Indians, deserve a few further remarks in this place relative to the curious modes of *pendent* and *pigment* ornamentation which they practise, and with effects perhaps more *bizarre* and more droll than even the blocks of wood worn in the lips, in the tribes where we are now halting.

Besides the ordinary way of painting with vermilion and other colours daubed on with the ringers, several of these tribes have a mode of *printing* the colours on their faces and bodies in the manner somewhat of theorem painting. On a certain sort of palm leaf, or a piece of parchment-dressed skin, the most curious and intricate arabesque devices are drawn and cut out, and this laid on one cheek and the other, and the forehead, and the colour, mixed with grease, covering the palms of the hands of the operator, a gradual pressure prints the intricate designs through the theorems upon the face.

There are often different patterns printed on the breasts, the shoulders, and arms, and legs, bewildering the beholder who does not understand the process, with astonishment at the apparent labour and artistic effect, produced on a figure in the morning to be washed off at night, little thinking that the whole effect has been produced in five minutes.

These theorems are prepared with oil and glue, so that they bear washing, and being once elaborated, can be used a thousand times; and the mystery that astonishes an artist is, that two and three colours are sometimes printed over and between one another, like chromo-lithographic printing, and the colours rubbed in with the ringers, effects are often produced that would test the skill of the best artist to copy.

The fat and round and solid cheeks of these people, and their peculiar colour, form the best possible ground for this curious art, which I am quite sure could not be practised with equal effect on any other substance.

The *pendent* ornaments of the face and ears in most of these tribes are not less surprising, and certainly are more completely unaccountable. Of the tribes that I have visited in that region, the most remarkable for these modes are the *Muras,* on both sides of the Amazon, above the mouth of Rio Negro, the *Iquitos,* the *Omaguas,* the *Ticunas,* the *Yahuas,* the *Marahuas,* the *Orejones,* the *Mayorumas,* the *Connibos,* and *Sepibos.*

These tribes all sever the rims of the ears and elongate the lobes, by wearing heavy weights in them; which accomplished, enables them to wear enormous blocks of wood and other ornaments in them, precisely like the Botocudos and Lenguas, whom we are yet amongst. By the process of elongating the lobe, it becomes enlarged, and often times is seen descending quite to the shoulder, and, from appearance, of half a pound or more in weight.

In Plate No. 18 I have given copies of three of my portraits made amongst those people, illustrating the principal and most curious of the above-named modes, (*a*) A *Mura* chief, his ears curiously mutilated and elongated, with ornaments attached, round plates of silver fastened to his cheeks, his chin, and his nostrils, and long thorns standing out from his cheeks and his chin.

For the supports of these singular ornaments of the face, incisions are made in the flesh in childhood, into which a large bead is forced, with a slight thong hanging out. The flesh heals around the cicatriced wound, and the bead is withdrawn. The elasticity of the flesh is such that the orifice is scarcely perceptible; and, at the times of ornamentation, for galas, festival days, &c, a bead, into which the butt-end of the thorn is pressed, is slipped into the orifice, and supports the thorns in the positions in which they are placed, and so the silver plates are supported on the cheeks and the chin, and feather and other pendents.

They dance, and sing, and yell, with all these ornaments attached, and if any one of them becomes the least deranged, the mere touch of the ringers adjusts it again. The portrait (*b*), same plate, an *Orejona,* is still more curiously ornamented with long feathers run through the cartilage of his nose, two splints fashioned from the branches of palm, attached by beads to the nose, and quills and beads suspended from his under-lip by the same means, and blocks of wood in the cartilage of his ears.

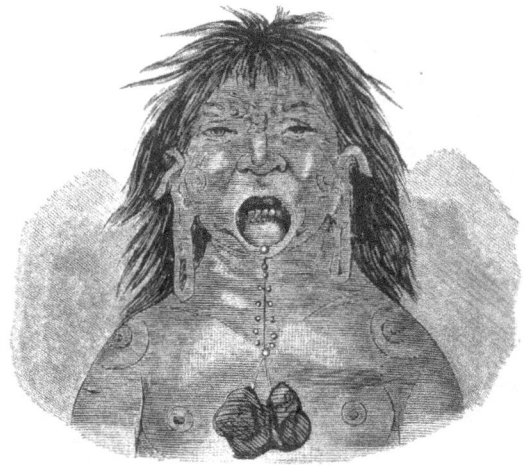

The portrait (*c*), same plate, of a *Ccocato* chief, with the same incisions, wears the blocks in his ears, and ornaments his face, on this occasion, with strings of beads only. And besides these *pendent* ornaments, their faces, and bodies, and limbs, were painted in a variety of forms and colours.

In Plate No. 19 I have given a copy of a portrait of a medicine man (sorcerer) in the Omagua tribe, who uses the perforation through his lip alternately for suspending strings of beads or shells, or beautiful plumes, or for suspending a boulder of flint of a pound or more in weight, supported by a large bead on the inner side of the lip, which he assured me was a habit that he could not dispense with, from the pleasure it gave him at times, and always after eating, of drawing the cool air upon the gums and through his teeth!

The habit of suspending strings of beads and feathers from the under lip is also practised by the females in many of the tribes, not only on the Amazon, but in various parts of South America, amongst the women of Venezuela, of Guiana, of Paraguay, and the mountains of Peru. The copy of a portrait of a *Gooagive* unmarried girl of Venezuela illustrates this mode amongst the females; and the long thorns projecting from her cheeks might almost be recommended for young ladies in the protectrice economy of civilized life (Plate No. 20). Finishing this curious episode amongst the Amazons, we return again to the Tobos and Lengua, whom we left on the Uruguay.

The passion for ornamentation seems to belong to all the human race much alike; whether they are clad in beautiful and costly stuffs, or are naked, the passion seems to be the same. The Indians in the northern latitudes of North America, who dress in skins, wear their ornaments in paintings and embroideries on their dresses. The Amazons, who wear no dresses, are equally vain, and expend their ingenuity and exhaust their means in ornamenting their naked limbs, without an inch of dress upon them. They load their wrists and ankles with bright and costly bracelets and rings, and their necks and breasts and hair with beads, and paint their limbs and faces with beautiful colours. And what can be more beautiful? what more proper?

But blocks, and thorns, and weights! What a mistake in taste! And last of all, to flatten and elongate their skulls, like the Flatheads and Peruvians, in order to look beautiful! Oh, Vanity, thy name is (certainly) - Indian! "Everything has its cause." It is easy to account for the love of ornament with paint and beads, and even blocks and thorns, but who can guess the cause of changing the shape of the skull to beautify "the human face Divine?" There *must* be a cause for this.

The Flathead tribe at the mouth of the Columbia, whose portraits I have shown (and also their mode of flattening the head) in Chapter 3. And the ancient Peruvians, as we learn by their skulls, are the tribes that have ventured

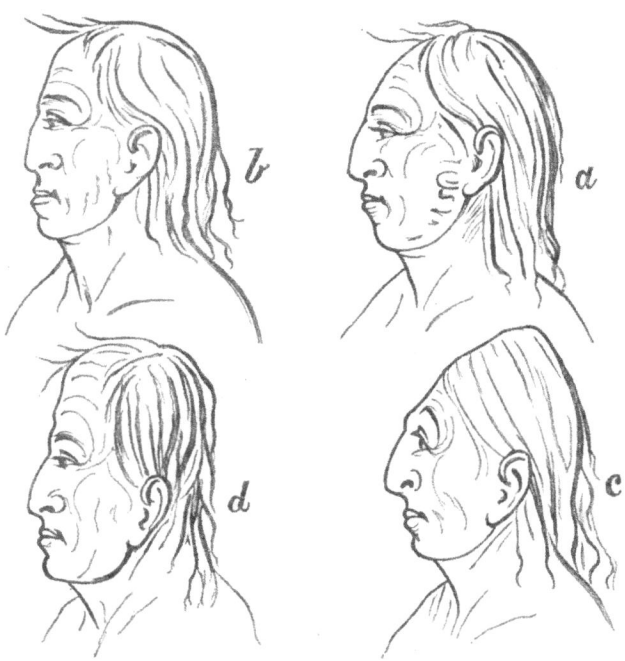

to *deform* nature for a form more beautiful in art. And is it exactly so? I do not believe it. I do not believe that any part of the human family would venture such a stride from nature as to flatten the skull as the Flatheads do, or to compress it into a sugar-loaf, as the Peruvians have done, without a model, without a fashion to follow - an Indian *beau ideal* to which they have aspired. Those *beau ideals* are seen in Plate No. 21 Letter (*a*), a Crow of the Rocky Mountains, and (*b*), an alto-Peruvian of the Andes, the two great original fountains of American man, to whom all the tribes point as their origin, and on whom, of course, all the tribes have looked as the *beau ideals* of the Indian race. The Flathead, letter (*c*), aiming at the Crow-skull (like the copyists of most fashions), has carried the copy into caricature; and the bas-Peruvian, letter (*d*), aiming at the elevated frontal of the mountain regions, has squeezed his up with circular bandages, to equally monstrous proportions.

Not to make this chapter too long, I shut my note-book on the Lengua and Tobos Indians around us; and shaking hands with them, a few days down stream showed us the little band of *Bocobies* at the mouth of the Rio Negro of Uruguay, and after that the beautiful city of Buenos Ayres, and where next?

"Patagonia and the Patagons, of course." The "Giants of Patagonia ten feet high!" and the "Cannibals!" I did not believe such things, but would go and look for them through the centre of Patagonia and Terra del Fuego. But here this chapter ends.

[1] If from any undue prejudice the superior quality of this soup should be questioned, it at least has this advantage over most other kinds, that it costs nothing, and is always at hand, and easily obtained in all the great western valleys of North, and in all the valleys of South America.

Chapter Seven - Buenos Ayres

Here, in a boarding-house, in a comfortable room looking on to the Plaza, and at home, of course, I was at work on my sketches.

Alza came in, and softly behind him, and wrapped in a scarlet mantle, a handsome young man, a half-caste, rouged to the eyes, and his glossy hair, parted on his forehead, falling back upon his shoulders, and without a quill upon his head; and in his wake, and more softly and timidly still, a young woman of the same colour, in a calico dress, her hair dressed in the same manner, the two looking effeminate enough, and enough alike, to have been sisters,

Alza, with his hat in his hand, "bowed and scraped," and introduced them as brother and sister, of the *Auca* tribe, living on the head waters of the Rio Salado, to the south of Buenos Ayres. Such was the suavity and gentleness of their manners as they advanced and both shook hands with me, that I felt almost embarrassed. Alza had no doubt given them a high-coloured description of me and my works, and they were approaching me with a profound respect.

Alza could speak somewhat of their language, and, what was better, the young man spoke Spanish very well, and his beautiful and modest sister well enough to be amusing and agreeable to me. They had learned enough from Alza to know the object of my travelling and the sincerity of my views, to enter into undisguised conversation about their own and other tribes of Indians in the vicinity, and conversation took place, for the time, of my painting, and my brushes were laid down.

I expressed my surprise at meeting red people in the city of Buenos Ayres, and particularly so beautiful a young lady, when *Til-tee* ("the Fire-fly" - I found that was her name) replied quicker than her brother was able to do, "Oh, we often come here, señor, and there's a plenty of us here now; my father, and my mother, and my sister are all up town."

Alzar then said, "This is a very respectable family, *Señor Gonzales Borroro,* he is a Portuguese gentleman, and his wife is an Auca woman. They live on the Rio Salado, and these are some of their children; and if you will permit me, señor - I know they will be glad to see your paintings." "Most certainly. Alzar, go and fetch them." Alzar was off, and I went to amusing my visitors with my sketches.

My portfolio of Indian portraits was giving so unthought-of and so exciting a pleasure to the two, and particularly to that beautiful little creature who became more beautiful every time she turned, that I was in the midst of a peculiar satisfaction being taken to myself, when Alzar came in, with the rest of the family.

This was the first day after my arrival in Buenos Ayres, and though I had several letters of introduction which I had not yet delivered, I spent the whole of that day with this interesting family, having learned, in the early part of my conversation with them, that their business was all settled, and their arrangements all made to start for their home on the Salado at an early hour the next morning.

I gained from them a great deal of valuable and reliable information respecting their own tribe, and of their neighbours on the south, the *Puelches* and *Patagons,* with both of which tribes I found they were well acquainted, and with which they were living on terms of friendship. The Puelches and Aucas, both coming freely into Buenos Ayres, and trading for guns, ammunition, cloths, hardware, cutlery, &c, which they sell at a profit to the Patagons, who are sworn enemies to the Buenos Ayreans, and never see them except on the field of battle.

My cartoon portraits, which they could not see enough of, gave an unspeakable pleasure to these people, and those with flattened heads, and those with blocks of wood in the lip, seemed to excite with a people who wear few ornaments, equally disgust and astonishment. They told me they never had thought that any Indians were such great fools.

Borroro and his son gave me such a glowing description of the country where they lived, of the beauty of the forests, the lakes, the prairies and pampas; of the chasing of ostriches, wild horses and wild cattle, which they kill for their hides and their hair, as well as the beautiful games of the Indians, and, at the end of all, so pressing an invitation to come and see, and to join in them, that I told them distinctly that Alzar and I would ride there before a fortnight was out.

This evidently gave them great pleasure, and the father said that both he and his son would join me in any or all of the sports of the country, if I would come. I told him I had long had an intention of making a journey through the middle of the Puelche and Patagon tribes, to Terra del Fuego, and he believed that from that place on the Salado, which would be 150 miles directly on the route, would be the proper point to start from; and that, if I chose, his son, who was an excellent horseman and hunter, and knew well the Puelches and the Patagons, should be one of the party, and could easily get me any number of first-rate young men around him to join me.

"Well done," said I, "Alzar, my troubles are all over, I see our way now clearly; we'll go through the centre of Patagonia."

Borroro was himself half an Indian (his father a Portuguese planter), and, therefore, with all the vanity that usually belongs peculiarly to the half-caste class, and with the strict traits of honour that generally characterize them also; and I thereupon said to him and his Indian wife, "There is one thing now that I want to ask of you - I want you to allow me to make a sketch of *Til-tee*, your beautiful daughter - the day is half gone, and I will not have time to finish it very well, but I will bring it with me and finish it when I come to see you; she is so pretty that I don't wish to forget how she looks."

The extreme overjoy of the mother seemed as if she had, in a measure, misunderstood the arrangement I had asked for, and no objections being made, and no conditions named, I went to work. The timid little girl said she was sorry that she had not her prettiest dress on. I told her that was no matter, it was not the dress I wanted, it was her pretty face and neck only, and if I could paint that part now, the dress could be painted when I should see her again.

The mother, sagacious enough to understand this, and flattered with my admiration of her daughter, stepped up, and pulling her arms out of the sleeves of her loose calico dress, which fell down upon her lap, exclaimed, "There! that's the way she is when at home." And oh! what a pretty creature, what a beautiful bust was before me! What an ugly veil was drawn from hidden beauty! and drawn by whom? by the hand of a *savage*; a savage who knew its worse than savage ugliness! And oh, how I worked. And when my work was done, "one thing more" I wanted, and they granted it. I wanted to walk with them to a jeweller's shop in the corner of the plaza, where, old man as I was, I could not forego the pleasure I had of buying, and placing in her ears, with my own fingers, a brilliant pair of pendents, for which she prettily tried to express (but could not well enough in Spanish) what her brother interpreted to me, "that her heart was thankful for the rich present I had made her." Night was at hand, and "Buenas noches," "a Dios," &c, and we parted.

I had commissioned the young man, *Gos-brok,* not to *buy,* but to look up, and have ready for my negotiation when I should arrive, the best horse in the country for my tour through Patagonia; an animal of the best bottom and speed, and well-trained to the chase of ostriches, horses, guanacos, or anything else; and the two or three weeks previous to our start I passed by working on my numerous sketches, and making the necessary preparations for our campaign.

My spirits were a good deal depressed during this time by reports, made to me by my friends, that there was a prospect of an approaching war between Buenos Ayres and the Patagon Indians, which would render my expedition to Patagonia impossible, as these people know no white people but the Buenos Ayreans, and would make no distinction between me and them, provided I were endeavouring to enter their country under such circumstances.

I nevertheless got my preparations made, and even against the advice of friends, with Alzar, started for the banks of the Salado. Our ride was a severe one, and much longer than we had apprehended, but the country one of continued interest as we passed. Not on the bank of the Salado, but a great way beyond it, we found the *rancho* of our new-made friends, and by and around them many families of the small and handsome *Auca* Indians.

The tribe is small, having been decimated by whiskey and the small-pox, and though partly civilized, are still living principally by the chase. Game of many kinds is always abundant in their country, and easily killed; and wild horses and wild cattle in countless numbers, which they kill for their hides and hair, which find a ready market in Buenos Ayres.

All were rejoiced to see us in performance of the promise I had made, and particularly so the pretty little *"Fire-fly,"* who was parading her sparkling eardrops and also the rather unfortunate mother, who, we learned (but not till some time after), had overheard, but misunderstood, the arrangement made between her husband and myself in Buenos Ayres, as to hunting ostriches, &c, and which arrangement, fearing an announcement of it for two or three weeks a-head would bring an unwished-for assemblage of Indian sportsmen around him, he had charged his wife *to say nothing about.*

Under the wrong impression which the poor woman got when I asked permission to take her daughter's portrait, which was that I had asked her hand in marriage, and afterwards under the injunction "to say nothing about it," she was keeping (as will be seen) the supposed important secret profoundly safe, and, as can be imagined, was not the least joyful of the family on our arrival.

The Aucas are not only a small tribe, but a tribe of small people, and, a singular fact, the men and women near the same size; and resemble each other so much in stature, in form, and features, and in the mode of arranging their hair on their always naked heads, that it is often difficult to distinguish one sex from the other.

They wear but little dress in the summer season, and that chiefly of civilized manufacture; of calicos and other cotton cloths. The men often wear ponchas, and the women, in the warm season, are naked as low as the waist, from which drops an apron of cotton extending as low as the knee; and wear a sort of sandal or half moccasin, made of goat's skin, or skin of the guanaco. In this really pretty way I found the handsome little *"Til-tee"* dressed, and freed from the horrible folds of pictured calico, she was free and graceful, and more beautiful than ever.

The young man, *Gos-brok,* lost no time in informing me that he had found the best horse in the country for me, without the least trouble - that it belonged to his father; a Mustang - taken by his own hand on the pampa, and trained in the chase by himself: that his father had ten horses, and this one, his favourite, he had resolved to sell to me. I gave him his price, 150 piastres, and the lasso was in my hand. A noble creature - an entire horse. I could imagine him "Charley" - but he wanted the colour; he was a silver grey, his mane and tail were black, and the latter swept the ground.

The sagacious animal seemed to know, from the moment his owner put the rein in my hand, that he had got a new master; and from my caressing, and combing, and trimming, evidently was soon convinced of the fact. A mutual understanding was soon established between us - several little excursions we made together about the neighbourhood, and yet there was one unthought-of and necessary condition to be understood and arranged which "Yudolph" (that was the name he answered to), nor his former master, had probably ever heard of.

Horses in that country, and ostriches and guanacos and other animals are taken with the lasso and bolas, and no guns are ever fired from a horse's back for anything. Colt's revolvers had not at that time travelled so far, and horses knew just as much of them as their masters; the amusement of which remained yet to be afforded to the one, and the alarm and astonishment to be presented to the other. In short, "Yudolph" had got to smell gunpowder, and the Aucas to understand revolvers.

"Sam," for the first time in that region of country, was taken from its case, and in the wigwam, in a little time, was partly comprehended; but for "Yudolph," it was to become a more inexplicable mystery. In the rashness and thoughtlessness of my *inexperience,* being then only fifty-seven years of age, it had not occurred to me that "Yudolph," though a bold hunter and warrior, as he had been, had probably never heard the sound of a gun; and, under this lack of intelligence, I mounted him with "Sam" in hand, in presence of his former master and Alzar, and the pretty little *Til-tee,* to see, as I said, how he would "stand fire," for *my* game had got to be taken, and my battles fought, not with lasso and bolas, but with gunpowder.

I certainly was a pretty good rider as well as a good shot, by this time; and galloping him around in a curve or two, I fired a cylinder to the left! - and the next thing that I was sensible of was that Borroro and Alzar had hold of me and were carrying me towards the rancho.

I said, "Hold on - I am not hurt. - Where's Yudolph?"

"He's yonder, Señor."

And at a distance of thirty rods I saw him standing broad-side - his head and tail up - a beautiful picture, as he stood gazing at us and wondering what had taken place. His master walked towards him and called him, *"Yudolph!"* when the faithful creature advanced, and met him half way. He led him up and put the rein again in my hand, and the trembling brute seeming to think there had been some *accident,* followed my motions as willingly as before.

"Where's 'Sam'?" said I.

"Here!" said Alzar, as he handed it to me in two pieces! the stock broken off below the guard, not injuring the lock in any way. "Where's the saddle?"

"Here, señor," said Borroro; "the girth is broken, and by that means you fell."

"I know that - saddles have thrown me many times, but no horse can do it."

"Is your rifle loaded, Alzar?"

"Yes, señor."

"Just give it to me then, and your bullet-pouch and powder-cartridges, if you have any."

Alzar handed me his rifle and three or four powder-cartridges, and placing my nose to the nostrils of the trembling animal, and exchanging a few breaths to inspire him with confidence, I threw myself upon his naked back, and galloping the same rounds as before, I fired the minié to the left kept the horse upon his course, re-loaded and fired again, and again, as if I were in a buffalo chase on the Missouri, or in mortal combat, and as easily, and with as accurate an aim, as if I had been firing from the back of "old Chouteau," my buffalo chaser at the mouth of Yellow Stone.

"Huzza! huzza! bravo! bravo!" exclaimed the bystanders; and trembling "Yudolph," as I rode him up, seemed to take one-half at least of the applause to himself. And last, though not the least complimentary and welcome, came the nice old lady, from where she had sat in the door of her house, who extended her hand, and showed me, by the expressions of her face, that she was taking to herself a *peculiar* satisfaction at the successful and laudable feats of her (as she still supposed) approaching son-in-law.

"Yudolph" now understood something of gun powder, and was ready for the chase. He had long since, under his former master, learned how to run and how to approach; and I, who had long since learned how to shoot, with "Sam" in hand and a six-shot revolver in my belt, was considered equal to a war-party. But where was Sam? Sent off by a little son of mine host to a small village on the river, some twenty miles distant, where a country blacksmith bound the two parts together, and it came back, not as handsome, nor as light, but quite as strong as ever.

After a few days spent in and about the little Auca village, the appointed day approached for a "grand hunt" - an *ostrich chase*. The young man, *Gosbrok*, had told me in Buenos Ayres that he knew of a fine brood that had been hatched and raised within a few miles, as yet unmolested, and just about old enough for sport. This he had told me in my painting-room, when the father and mother were sitting by, and just when I had obtained their consent to *have the daughter,* painted; and the old lady, from her imperfect knowledge of Spanish, understanding but a word or two of what he had said, nodded assent, as in the other cases, supposing we were still talking of *Til-tee,* whilst the "rest of us were thinking of ostriches.

This "hatch" was also known to Gonzales Borroro (his father), who now told me they would be found in the edge of the thistles, near the head of the "red water," one of the extreme sources of the Salado, and in the pampa.

The pampas in various parts of South America are vast level plains, not unlike the great prairies of the Platte and the Arkansaw, excepting that they are covered with high weeds instead of short grass; and amongst these weeds, of which there are many kinds, there are wild flowers of all colours. And on the eastern borders of the great pampas, stretching off from Buenos Ayres to Patagonia on the south, and to the base of the Andes on the west, there are vast forests of thistles, which, sometimes for a great many miles together, though they grow in patches, and as high as a horse's back, are almost impassable, even for a man on horseback.

These thistles are the covers and asylums for the ostrich, which feeds mostly out in the open plains and in the ravines; and when pursued, runs to the thistles for cover, where it is excessively difficult to follow it.

The plan of our day's sport was to ride about ten miles before sunrise, and break upon the brood whilst they were feeding in the open plain; and if not successful in that, to drive a thistle patch of several miles in circumference, forcing the game to cross an intervening prairie of two or three miles to enter another thistle cover, and in which plain our run would take place.

Borroro laid the plans and took the lead, riding a beautiful pied horse, his bolas coiled upon his left arm, and a lasso, in loops, around his horse's neck.

His son, *Gos-brok,* and two other young men, well mounted and equipped in the same way, and Alzar with his minié rifle, and I with "Sam" in hand, and a six-shot revolver in my belt, formed the "hunters" of the party; and some six or eight Indians, mounted but not armed, followed in our train, as drivers of the thistles.

I have before said that sportsmen in this country hunt without guns. The bolas the "deadly bolas!" a thing imagined in the powder-burning world, and yet but little understood. Let us know more about it and its deadly powers before we go further before we see these true sportsmen playing with the flock of birds before us. (We will come back to this play-day anon).

"Borroro lives by killing and by catching horses, and others of my people live by killing cattle." So said Borroro to me; and two weeks after this playday on which we have commenced, I went with Borroro and party of ten, to see the deadly works of the bolas amongst a band of wild horses that had been reported on the plains near the head of the Rio Saladillo.

Driven by drought upon the vast pampas, these animals often come in thousands together to the extreme sources of the river's rising in the plains, to get water; and sometimes, the Indians tell us, die by thousands and rot upon the pampas before they reach it.

A circuit of ten days, in which I lost much flesh, though I had no flesh to spare, satisfied all the passion I ever had to witness the extreme of Indian endurance, the deadliness of the bolas, and its havoc amongst the noble tenants of the pampas.

Killing Wild Horses with Bolas

The bolas is a raw-hide cord (and, of course, of great strength, though very small), somewhat in the form of the capital letter T; each of the three branches being some eight or ten feet in length, and having a leaden ball of half a pound weight at its end. This is carried in a coil on the rider's left arm, or on the horse's withers, and when in the heat of the chase the rider raises it and swings it in a rotary motion around and above his head, by holding one of the balls in his hand. His horse is trained to approach its game on the right hand side, that the missile may be thrown with its fullest force and accuracy; and at the proper distance, the balls are sent forward with a force and tact that keeps them revolving in the air, and their centrifugal force keeping the cords straight, till one or the other of the cords strikes the animal's neck, it matters not which, for in an instant they all wrap around its neck and legs, and binding both and all together, the animal falls upon its head, and generally the neck is broken by the fall; if not, before the instant is out its hamstrings are cut by a long and semi-circular-bladed lance, .and its chances for life are ended. (Plate No. 22).

In battle, an enemy's arms are thus wrapped to his sides, or his body wrapped to the neck and the legs of his horse, and both go to the ground together! In this hunt (or massacre), to which I have no more space to devote, twenty horses were killed; their skins, with the manes and tails attached, were stripped off, and on the backs of mules were transported to the Indian village.

This chase was for skins and hair only, and the lassos were not used. When death is wanted, the bolas is taken in hand. When the Auca or the Puelche

Indian wants a horse for service, the affectionate lasso is dropped over its neck, and it is broken in and domesticated much in the manner of the North American Indians, described in the first volume of this work.

Mounted and equipped, as has been related, for the ostrich chase, we were assembled at and around the rancho of Gonzales Borroro, a little before the dawn of day.

Til-tee was up and dressed (the little she had was soon put on), and her fond mother was there too, and, from a wooden bowl, filled my pockets with dried prunes, delightful to eat in the chase, when water is scarce. She patted Yudolph on the neck and the nose, examined the girth of my saddle closely, and saluted me with a waive of the hand, and a long "ya-ya-a" as I rode off, evidently afraid that I should be thrown from Yudolph's back, and perhaps my neck broken.

At that time I could not more than half comprehend such marked kindness, and such *peculiar* solicitude, but gave the good woman credit for it, and received it as *a very strong expression* of hospitality.

We were off, and galloped over our ten miles pretty quick, and getting near to the ground for our sport, it was necessary to follow up for a mile or two the bed of a small stream, forming a little grass-covered valley, lower by some twenty or thirty feet than the surface of the level platform on which our game was expected to be discovered.

Borroro and myself, leaving the rest of the party in the valley to await our signals, rode up the embankment as quietly as we could, under cover of some hazel-bushes and thistles standing on a projecting point, to reconnoitre the plains about, of which we had a perfect view for several miles.

Discovering nothing, after a careful search, we stepped our horses out into the open prairie, and hearing the signal whistle of his son, which he understood, "here they come!" said Borroro, as he was wheeling his horse about, and the whole troop, with their necks stretched, and their wings up, were breaking from a copse of willow on the bank of the stream, where they had been for water, had passed our companions, who were mostly dismounted, and were now steering for the thistles, exactly in a: straight line towards us, and with our fellow sports men in their wake, as fast as they could get their feet in the stirrups.

"Stand!" said Borroro, "we can do nothing in meeting them, we must get behind them." And moving his horse back into the bushes, at his signal I followed him.

It was a beautiful sight, there were about twenty in the troop, two coveys united. They rose the. hill within a few rods of us, and the plunging chevaliers were a long distance behind them. "Now!" said Borroro, "don't try to shoot, but lay out: Yudolph to his utmost, we must cut them off before they reach that thistle patch, or we lose them!" Both Borroro and myself were at our extremest, and side by side, as if on a race-course. The "thistle patch" was half a mile or more. Yudolph headed him by several lengths, and yet the running-flying troop, on their tip-toes, turned the point of thistles before us, and were out of sight in an instant.

All hands again together, and out of breath from the sudden brush, a dismount and a "council of war" was the next thing. That we should have passed the whole troop in so thoughtless and careless a manner within two or three hundred yards, in the valley, was an affair so provoking, and so humiliating to all, that the first part of our counsel was taken up with groans and exclamations of disappointment and regret, and afterwards we proceeded to plans for bringing our labours to better results.

If Borroro and I had been a few rods further ahead in our chase, we should have cut them off from the thistles, and turned them loose upon an open prairie of several miles, where the ground was good, and where our sport would have been of the first order. "However," said Borroro, "we'll have it all right yet - there's the south prairie - we'll turn them into it - it's just as good."

The "south prairie" (or llano, as they call it) was another open, grassy plain of several miles in extent, stretching off between the forest of thistles into which our game had plunged, and another similar forest further to the south. Our plan now was for the hunters of our party to ride around some five or six miles, and in this prairie, on its northern border, to take our positions at equal distances, under cover of the edging thistles, and await the breaking of cover, which was to be produced by our staff of "drivers," who were to enter the thicket, and work their way through it from the north.

Signal whistles were to be blown when the birds were well entered on the prairie, for the drivers to appear as soon after as possible on the prairie's border, to prevent them from returning to the thistles, and not until their appearance was the chase to begin.

We all sat close and silent, and at length (it was a curious sight) the older and wiser birds appeared first, and led the way, tilting and crouching along as they cautiously emerged, and their long necks stretched, examining the prairie before them to see if an enemy was on it; moving as if they suspected the plot, and, the younger of the broods following, they advanced a long distance into the prairie, and laid down, some upon their bellies, and others upon their sides, hiding their heads behind bunches of leaves and tufts of grass, whilst the whole of their fat and round bodies loomed up in full view and exposed.

Our "drivers" came out and showed themselves at different points, and at the sound of Borroro's whistle we all started. The poor birds (which Borroro subsequently assured me had all shut their eyes), from the tramp of our horses, which they heard with their heads on the ground, announced our approach, and they were up and off. We were now in the chase, - "an ostrich chase."

They started in a group, and ran, not in a circuit or a curve, but stretched their necks in a straight line for the nearest thicket, perhaps at a distance of two miles. No maneuvering, and nothing but a fair and a straight race offered us any chance, and for the first half a mile was thus contested with equal speed, when the tremendous strides of maddened Yudolph, in spite of all the poor creatures could do, brought me into the midst of them, with Borroro but a length or two in arrear, and on their right flank. At my first cylinder one of them fell, and, probably, from the sound of the gun, they broke and run in all directions. The sport then became beautiful, each rider, crossing their curves, came upon them. I saw them writhing and struggling in the deadly coils of the bolas, and recognized the "old minié's" voice in the *mêlée*. It was now a "running fight," a leaping and dodging for life with some, and others were leading off in straight lines for the thicket, and some got there - but few. Every one was attending to his own business, and it was difficult to see or to know exactly what was actually progressing.

When the field was cleared, however, and there was nothing more to be done, though we were separated, in some instances, several miles apart, we got breath by resting awhile in our saddles, or by dismounting and lying on the ground, and at length got together on the field, our drivers having been whistled up to carry our game.

I have joined in the buffalo chase in all its forms, but never before took part in a chase so difficult as this. After the brood was separated, they ran in all directions, darting in zig-zag and curved lines before and around us, leading our horses into angles difficult to turn, and the rider into positions from which he could not use his weapons. Our horses, at the end, as if they had run a five-mile heat, like ourselves, were ready to lie down upon the ground for rest.

My two first shots killed, but I discharged the other four cylinders all upon the same bird, but without effect, owing to its shifting courses, and the consequent irregular and violent motions of my horse. My two first shots, which were fatal, were given while both the bird and the horse were running on a straight line, which made the aim more steady and more sure. My third bird worried me and my horse by its crooked lines until it reached the thistles, and I returned without it.

Borroro picked up three, and his son brought in two. The other two Indians had three between them taken with lassos, and Alzar had fired once and missed.

Our birds, therefore, counted up, were ten. The ostriches that we killed, called in that country "nandu," were about one half the size of the African ostrich, with three toes instead of two; and their feathers comparatively of little value. Their wings were cut off and carried, and their legs for the sinews; and the skins of several of them were taken for sacks, useful for many purposes, and their carcasses were left on the field.

The ten pairs of wings were elevated on two long poles by two of the Indians, as we rode triumphantly into the village under shouts of applause. Little *Til-tee's* voice and hands were raised amongst the number, and the good mother, when she heard from her husband how I had performed, patted me on the shoulder, exclaiming, "Bueno! bueno! - *muy* bueno, Señor!" thinking perhaps to herself of what nobody but herself had yet thought of.

The grand features of this vast and untilled country, in addition to its pampas and prairies, are its lakes, its salines, and its sables. Its sandy (or "cedar ridge"), lying off towards the Rio Negro, is full of guanacos, a species of llamas, beautiful for chasing, and almost the only sport and living of the Puelches and Patagons. Its flesh is equal to that of venison, and the skins form leggings and robes for clothing, and, sewed together, form coverings for their tents. We planned a run amongst them, but now are taking a look at the "Grand Saline."

Gos-brok, the chief's son, was to lead us. Alzar was going, and two Indians. The ride was thirty miles - one day's work. One day to be spent there, and two days to come back, examining the "talking lake" and shooting ducks on our way. We laid in salt (we actually required nothing else). I promised the little *Til-tee* to bring her some beautiful feathers, which could not be reached by bolas or lasso, and she was in raptures, and the mother again stuffed my pockets with dried prunes.

Our horses were led up, but not yet saddled, and Alzar's nag from Buenos Ayres, ruminating perhaps on the uncouth manners of people in this part of the country, slipped its head out of its bridle, and evidently was turning its face towards the civilized city. Alzar mounted on to one of the Indian's horses, and, with a lasso in his hand, with which he was tolerably expert, he galloped off after it. A broad prairie was before us, and making a circuit, to get a head of his eloping horse, and making several passes at it, the cunning animal showed its heels, and effectually kept out of his way.

The scene was an amusement for all, and all were astonished at the desperate bolts and curves made by both, to no effect, excepting the complete discouragement of Alzar, who seemed to be abandoning the chase in despair, to return to the village.

I stood at the moment holding Yudolph, yet unsaddled, with the bridle in both hands crossed behind me, and feeling a gentle pressure upon the rein, I looked around and met the sparkling eyes of the smiling little *Til-tee,* by their very expression emphatically and silently asking consent as she was timidly drawing the rein of Yudolph out of my hand. The instant allowed me was just enough to yield consent, and to see that she had a lasso coiled on her left arm, when Yudolph had her astride of his bare back, and was off, in his clear and flying bounds!

A shout of surprise was raised, but no one had fears but myself. The father smiled, the mother gazed, and the child rode on! And as her floating black hair and narrow shoulders of demi-red were alternately rising and sinking above and in the waving grass, I thought, "Oh, lucky, envied horse! Were I in Yudolph's place with such a prize, I would gallop to the golden coast." She seemed troubled; her hair had lost its pin, and fell in two parted waves over her shoulders; and, dropping the rein to adjust it (for it was in her way), oh, how gracefully she balanced, and how prettily her pointed breasts and her elbows stood out, as she was wrapping and tieing it around her neck!

Yudolph, though knowing his errand and his rider, had kept his speed, but not exactly his course. The rein was lifted again, and the mile that she and Yudolph then made in a straight line was like a flying arrow, leaving a tinged train from its reddened feather. Alzar was passed, and stood astounded, as if a meteor had gone by him! The Buenos Ayrean steed, aware of what was behind him, steamed at his highest, and just before they would have slipped from our view, the delicate arm of the little Amazone (for with my pocket-glass I could see it distinctly) made a circuit around and over her head, and the fatal noose was seen to fall! A shout was raised, but she was too far to hear it. Yudolph was seen galloping a curve or two with the Buenos Ayrean nag by his side, like a boat picked up on the waves of the sea, and taking Alzar in tow, all came trotting in together.

Alzar looked distressed, but said the Indian horse he rode knew he was not an Indian; his Buenos Ayrean steed showed an expression of utter despair, and a full conviction of Yudolph's superior mettle; and ever-beaming little *Til-tee* dismounted, and with her smiling cheeks and heaving breast received the applause of *all,* and from *me* a kiss - I could not help it - and a beautiful pocket looking-glass, set in silver.

Our ride to the *"Grand Saline"* was yet before us, and, our saddles on, we started. An hour or so, and we were at the shore of another branch of the Salado; into it, and through its clear waters, and over its pebbly bottom we waded - reminding me of Caesar and me in the Snake River. As we passed over these clear and transparent waters quietly on their way to the ocean, I contemplated the vast and unknown solitudes of grass and thistles in which they had their origin, and rising the terraced banks and slopes on the opposite side, the ancient turns and motions of the elements when these vast excavations were dredged out.

We were beyond it, and on an elevated plain of grass, with wild-flowers that no pencil could portray and no pen could describe. We were evidently on a divide - a water-shed, and looking to the south convinced us; a vast and interminable lake or sea seemed to be lying in distance before us, here and there spotted with green, like islands, which proved to be shrubbery, but at last terminating, like every thing else, blue in the distance, and yet not all blue - there were streaks of white. And in the sky, what's that? An army of soldiers? Soldiers are not in the sky. It's a mirage. It's the mirage of a war-party; and yonder is another, drawn out in Indian file! It must be so! But stop! these soldiers are pouring down like a stream into the lake of blue and white below; and now this shadow passing by us!

"Now look up, Señor; here is another war-party right over our heads!"

"And so it is. And now I understand; these are the beautiful birds, the *flamingos,* that you are taking me to see."

"Yes, Señor; that blue lake that you see in the distance is the *'Grand Saline,'* and the streaks of white are the beautiful birds hatching out their eggs. This is just the season, and to-morrow you shall have fun enough."

From the summit of the graceful swell upon which we had mounted we gradually and almost imperceptibly descended for several miles, until we were near the border of this vast saline; when, whispering, Alzar begged us to halt for a moment. I held his horse as he dismounted, and cautiously advancing a few rods, he raised his rifle and shot down a solitary guanaco that had stood its ground and was looking at us, precisely at the place where we were going to sleep, and when fresh meat was wanted.

We were now on a level with the saline, and could see little but the constant flocks of flamingos sailing about like infantry, or like war-parties on the march. These, constantly rising and get ting high into the air, were steering off to other parts, or were streaming down into the saline to spend the night.

We collected great quantities of dried willow-stalks for fuel, and with a rousing fire on each side of us, and a smoke from burning rotten grass, we kept off the mosquitos, but greatly to their disappointment. Their hour arrived, about ten o'clock, they were silent, and we walked forth in the cool air unmolested, and unattracted or amused, except by the clacking and chattering of the wild-fowl of these saline solitudes and the incredible beauty of the firefly halos that were here and there glowing like the light of hidden lamps.

Everywhere and all around us these little insects, each one carrying his beautiful phosphor lamp, were making their curves, and swinging, and dancing under our noses, and sometimes against them; and here and there, in the distance, swarms with myriads in a little space moving in the air, or settled and hovering in the grass and around the bushes, where my note-book was read as easily as by daylight, or under the brightest lamp.

These swarms, some stationary and others travelling, could be seen in the distance until their numbers became countless, and a general flood of light near the ground almost extinguished the dark ness of night. [1]

The salines, of which there are many on the head waters of the Salado and Saladillo, and also further south, near the Colorado, and between that and the Rio Negro, are evidently the remains of salt lakes, in time filled in with growing and decaying vegetation. There are still, around the extreme sources of the Salado, a great number of salt lakes without any connection with running streams, either into or out of them.

These salines, in the winter season, are generally covered with several feet of salt water, which rises from the earth, and in the summer season this water is evaporated by the rays of the sun, leaving an incrustation of the muriate of salt over much of the surface, and other parts a slimy mud associated with salt, so excessively difficult to travel on and so nauseous that no animal whatever will venture into it, and none of the feathered tribes except the stork species, of which are the flamingos. They build their nests and hatch their young in it, in perfect security from molestation by animals of the country.

It is probably owing to this perfect security to their eggs and their young, that incredible numbers of these birds are seen in that country, often settling down, and rising, and wading in these salines, and sailing about over them in millions at the same time.

The flamingo, which is one of the most delicate and beautiful birds in existence, varies from four to five feet in height; its chief colour is pure white, with parts of its wings of the most flaming red, and another proportion jet black.

They gather grass and weeds, with which they build their nests on the ground, and stiffen them up with mud, much in the manner that swallows build. These nests stand in the mud, and are generally about one foot high, open cones, and from two to three feet apart; and sometimes cover hundreds of acres, looking from a distant elevation like a mass of honeycomb.

In the winter season these nests are all under water, and not seen. In the summer, when the water is evaporated, they re-appear, and the birds, taking possession, fit them up, and hatch their broods in them again. The birds are always paired, and the male is busily engaged in hunting and bringing food, or standing by on one leg and sleeping whilst the female is sitting on her eggs. Domestic rights seem to be guarded with the greatest jealousy, and, from their frequent encounters, one would suppose they were protected with the most obstinate and heroic gallantry.

From our bivouac we saddled up in the morning, and rode to a slight eminence, the nearest we could see to the nests, and from that, overlooking the scene with a good field-glass, the picture was one of interest for hours to look upon; it was truly a "Grand Exposition" - grand for its industry of millions, all busy, building, hatching, and feeding - grand for its proportions, extending, perhaps, some twenty miles in length - and grand for the beauty of its colours; for the sun was just up, and its horizontal rays, catching upon the bending columns soaring in the air, and on the never-ending group, where thousands were constantly playing on tip-toe with up-spread wings, and all, the red, the black, and the white, glistening, like the slimy mud they walked and run and played upon, with the sun's refracted rays.

My glass was good, but perhaps I am more inquisitive than other folks - I wanted a nearer view. Reconnoitring the ground closely, though we were full a mile from the nearest part of it, I discovered a sort of promontory of grass and bog, with now and then little tufts of willows, extending into the saline, and very near to where the nests commenced. One of the little Indians who had accompanied us (half negro) told me he could lead me near enough to shoot amongst them. He said he had sometimes walked up so near to them as to catch them with the bolas. "Come on, then," said I. We left the rest of the party to overlook us; we were in the chase (or rather ruse).

Advancing about half the way, we came to a bunch of alder and willow-bushes, and in a few minutes he had cut and so arranged a screen of those, to carry in both hands before him, as completely to hide him from their view, and also to screen me, as I was to walk close up to him, step ping in his footsteps. My hat was left behind, and my belt was filled with boughs rising higher than my head, and with others descending to my feet, so that we were ostensibly (at least for silly birds) nothing but a bunch of bushes.

My cylinders, which my friend Colonel Colt had shaped expressly for shot and ball, I had filled with duck-shot, and we began to move forward in a straight line, but very slowly. Full half a mile, almost inch by inch, the bunch of bushes moved. Sometimes we were on, or astride of, bogs, and sometimes up to our waistbands in mud, and ignorant of the moment that might have taken us to the chin.

However, "nothing risked, nothing won." We kept on, and at length came within some five or six rods of the nearest nests, where the females were setting on their eggs, and the husbands standing on one leg by them and fast asleep, whilst others were gathering worms from the mud and bringing to feed them!

The silly things looked hard at us as an unaccountable appearance, but the bunch of bushes not apparently moving, they seemed to think it was but the natural. I had no chance to sketch, as "Sam" was before me in both hands, and motions would have been imprudent; but I had the most perfect chance to see and to study (to sketch in my mind) every attitude and every characteristic

At length one of the tallest of the throng, with his mouth full of collected worms, seeming to be suspicious, advanced quite up to take a good look at us, and poked his long neck forward, and began to walk around to get a side or back view of us. His motions and expressions were so droll, as I saw him across the bridge of my nose? that I burst (which I could not avoid) into a loud laugh. He screamed, and I fired through the group, a raking fire, and another cylinder as they were getting on the wing; and of all the curious hunting or other scenes that I have seen on earth, that scene was the most curious. Those that were near were wheeling about in the air, like a cloud above us, and shadowing the earth around us; and as the alarm was general, those rising more slowly in the extreme distance looked like a white fog streaming up from the ground. We stood still, and the whirling multitudes in the air formed into lines like infantry, and each, with its leader, was moving around and over our heads, not knowing what the matter was, or where the danger was, or where to go.

One of these lines came so near that I brought the leader down. He descended with outspread wings, and fell within ten feet of me, and down came his troop, faster than I could count them, all in a mass, one upon the other, not knowing what was the trouble, stretching down their long legs and flapping their scarlet wings actually against me and in my face! At the struggling of their dying leader, they all saw there was some mistake, took the alarm, and were off in confusion. Still, brigade after brigade came sailing around us, and I soon discharged all my cylinders, bringing down one at each fire.

From my two first raking shots, where in range they looked like a solid mass, seven or eight were lying dead, and others were hobbling off with broken wings; and of all together we picked up thirteen. But, before picking up my birds, I had been obliged: to pick up my negro Indian boy; he had had no idea of my firing more than once, and my agitation and somewhat of confusion in turning to fire right and left, and withed up in a bunch of bushes filled with smoke, the sharp breech of my rifle had struck him on the temple, and knocked him helpless down, without my knowing it. He had fallen backwards, entangled in his bushes, and was lying on his back, imploring me to be merciful. He thought I had shot him, and that I was going to shoot him again.

I got him up, and soon explained, by signs, the accident, and then we observed our companions without their horses, coming at full gallop, to join us. We were a nasty group, up to our waistbands in the mud and slime, on which the birds walked with scarcely wet feet.

The scene now before us was strange in the extreme, a landscape, a perspective of nests, with the heads of young birds standing out, as far as the eye could discern, and nothing else. Nests with eggs, and nests with young; the very young heads up and gazing, the older young, but without wings, pitched out of their nests, and sprawling, and trying to fly or to hide themselves on the ground. We replaced the little chicks in their nests as, well as we could about us, and left them.

Two pair of the handsomest wings I cut off with my own knife for little *Til-tee,* and the rest were taken by the others of the party. These wings, for military feathers and other uses, are objects of commerce, and always find a ready market in Buenos Ayres and Rio de Janeiro.

Now, why should I lose space by telling how we got back; how we spent the day amongst the birds, the worms and snakes that infest in myriads the shores of the "Grand Saline," how we recrossed the sandy plains, rode to the "talking (echoing) lake," and after shooting ducks and geese till we were tired, we returned to the happy little Auca village.

Til-tee was the first to meet and to greet us, a half a mile from the village. I then gave her the beautiful red wings of the flamingos, and others of green and blue, of the wood-ducks I had shot at the "lake that talks." *Yudolph* knew the little maid, and he trembled with his love for her when she came up and patted him on his nose. She bounded with joy, and was in the village before us.

The villagers were gathered around us, and what was the first that we heard? Borroro had gone to Buenos Ayres, with two Puelche chiefs, who had arrived from the Colorado with information that a large war party of Patagons was assembling on the Rio Negro, for a war with Buenos Ayres! Borroro had left word that I must not think of going to Patagonia yet, and that his son *Gos-brok* should accompany me to Buenos Ayres.

I was very liberal now with the little store of presents I had laid in for the Patagons. *Til-tee* got many strings of beautiful beads, of ribbands, needles, &c; and her mother several vari-coloured cotton shawls, for which she had a peculiar passion; , and with *Gos-brok* for our guide, we started for Buenos Ayres.

And what in Buenos Ayres? All was for war, "war, war, with the infernal Patagons!" Men were enlisting, and soldiers were drilling; and I saw at once the impossibility of a tour through Patagonia under the present circumstances, and why should I say more of my dreamed and fancied expedition which did not, and could not, take place?

Faithful Alzar, who had become very much attached to me, and I were obliged to take leave of each other, and shaking hands for the third and last time, he was saved, perhaps, from shedding any tears, by the "old minié," which I had promised him, and now placed in his hands.

[1] What an ornament these beautiful and harmless insects would be to a nobleman's or gentleman's grounds in England; how beautifully they would light up his lawn. They could easily be imported, and the climate of England would, no doubt, be suitable for them.

Chapter Eight - Tierra del Fuego

My "occupation (again) gone," I dwelt no more on Indians, but thought again of *"Rocks."* "How much more grand, how sublime! Indians are, after all, poor things, and soon to become extinct but rocks! *rocks!* the eternal landmarks and boundaries of the globe!"

"*Tierra del Fuego* (the land of fire), the perpetual snow-covered mountains of the *land of fire!* how harmonious and how inviting. And the fire-vomiting Cotopaxi (Cotopaçi), that coughs up a rock of sixty tons weight, and only throws it 15 miles! and 600 miles the greatest extent to which its awful bellowings are heard; and the snow and cloud capped Chimborazo! (Tchimborācho); these are said actually to exist, and the great Baron de Humboldt has even said so, and also that he saw them; but how much more satisfactory to go and see and *feel* them."

With such contemplations, could I stop in Buenos Ayres? I was going on board the *"Gladiator."* She was bound to Valparaiso, on the Pacific coast. From day to day the palisaded coast of Patagonia, like the cliffs of the Kentish coast in England, were tantalizing us as we passed them. And the ragged, and black and white, and smoking heaps and piles of lifted mountains and mountain-peaks of *"Magellan"* and *"Fuego"* were ahead of us, but as yet in imagination. Cartoons were ready, and colours and pencils, and two days of sleep, ahead, so as to be wide awake whilst passing them.

We are in the Strait of Magellan - and those mountains, blue on our left and before us, and some over them and higher, glistening like the tin roofs of Montreal - the sun's rays are on them, and they are covered with snow!

"Captain, you know all about these?"

"Well, I ought to know something of them; I have seen them from all sides."

"And these black and frowning walls on our right, they look as if they had been broken off with mighty sledge-hammers; and these two, right straight ahead - how immense and how grand! They look as if they had been shoved up from the bottom of the ocean on the back of some terrible monster! Surely the Andes has been broken in two here! what an awful struggle there has been! The Indians tell us that the Andes was once a great serpent - that its tail was here, and these huge rocks were its rattles! how sublime! what a rattle snake! I have crossed over the back of this reptile, and also of its mate, in North America, the Rocky Mountains, in their largest parts."

"I think you are fond of rocks and mountains, sir?"

"Yes, captain, there is nothing else on the earth's surface so sublime, so grand, and so interesting for the study of man. I think of nothing else - but here - how is this? you are anchoring in this cove - what for?"

"Why, sir, the wind is dead ahead around that point yonder, and blowing fresh we'll have to lie by a bit here. We are in 'Pecket Harbour;' vessels are often wind-bound here, and take in water and provisions. There's a sutler here, and he's just come on board, and this is he, sir."

"Ah! where's your town, sir?"

"That's all, that you see yonder, sir, and a few houses around the point there's nothing here but a few of us, and some poor devils, Indians, encamped around us -"

"What! Indians? Well, that's droll; I thought I had finished with Indians. What Indians are they?"

"Well, sir, there's a little encampment of Patagons, and a dozen or so of Fuegians."

"The deuce take the rocks and mountains of snow! they can be seen a hundred years hence as well as now. Captain, I am going ashore, and you must send the yawl with me after breakfast; and let me have one of the cabin-boys to carry my portfolio."

"They shall be at your service, sir."

Ascending the little hill at the back of the village to reach the Indians' camp, and near it, with a mulatto boy carrying my portfolio, I met a large and very fine dog hobbling along towards me, and yelling in the most piteous manner, with an arrow driven into its side quite up to the feather, and two Indians were following it with guns, and evidently intending to shoot it. My first impression was that it was *mad,* and I was raising my rifle for self-defence, when I observed by its crouching position and the wagging of its tail as it was approaching me, that it was seeking a friend in me, and evidently was approaching me for protection.

I answered its supplication by beckoning with my hand, and the poor creature understanding me, crept up and laid down at my feet; but the link of sympathy was severed the next moment, by one of the Indians advancing and shooting the poor creature through the head!

I had no interpreter, and of course no means of getting an explanation; and taking it by the legs, the Indians dragged it into the camp. This was entering an Indian village for once in my life under an excited and rather hesitating feeling, but it would not do to turn back at this point, where the eyes of all were upon us. I was met, however, and luckily, in this dilemma, by an interpreter who was sent to speak with us.

The first thing I asked, and the first thing explained, was the object for which the poor dog had been shot; it was required, by the singular custom of the country, to be placed in the grave with its master, whose body was then just being buried, and whose tent, at a little distance, containing all its furniture, clothing, &c, was then burning!

In the middle of the night before, the poor man had gone out from his tent to move the picket of his horse, when he was bitten in the leg by a rattle snake that he had disturbed. The villagers were all up, with torches in their hands, and the reptile being found, was killed, and the man died in a few hours.

I had sat down with this interpreter, who was a Portuguese half-caste, and also spoke Spanish tolerably well. I told him I feared it would be an unlucky time to visit their little camp, and he said, "No; the occurrence which had just happened would present no difficulty whatever;" and he then conducted me to the chiefs tent, where I was politely received, and easily explained my views, - that I had come ashore from a vessel just arrived, and having learned that a party of Indians were there, I had come to make them a short visit, probably for the day only.

I told him that I had spent the best part of my life in visiting numerous tribes of red people like himself, in various parts of the world, and, like a practical and reasoning man, and a real gentleman, he evidently appreciated my motives in an instant, and began to ask me questions about the various races I had seen, faster even than I could answer them.

This man, though a chief, was but the chief of a band, or perhaps, only of the little encampment over which he had control. His questions were rational and judicious, and after answering them awhile, I took the initiative by opening my portfolio of portraits, which seemed to answer a thousand questions, and evidently to suggest as many more.

I explained to him that I had visited more than one million of red people in their various villages; and on a small map of North America, I pointed out, so that he clearly understood their relative positions and distances from where we were then sitting. He expressed no astonishment whatever-' in his looks or actions, nor made ejaculations, but calmly told me there was much more for poor Indians to learn in this world than he ever before had thought of.

By this time his tent was becoming too small for the crowd that was getting into it, and it became necessary for my mulatto boy to hold up each portrait in turn so that all could see them, whilst I, with the aid of the interpreter, descanted on them.

These people never flatten the head, nor cut and maim the flesh in any way for the purpose of ornamentation, and when I showed them the Flatheads, and explained the process of flattening the head, and the Botocudos and Nayas portraits, with blocks of wood in their lips, a tremendous laugh was raised, and the chief very coolly remarked that "they were very great fools."

For want of space I was now obliged to take up a position outside of the chief's tent, where all comers could see and hear; and amongst others that appeared, there soon came from two grasscovered wigwams, at a little distance, several Fuegians, and amongst them an eccentric character whom the interpreter told me was a medicine-man (a sorcerer), his body and limbs curiously painted, and his head and neck as white as pipe-clay could make them, and surmounted by two white quills of the largest dimensions. This strange looking being, either from jealousy of my works (which of course were considered great *medicine*), or from disbelief in my wonderful relations, took it in his head to raise objections to the "spectacle" that was going on. The chief, however, telling him that I would most likely have his frightful face put in my book, caused him to haul gradually off, whilst the crowd were laughing at him.

I felt at once amongst this little group as if I were amongst a group of Comanches of North America. Not only are they mounted, equipped, and armed, like the Comanches, with bows and arrows, and long lances, and like them in their modes of dress and ornament, but strikingly resemble them in physiognomy and physiological traits.

The men chiefly divide their long hair in two parts, separated on the forehead and thrown on to the shoulders and back by a silver-plated band or hoop, which is crowded down from the top of the head and over the hair, near to the eyebrows, holding the hair in its place, clear from the face and back of the ears. Their faces are always (in full dress) painted red from the eyebrows to the mouth, including the ears, and the other parts of the face painted in a variety of shapes and bright colours, and they wear no head-dresses, and very seldom ornament the head even with a single quill or feather.

Their dress at this season - the middle of January, and therefore midsummer - is very slight. The men wear a breech-cloth around the waist, and the women a sort of apron of cotton-cloth or of bark, extending down to the knee, and mocasins beautifully embroidered, made of the skins of deer or goats; and, in the colder season, both men and women dress the leg with skins and wrap them selves in robes made of the skins of guanacos, and curiously painted; and their tents, which are small and light for the convenience of transportation, are made of the skins of the same animal, or of wild cattle and horses, with which the vast plains of their country abound.

Observing on the chiefs face the marks of small pox, I questioned him about it, and he informed me that when he was a boy he was near dying with that disease, and he told me that, about 1812 or 1815, as near as I could ascertain, that awful disease was communicated to his people by some white people on the coast, who were selling rum and whiskey and other things to the Indians, and that more than one half of the great and powerful tribe of Patagons were destroyed by it.

"We are poor," said he; "we want many things that the white people make - their cloths, their knives, their guns, and many other things - and we come here to buy them, and many of my people, who are foolish, will buy whiskey, and it makes them mad, when they will kill even their own mothers and their little children. We do all we can to prevent this, but still it is not stopped, and we are afraid of getting the awful disease again."

One can easily see that I had enough to do this day without painting, and we returned on board full of fatigue and hunger, the chief having agreed to sit for his portrait the next day, if the vessel would wait for me.

My conditional appointment with the chief being explained to the captain, and the portfolio opened to him, which he had not before seen, he agreed to wait another day, whatever the wind might be, for the satisfaction of gratifying me, and the pleasure he would have ashore with me.

Captain Ford proved to be a real *"bon homme,"* and, becoming as much taken up with me as the Indians were, went ashore with me the next morning, on condition that he could have the pictures to lecture on amongst the women and children, who had not yet seen them, whilst I was sketching my portraits. And when night came, and we were safe on board again and our craving stomachs pacified, he said to me that this had been to him the happiest day of his life that he ever had spent.

My sketch of this rational and intelligent chief was followed by that of his wife and a warrior; and then hasty sketches were made at the little and more humble demure of the Fuegians, at which the famous doctor, with his white head, was *minus,* he having withdrawn himself, probably with absolute disgust.

The reader will easily imagine with what excitement, and with what *éclat,* and with what security and success, from this point I could have penetrated and passed through the centre of Patagonia, with the introduction of this little returning colony, had there been no rumours of war, and I had had my faithful Caesar, or even Alzar, with me; but here I stood alone, and the barren coast could have furnished me no reliable companions. But it may happen yet that I shall be able to see the way and a proper time to pass through the midst of these interesting people; and then if it happens I shall be able to say more of them and their customs than I now can.

Yet, from this little caravan, who had travelled several hundred miles to visit the coast, I learned many things of interest, and was enabled to learn them in a little time. As to the fabulous accounts of "giants," men "eight and ten feet high," as related by some early writers, I learned from this chief that there actually existed no such monstrous persons in the tribe, though there were some parts of the country where the men were very tall, considerably taller than himself.

From this man I learned that the government of the Patagons resembled very closely that of most of the North American tribes - a head chief, and a council of subordinate chiefs, or chiefs of bands, forming the government of the tribe. He told me they could muster 8000 warriors, well-mounted and well-armed, and were abundantly able to defend themselves and their country from assaults of any enemy they had.

That the tribe of Puelches on the north of them, between them and Buenos Ayres, were their relations, and that through them they traded horses and hides for guns and ammunition, to the Buenos Ayreans, and in that way could equip all the warriors of the tribe. They catch their horses wild on the prairies, and train and ride them, in the same way, and as well, as the Comanches do.

Their saddles and stirrups are made with great skill, and the stirrups for women (who ride astride, and as boldly as the men) are suspended by a broad and ornamented strap crossing the horse's neck; and for both men and women these stirrups, which are made of wood, and curiously carved, admit but the two largest toes to enter, to guard against fatal accidents which too often befall horsemen in the civilized world.

Their dead are always buried in a sitting posture, and with them their pipes and their weapons, and by the side of them their dogs and their horses; and everything else that they possess is burned with their wigwam.

The Fuegians are a tribe of some five or six thousand, inhabiting both sides of the Strait of Magellan; living entirely on fish and wildfowl, and their lives are spent chiefly in their canoes, made from bark of trees, sewed together and glued, some what like the canoes of the Ojibbeways of North America. In the summer season they go chiefly naked, both men and women, wearing only a flap covering the hips; and in the winter, cover their bodies with robes made of the skins of the sea-wolf, which they kill with their spears and arrows.

Their manufacture of flint spear and arrow heads is not surpassed by even the Apachees, or Snakes, or any other of the North American tribes, and they are made in the same forms, and by the same process, which has been described. And their wigwams, which are very small, are made by setting a number of slender poles in the ground in a circle, and bending the tops in, forming a cone, which is covered with long grass, or with skins of the sea-wolf.

These people are unquestionably a branch of the Patagon family, speaking a dialect of the Patagon language, and living in harmony and friendship with them; and living by the side of and adjoining them, and still so entirely unlike, both in physiognomy and in symmetrical proportions, furnish one of the most striking and satisfactory proofs of the metamorphose of *man,* by men's different modes of life.

Wind-bound a third day, I went again ashore, and drew, through the interpreter, which he pronounced with distinct emphasis, the following brief vocabulary of Patagonian translations of English words, which may be interesting to the reader:

English.	Patagon.	English.	Patagon.
I	ya	good	getenc
you	mushma	bad	sterone
he	da	large	stsanic
they	dushda	small	stsalenc
this	win	hot	borshenc
that	miro	cold	curshenc
dry	arenc	girl	carsen
wet	etshaksh	father	yanco
high	sebenick	mother	yan
low	tsamnick	brother	den
sweet	goosh	sister	denon
bitter	stark	husband	hausenk
clean	jet	wife	shay
dirty	startenk		
sick	shoyu	head	eru
much	tsait	hair	hon
little	stalco	nose	or
red	gabenk	eye	otl
yellow	waitenk	mouth	consen
blue	caltenk	tongue	stal
white	orenk	ear	shan
black	polnk	knee	tepen
before	wieeker	foot	shawkenue
behind	aucenker	arm	hensh
below	anunk		
here	nane	horse	caul
there	hemai	mule	molo
yes	hooi	dog	shamenoo
no	gom	fire	yaic
		water	hamin
man	alen	wind	kurshun
woman	naac	sea	kono
baby	amel	sky	coche
boy	stalsen	cloud	pawin

gold	pothamic	star	sterke
silver	pesho	night	stenon
iron	akels	morning	wiec
stone	yaten	noon	catese
knife	paiken	evening	sterker
pipe	anu	before	seuco
tobacco	golgi	to-day	ma
spoon	coyu	to-morrow	nashgut
gun	yalbok	to-morrow morning	} hatyunk
pistol	yalbok-chame		
powder	yalbok-shepen	yesterday	nashensh
		now	yomeno
sun	senisensin	always	gelooni
moon	senisenson		

Numerals

One	choche	Seventeen	caoc-caur
Two	wame	Eighteen	winecage-caur
Three	caash	Nineteen	kamektsen-caur
Four	cage	Twenty	wameno casen
Five	tsenon	Twenty-one	wameno casen choche-caur
Six	winecash		
Seven	caoc	Thirty	casheno casen
Eight	winecage	Forty	cageno casen
Nine	kamektsen	Fifty	tsenono casen
Ten	casen	Sixty	winecasheno casen
Eleven	choche-caur	Seventy	caocono casen
Twelve	weme-caur	Eighty	winecagono casen
Thirteen	caash-caur	Ninety	kamektsenono casen
Fourteen	cage-caur	Hundred	patak
Fifteen	tsenon-caur	Two hundred	wame palak
Sixteen	winecash-caur	Thousand	warank

Chapter Nine - The Indians, Where From?

Having in this and the former volume introduced my young readers in a cursory manner to most of the principal tribes of the American Indians and their leading customs and modes of life, from the highest latitude in North America to the southernmost cape of South America, there yet remain to be made, within the original conception of this little work, some general remarks of interest, which are suggested by the queries naturally arising in the minds of the readers - *"Who are the American Indians? - from whence did they come? - and, where are they going?"*

These questions involve matter of very great importance to ethnology and to human education generally, and deserve a much greater space than can be allotted to them in this little book, in which all that is to be yet said must necessarily be concise.

If we should look to the Indians themselves to answer the above questions, they would decide for us very briefly (having no history, sacred or profane) "that they are the favourite children of the Great Spirit, created on the grounds on which they live," and that they are "going to the setting sun."

The first of these beliefs is the unexceptional instinct of all the American tribes; and the second, no doubt the poetical figure raised by the continual and never-ending encroachments of civilization upon them, forcing them from their hunting-grounds, and consequently driving them to the west, towards the "setting sun."

Some of their various theories of their creation will be given, but science demands some better solution of questions so important. And if with that view the suggestions hereafter to be made should fail to settle those important facts, they will, like other theories that have been abundantly advanced, tend towards an ultimate solution of questions which science as yet is a great way from having determined.

Various theories have been advanced, and by very eminent men, as to the origin of the American Indians, who were found, on the first discovery of the American continent, to be inhabiting every part of it from pole to pole, and every island contiguous to it in the Atlantic and Pacific oceans.

These facts put the question at once - "From whence did these people come? and by what means and by what route did they come?" These questions are based upon an established *presumption of necessity* (which may yet.be questioned), and ethnologists and geographers have indicated Bhering's Strait and other points as the probable routes by which they arrived from the "Old World." All have suggested routes and modes by which it was *possible* they could have come, and their theories there all stand on the slender ground that not one of them has produced a particle of proof that they *did come,* or that it was *necessary* that they *should have come.*

When the science of human ethnology, which has been for some thousands of years travelling to the west with the advance of civilization, gets quite around the globe, it will probably be seen whether there has not been some error at its starting-point - error as its basis, and, consequently, error heaped upon error as it has advanced. Whether erroneous dogmas, travelling with the wave of civilization, have not been too much the established rule by which all things ethnological in the New World should be measured; and whether true ethnological knowledge of a people is best drawn from an independent study of those people and their habits, or from the application of an ethnological education drawn from books, *made from books,* with all the dogmatical rules that have been made for, and applied to, other peoples?

Is it *necessary* that on the last quarter of the globe a whole continent of human beings, independent, and happy in their peculiar modes of life, and never heard of or thought of until the fourteenth century, should be traced when discovered, back to the opposite side of the globe, because civilization happened to come from there? What an ill conceit of civilized man to believe that because his ancestors came from the east, all mankind on a new continent, a new world, must have come from there also! And what a pity for science, and what a blunder *in* science, if such a fact be established before it is proved; and what proof of it is there? I have said, "None whatever."

Ethnologists and other savants find amongst the American Indians some resemblances in physiological traits to some foreign races. How strange if there were not such! Once in a while, a word in their language resembles a word in the Hebrew or other eastern language. How extraordinary if in any two languages there were not some words bearing a resemblance to each other! And then these savants say, "Not only in the resemblance of language, but in the *structure* of language." But how trivial is all such evidence as this, when all languages are constructed to suit the organs pronouncing them, and which are the same in all the human race, leaving us to wonder that the resemblance in the construction of languages is not greater than it is.

One distinguished ethnologist of England recites in his work on Ethnology one word of only two syllables, found in use amongst an American tribe on the Pacific coast, the same as spoken by a tribe on the opposite coast of Siberia, as an evidence that the American tribe came from that coast, probably by the way of Bhering's Strait!

What a monstrous way to prove a theory, and how bad the theory that grasps at such proofs! If such an isolated word was worth a notice, why not better suppose that probably some poor fisherman of Siberia had been driven in his canoe to the Columbia coast, and that the American Indians who picked him up adopted from him a dying word to recollect him by?

As has been said, that I went to Petropotrovski, to the Alaeutian Islands, and to Kamskatka, on the coast of Siberia. I found many words of Siberian languages spoken on the American side of the Strait of Bhering, and as many, or more, on the Siberian side, of the American languages. What did this prove? Nothing - except that there had been a mutual crossing of Bhering's Strait in their canoes or on the ice (both of which at certain seasons are feasible), and that there had been, to a certain extent, a mutual adoption of words in their languages. It proved that those opposite people sometimes cross the strait, while the total absence of resemblance in physiological traits as positively disprove the fact of emigration (or peopling a continent) from one side or the other.

The ethnologist enters the wildest tribes on the United States frontier, and to his astonishment finds the Indians there using occasionally French and English words, and now and then meets a half-white Indian, with a French face and a French beard. This is no evidence that these tribes are Frenchmen or Englishmen, but proves only that Frenchmen and Englishmen have been there a hundred years before him.

He finds these people using bows and arrows, the same precisely as were anciently used by the ancient Saxon race, the flint arrow and spear heads precisely the same as those of the ancient Britons, and he is astounded! but why astonished? What do these prove? Not that the American Indians emigrated from the British Isle, or that the ancient Britons came across the Atlantic in their canoes from America, but it helps to prove the truth of the old *adage,* that "necessity is the mother of invention," that the nations of all the earth, without the use of iron, having necessity for food and means of getting it, and implements for war and defence, have had alike the ingenuity to take the sharp edge of broken flints for knives and arrow-points, and by the aid of their inventive powers, granted them alike by the Great Spirit, they have everywhere improved them much in the same shape, not from each other, but led to the same results and same forms by the peculiar fracture of the stone, in all countries the same, and the similar objects for which their knives and arrow-heads were formed.

The flint arrow, therefore, and the bow to throw it, have been not necessarily the gift of one nation to another, but the native invention of every people. They certainly came not from Adam. Adam was a gardener, and his sons farmers and tenders of flocks. These things, then, were purely of human invention, and growing out of necessity; and if one race invented them, another race, from the same necessity, could as well do it.

Savants who have grown up ethnologists in their fathers' libraries of books, also tell us that some portions of the splendid ruins at Uxmal and Copan, as well as ancient sculptures found in Mexico, and the relics found on the Ohio and Muskingum are of Egyptian origin, because they resemble Egyptian monuments.

How weak is such evidence, that merely because these ruins and these sculptures happen to resemble some edifices or some sculptures of the Egyptians, that they are of Egyptian origin. They admit that they were built by savage tribes, for they bear no Egyptian inscriptions or hieroglyphics, but the inscriptions and hieroglyphics of savage races who must have brought their art of building and sculpture from Egypt!

How astonishing that such stupendous ruins are actually there, and were built there, and left there, without a living soul to tell their history, or who built them, and covered with inscriptions and hieroglyphics, no doubt telling their own history if they could be read, but no corresponding living language in the old world or the new, to prove that their origin was Asiatic or Egyptian.

Egyptian sculpture and Egyptian architecture were not taught the Egyptians; they were the inventions, and in their grandeur and magnificence were but the progress of, native art; and so the ruined temples and palaces of Palenque and Uxmal.

Talents for art and design are inherent in all mankind, and as wealth and luxury and civilization increase in all countries, so will sculpture and architecture advance in grandeur and in beauty of. design; and these advancements, like those in Indian weapons, suggested by the demands of elegance and comfort in buildings, or of beauty and nature in sculpture, with nature everywhere the same for its models, will necessarily, in all countries, arrive, sooner or later, at more or less resemblance.

A sculptured statue, found amongst the antiquities of Mexico or Yucatan, if it resembles ever so closely an Egyptian statue, it is no evidence whatever that it was transported from Egypt to America, or that the sculptor of it came from that country, bringing his tools and his models with him; it only proves that in both countries men have alike an inherent talent for art, and that working from similar models, and in similar material, they have arrived at equal perfection, both copying closely their model, and their works, consequently and necessarily, resembling one another.

An ethnologist finds amongst the American Indians a wooden spoon, precisely the same in proportions and shape as the wooden spoons brought from the Kalmuk Tartars, in Asia. This, though only evidence for a bad theory, proves just as much as resemblance in statuary, or of façades, door ways, &c. in ancient palaces; it proves that man's ingenuity and necessities in both countries led him to build façades and doorways, and to adapt the length and shape of his spoon to suit the motions of his arm, and the bowl of it to fit his mouth.

The ancient Egyptians, before the construction of their stupendous monuments, and their grand groups in sculpture, which now stand to astonish the world, lived in tents like the Aztec Indians previous to their building the cities of Palenque, Copan, and Uxmal. And the two native races, developing the talent with which nature had endowed them for those grand purposes, probably constructed those vast edifices on the two continents about the same time.

In the two countries the wonder is, not that there should be a resemblance in their monuments, but that the people who built them, and arose by their own talents to such grandeur in art, and such luxury, should have fallen short of all history which should have recorded their greatness.

To the theory so often and so strongly advanced of an Egyptian or Asiatic origin of the American Indians, there are yet other and stronger objections to be produced before the subject is disposed of.

The theory of such a mode of peopling a whole continent involves, as will be seen, difficulties and objections (considering the time at which such supposed emigrations took place), in effect equal to *impossibility* itself. I say *impossibility,* because the Aztec ruins in Yucatan and Guatemala, which speak a language, which no one can deny, are as old as the most ancient monuments of Egypt, and are unquestionably the results of the growth of a civilization from savage native tribes, which growth itself must have required some thousands of years.

The evidence that those monuments were not the works of Egyptian architects, is, that, though in some respects they bear a resemblance, not an Egyptian inscription or hieroglyphic mark is to be found amongst them, and also that if the Egyptians, in so advanced a state of civilization and art, emigrated to the continent of America, and built such stupendous palaces and other edifices, it is quite impossible, though the people have perished, that history should have been, until the date of Columbus, in ignorance of the American continent.

From the above dates and evidences of dates, we are bound to infer that the American native races are as ancient as any of the races of the "old world," whose antiquity is known by their monuments.

Then let us see, if the builders of those monuments were Egyptians or Asiatics, what objects they had in coming to America - how they found the way there - and how they got there (at least 6000 years ago, if at all), when civilization, with the art of navigation, and stimulated by commerce, by science, and the thirst for gold, never reached there until within the last 400 years..

There is nothing in history, sacred or profane, to prove a peopling of one continent from the other, and probably forever, as at the present time, *presumption* will be the only ground on which such a theory will stand; and if the fact could be proved to have transpired, there is nothing yet to show that it might not as well have been from west to east, as from east to west.

The most enthusiastic theorists on this subject have never yet entertained the idea of a savage emigration across the Atlantic or the Pacific Ocean, but look to Bhering's Strait, where, by possibility, at certain seasons of the year (as has been said), they can cross from continent to continent on the ice, or in canoes, but what motive for doing that, in the state in which savage society in the frozen regions of Kamskatka, 6000 years ago, when at the present time, with all their modern improvements in boat building, in weapons, and with some ideas of commerce to stimulate them, no Indian, on either coast, ventures across, except under the advice and escort of civilized men who accompany them.

Savages, of all the human family, are the least disposed to emigrate, - like animals, their instinct is against it; driven from their homes, like animals, they will return to them, and without the stimulants of science, of commerce, or of gold, like animals, they are contented to remain in them.

If the barren and frozen coast of Siberia had been overstocked with a surplus population, and the American coast opposite, a luxuriant garden, instead of a coast equally barren and desolate, such an emigration might have been a possible thing for Asiatics, and in the space of 6000 years they might possibly have increased and spread over North America, and perhaps through Central and South America, to Terra del Fuego, but if so, where are they?

In the whole extent of the whole American continent, from Bhering's Strait to Terra del Fuego, there is not to be seen, amongst the savage tribes, a Mongol, a Kalmuk, or a Siberian Tartar, nor a word of their language to be heard. Languages, to be sure, may be lost or changed, but physiological traits of people are never lost whilst the race exists.

Some travellers through South America, as if to aid the theory of Asiatic emigration, have represented the tribes of the Upper Amazon with "bridled" eyes, like the Chinese, and even caricatured the Chinese obliquity, and put these more than Chinese peculiarities forward as "types." But I have seen most of the tribes on the Amazon and its affluents, and though the natives in those regions are *generally* a low degree of American aborigines, they exhibit nothing of the Mongol general character of face, nor Mongol obliquity of eye, other than the occasional muscular approach to it produced by their peculiar habits of life, living mostly, in their fisherman's lives, in their canoes; their eyes affected by the refraction of the vertical rays of the sun on water, on which they are looking; and on land, walking with naked feet, requiring their eyes to be constantly on the ground before their steps.

The effect thus produced in the expression of their eyes is very striking, but is neither Mongolic nor a "type," but *aberration from type,* produced by the external causes above named.

I have said above that if an Asiatic population had crossed at Bhering's Strait, they might in time have advanced through North and South and Central America, and have stocked the whole continent; and this has been claimed by the advocates of Asiatic immigration. This is a *possibility,* and therefore, they say, is *probable;* but here possibility stops, and certainly *proof* with it.

The Sandwich Islands, with a population of 500,000, are more than two thousand miles from the coast of South America. How did the population of those islands get there? Certainly not in canoes over ocean waves of two thousand miles. But I am told, "The Sandwich islanders are Polynesians." Not a bit of it; they are 2000 miles north of the Polynesian group, with the same impossibility of canoe navigation, and are as different in physiological traits of character and language from the Polynesian as they are different from the American races.

However voluminous and learned the discussions may be on the mysterious subject of the origin of races, they must all come to the conclusion at last that, even if Asiatic, or Egyptian, or Polynesian populations found their way to the American continent, at whatever date, they found, and intermingled with, an aboriginal American race as ancient as, or more ancient than, the races they descended from.

Some have contended that the American Indians are Jews, and that the "ten lost tribes of Israel," got to the American coast, and gave a population to the continent. How chimerical is this. At the date of the disappearance of the "ten tribes," the ruined cities of Yucatan and Guatemala were in full splendour; and with no advantages of navigation, the ten tribes would have had to wander through the barbarous and savage tribes of Chinese, Kalmuk, Mongol, and Siberian Tartary to the snowy and icy regions of Kamskatka and Bhering's Strait, a distance of more than 10,000 miles; and for what? for a new continent they never had heard of, for, if any one had ever reached it, certainly no one had ever gone back.

This interesting but unimportant question of, "Where the American Indians came from," has been elaborately and ingeniously discussed by able writers, and still will probably continue to be discussed for centuries to come, without being further understood than at the present time; and enough has been said of it in this little work to prepare the minds of its readers for my own opinions, which I am about to advance, as to that part of the question put in the beginning of this chapter, not *"Where they came from,"* but *"Who are the American Indians?"*

Chapter Ten - The Indians, Who Are They?

The reader has learned, by following me through these two little volumes, that I have, during fourteen years of research, not amongst books and libraries, but in the open air and the wilderness, studied the looks and character of the American native races in every latitude, from Bhering's Strait to Terra del Fuego; and here he will learn that, from the immutable, national, physiological traits with which the Almighty stamps this and every other race, I believe the native tribes of the American continent are all integral parts of one great family, and that He who made man from dust created these people from the dust of the country in which they live, and to which dust their bodies are fast returning.

I can find nothing in history, sacred or profane, against this; and from their colour and physiological traits, which are different from all other races on the earth, as well as from reasons advanced in the foregoing chapter, I am compelled to believe that, in His boundless and unerring wisdom, the Almighty, who "created the cattle of the fields, the fishes in the sea, and fowls of the air" of this vast and glowing continent "for man's use" (not that they should grow and decay for thousands of centuries, until man should accidentally reach them to enjoy them), placed these red children there, and said to them, in some way, "I am your Father, your Maker; I give you these things; go forth and enjoy them." And that in the undisputed enjoyment of this rich inheritance given them, of unlimited fields and forests abounding in game, and unbounded liberty for using it, they were, in Mexico, in Yucatan, and Perou, duly and successfully using those faculties which God had given them, and intended for raising them gradually into civilization and splendour, when cataclysms sunk the splendid edifices and the people in one, and more than barbarous or savage cruelties of mercenary men, crushed their rising power, robbed them of their gold, and carried the sword and death amongst the others, and sent a drowning wave of discouragement through the remotest tribes of the continent.

The American Indians are as distinct from all the other races of the earth as the other races of the earth are distinct from each other, and, both in North and South and Central America, exhibit but one great original family type, with only the local changes which difference of climate and different modes of life have wrought upon it.

I believe they were created on the ground on which they have been found, and that the date of their creation is the same as that of the human species on other parts of the globe. This belief is founded on the reasons advanced in the fore going chapter, supported by the traditions of the Indians, which will be noticed, and a strong and unavoidable, intuitive disbelief that all the races of man, of different colours, have descended from one pair of ancestors, involving, from necessity, the crime of *incest,* after the holy institution of marriage, as the means of peopling the earth; and the inconceivable plan of the whole surface of the earth teeming with luxuries, "created for man's use," vegetating and decaying for tens of thousands of years, until wandering man, from one point, and from one pair, by accident, arrives there to use them.

Some writers have advanced the belief that South America and the continent of Europe were anciently united, and that the American continent received its population in that way; but as this is mere hypothesis, and probably will forever remain so, it refers us for a last remaining remark, to Bhering's Strait, by which route, if the American Indians are the descendants of "Adam" and "Eve," at the rate that an infant savage population would spread over an uninhabited and desolate country, several thousand years would have been required to populate and move through the vast regions of Kalmuk Tartary and Siberia to Bhering's Strait, a distance of more than 10,000 miles; and from Bhering's Strait to Central and South America, and Terra del Fuego, 10,000 miles more, and an equal time required - one thousand years at least for a civilization to arise sufficient to have built the splendid monuments of Yucatan, and the vast space of time that has transpired since those monuments were depopulated; in all, a space of time far transcending that allowed by sacred history, or even by geology, for man's appearance on the earth!

The American Indians know nothing of this, yet their traditions and monuments prove beyond a doubt their great antiquity; for, of 120 different tribes which I have visited in North and South and Central America, every tribe has related to me, more or less distinctly, their traditions of the Deluge, in which one, or three, or eight persons were saved above the waters, on the top of a high mountain; and also their peculiar and respective theories of the *Creation.*

Some of these tribes, living at the base of the Rocky Mountains, and in the plains of Venezuela, and the Pampa del Sacramento in South America, make annual pilgrimages to the fancied summits where the antediluvian species were saved in canoes or otherwise, and, under the mysterious regulations of their *medicine* (mystery) *men,* tender their prayers and sacrifices to the Great Spirit, to ensure their exemption from a similar catastrophe.

Indian traditions are generally conflicting, and soon run into fable; but how strong is the *unanimous* tradition of the aboriginal races of a whole continent, of such an event! how strong a corroboration of the Mosaic account; and what an unanswerable proof that the *American Indian* is an antediluvian race! and how just a claim does it lay, with the various modes and forms which these poor people practise in celebrating that event, to the inquiries and sympathies of the philanthropic and Christian, as well as to the scientific, world!

Some of those writers who have endeavoured to trace the American Indians to an Asiatic or Egyptian origin, have advanced these traditions as evidence in support of their theories, which are as yet but unconfirmed hypotheses; and as there is not yet known to exist (as I have before said), either in the American languages, or in the Mexican or Aztec, or other monuments of these people, one single acceptable proof of such an immigration, these traditions are strictly American - indigenous, and not exotic.

If it were shown that inspired history of the Deluge and of the Creation restricted those events to one continent alone, then it might be that the American races came from the eastern continent, bringing these traditions with them; but until that is proved, the American traditions of the Deluge are no evidence whatever of an eastern origin.

Though there is not a tribe in America but what have some theory of man's creation, there is not one amongst them all that bears the slightest resemblance to the Mosaic account. How strange is this, if these people came from the country where inspiration was prior to all history!

The Mandans believed they were created under the ground, and that a portion of their people reside there yet. [1]

The Choctaws assert that "they were created crawfish, living alternately under the ground and above it, as they chose; and coming out at their little holes in the earth to get the warmth of the sun one sunny day, a portion of the tribe was driven away and could not return; they built the Choctaw village, and the remainder of the tribe are still living under the ground."

The Sioux relate with great minuteness their traditions of the Creation. They say that the Indians were all made from the "Red Pipe Stone," which is exactly of their colour - that the Great Spirit, at a subsequent period, called all the tribes together at the Red Pipe Stone Quarry, and told them this: "that the red stone was their flesh, and that they must use it for their pipes only."

Other tribes were created under the water; and at least one half of the tribes in America represent that man was first created under the ground, or in the rocky caverns of the mountains. Why this diversity of theories of the *Creation,* if these people brought their traditions of the *Deluge* from the land of inspiration?

How far these general traditions of a flood relate to an *universal Deluge,* or to local cataclysms (of which there have evidently been one or more, over portions of the American continent), or whether there HAS BEEN *an universal Deluge,* and at what period, it is difficult to determine.

One thing, however, is certain - the Indian traditions everywhere point distinctly at least to *one* such event, and amongst the Central and Southern tribes, they as distinctly point to *two* such catastrophes, in which their race was chiefly destroyed; and the rocks of their countries bear evidence yet more conclusive of the same calamities, which probably swept off the populations in the plains, and, as their traditions say, left scattered remnants on the summits of the Andes and the Rocky Mountains.

Since that epoch (or those epochs), their descendants have wandered off into the fertile plains where climate and a greater abundance of game and fish have invited them, peopling in time the whole continent, from the Atlantic to the Pacific coasts, and the West India and other islands.

These scattered people have arranged themselves into different tribes, with languages dialectic or idiomatic, but without exception bearing evident physiological traits of the ancient parent stock, with local and tribal differences produced by different habits of life, and varieties of climates, and differences of food on which they subsist.

The Crows, of whom I have spoken in a former chapter, and also at greater length in the first volume of this work, still inhabiting a part of the Rocky Mountains in North America, with the Apachees and several other tribes in New Mexico, still exhibit in bold relief the original type, which is seen so well preserved in the stone monuments of Yucatan and ancient Mexico, and the same unmistakable, though less conspicuous, is traceable through the alto-Peruvian tribes; the *Moxos,* the *Chiquitos,* the *Cochabambas,* and others yet to the south.

The Crows are living Toltecs (or Aztecs), and history abounds in proof that the Toltecs in Mexico and the Aztecs in Yucatan and Guatemala came from the mountains in the north.

The Aztecs emigrated farther to the south and east than the Toltecs, and to a more fertile country, but lower in position, by which means, in the second cataclysm, their magnificent cities were submerged, and their populations exterminated, but their imperishable monuments record the truth that such a race then and there existed, as well as the physiological traits of its present population prove that the Mexicans are remains of the Toltec race.

The history, which establishes beyond a doubt the migration of the Toltecs and Aztecs from the mountains of the north-west into Mexico and Yucatan, is extremely vague as to time, and from the similarity of their monuments, it seems probable that they were portions of the same race, who have taken different names from the different periods of their emigrations, or from the positions to which they respectively went, the word Toltec (or Toh-tec) being still applied by some of the northern Mexicans to the people of the mountains (mountaineers), and the word Aztec (or Ah-tec), to the people of the low countries (lowlanders), and Ah-na-tec to the people beyond the lowlanders (the white people). Subsequent to the second cataclysm, which destroyed the Aztecs, and deluged their stupendous monuments, the Toltecs built the city of Mexico in a high and sterile region, from fear of a similar fate to that of their neighbours, the Aztecs.

In the second cataclysm the summits of the mountains in the West Indies, then forming a part of the main land of the continent, protected a portion of their inhabitants, who, from the fear of another calamity (and later from the cruelty of the Spanish invaders, since the discovery of America), have emigrated in vast numbers to the coast of Venezuela, Guiana, and Yucatan: such are the *Caribbes;* and from the north and the west of Guatemala and Mexico, the *Maya* and other tribes have migrated to the east, spreading over the promontory of Yucatan, Honduras, &c.

Amongst all of these tribes, as well as amongst the present Mexicans and the numerous tribes to the north, even to the Kiowas and the Comanches, I have found distinct traditions of *three* successive cataclysms - two by *water,* and one by *fire.* And in the rocks and mountains, both in the West India Islands and on the Mexican coast, as well as in Yucatan and its ruins, I have found, from chemical and geological tests, undeniable evidences of the same catastrophes.

Nothing is more certain than that the second cataclysm in those regions was produced by the volcanic actions underneath, causing a subsidence of a large tract of country, including the whole range of the greater and lesser Antilles, the promontory of Yucatan, the eastern and lower parts of Mexico and Honduras, and even extending to the coast of Venezuela.

At a later period (perhaps some thousands of years) this subsided country, or a great proportion of it, has, from an opposite action of similar causes, risen to a sufficient extent towards its ancient elevation, to show, in the granite and volcanic tops of the Antilles which have reappeared above the ocean, the continuation of the Cordillera, and also to expose to view the Aztec ruins of Guatemala and Yucatan; leading us to the rational and unavoidable conclusions that a people so far advanced in civilization and the arts as to build such populous and magnificent cities as Palenque, Uxmal, and Copan, were never confined to three cities, but that other cities of equal or greater extent were spread , over the plains, which, in the days of the Aztecs, extended from the ruins of Yucatan to the base of the West India mountains, and which lost cities may now be said to be *ruins under the sea.*

What is now the Caribbean Sea and the Gulf of Mexico were, in the days of Uxmal and Palenque, vast and fertile plains, through which the Rio Grande del Norte and the Mississippi wended their long and serpentine ways, and, uniting their waters near the base of the mountains, debouched into the ocean between Cuba and the Bahama Islands.

This vast space, in area much larger than the kingdoms of France and England together, teeming with luxuries the most inviting to man, with the richest soil and the most salubrious climate of the world, would consequently have had its portion of the Aztec race, and probably the ruins of million? and millions are there, still embedded under the sea. [2]

The reader who does not travel may easily trace on his map the Cordillera range, through Grenada, and pointing out at Santa Martha, on the coast of Venezuela, and follow it through the lesser and greater Antilles; and he who travels may see with the naked eye, on the northern face of the Silla, at Carraccas, the sublime vertical grooves cut when that mighty subsidence went down.

From those points, the chain of the lesser Antilles, as now seen, is a succession of mountain peaks, some volcanic, and others not, continuing the course of the Cordillera; and from chemical and geological tests, I have found that they have anciently occupied positions equally elevated as the highest parts of the Andes at the present day!

In my descent from the tribe of Crows in the northern ranges of the Rocky Mountains (as has been described), through the other Toltec tribes, to Mexico, in 1854, and gathering their traditions all pointing to the sunken countries, I was forcibly struck with the importance of these great changes, in their probable effects on the distribution of races.

I contemplated *tests* by which to determine the extent of those subsidences, and the depths to which they had sunk; and also, the partial elevations to which they have again arisen; and with examinations I then made, partly establishing my theory, I visited the Baron de Humboldt, in Berlin, in 1855 (the same visit alluded to in page 204). And after having fully explained my theory to him, and the tests which I brought him, when I was about starting on a second voyage to the lesser Antilles, I received the following complimentary and approving letter from him:-

"To Geo. Catlin, Esq.

"My Dear Sir,

"I have read with profound interest the papers you left with me. I believe with you; that the Crows are Toltecs; and I was instantly impressed with this belief when I first saw your portraits of Crow chiefs in London, some years since. But I am more struck with your mode of determining the sinking and rising transits of rocks, and the probable dates and extent of cataclysmic disasters. I believe your tests are *reliable,* and perfectly justify you for making the contemplated voyage to the lesser Antilles. The subject is one of vast importance to science, and if I were a younger man I would join you in the expedition at once!

"I believe your discoveries will throw a great deal of light on the important subject of the effect of cataclysms on the distribution of races.

"I return to you with this, the papers you left with me, and I enclose you a *memorandum* for your voyage, which may lead you to examinations that you might otherwise overlook.

"Let nothing stop you - you are on a noble mission, and the Great Spirit will protect you.

"Your sincere friend,

"A. V. Humboldt.

"Potsdam, Sept. 12th, 1855."

Armed with this encouraging letter, and the in valuable *"memorandum,"* from that great philosopher, for my further guidance, I made my second visit to the West Indies, and carried my tests, and applied them to the summits of the Ando Venezuelan mountains on the coast of South America; and with facts which I then gathered, I re-crossed the ocean, and was traversing the continent to lay the results of my researches before my noble friend, as he had desired, when the news of his death met me, but in no way depreciated the important facts with which I was freighted. [3]

The migration of the Toltecs and Aztecs, from the north, and the cataclysmic events so well proved by Indian traditions, and more positively established by the tests I have alluded to, account for the total extinction of a race so numerous, and so far advanced in civilization and arts, that they could not have fallen by the hands of native tribes; nor is it possible to believe that the whole of such a race could have been destroyed by an epidemic disease.

All traditions of the contiguous mountain tribes are against this, and point distinctly to a flood in which the tribes of the lower countries perished; and the ocean sands and deposits covering the whole surface of Yucatan and its ruins, with other evidences equally strong, help to establish, beyond a, doubt, the same calamity.

The cataclysm by fire, forming a part of the traditional catastrophes of Central America, and equally well established, was less extensive and less disastrous in its effects, and probably took place at the same time; and from the same commotions which caused the subsidence of earth, and consequently flood of water. And that such eruptions of flame have been of repeated occurrence, and that they accompany most earthquake commotions, there is abundance of evidence in their marks on the rocks in the crevices of the mountains of Central and South America.

The great antiquity of the Aztec ruins is questioned by some, who find amongst them painted frescoes, painted tablets and statues, and lintelled roofs, and Maya and Mexican inscriptions.

The Maya Indians, who, it has already been said, migrated from the west, and took possession of those ruins after they arose from the sea, found convenient shelter within their walls, which they defaced, and to which they added inscriptions; and centuries after (and for centuries previous to the reign of Montezuma), a succession of Mexican princes occupied the same ruins - lintelled and roofed the palaces - painted the frescoes and tablets and added Mexican inscriptions, until the ablest archaeologists are unable to expound them; but the very sands which cover them and the whole country around them, not blown there by the wind, but deposited by the waves of the ocean, show that neither the Maya Indians nor the Mexicans had anything to do with their original construction.

[1] See an account of their astonishing mode of celebrating annually the subsiding of the Deluge, accompanied with their various modes of voluntary torture, recently published by Trübner. 60, Paternoster Row. "O-kee-Pa: a Religious Ceremony of the Mandans. 13 Coloured Illustrations. By George Catlin."

[2] For the young readers of this book, who have long lives before them, these are but *suggestions,* pointing to *proofs* that they will sooner or later read on these interesting topics.

[3] The last few years of my wanderings have been more amongst *rocks* than amongst *Indians;* and a work which I am preparing, to be entitled *"The Lifted and Subsided Rocks of America,"* will carry this subject much further than space will allow in the compressed remarks of this little work.

Chapter Eleven - The Indians, Where Are They Going?

If the brief remarks advanced in the two preceding chapters leave the reader's mind in any doubt as to the *origin* of the American Indians, there need be no uncertainty in answering the second question, "Where are these poor people going?" It requires no archaeologist, no historian, nor antiquarian for this - "to the setting sun," knowing, from the irresistible wave of civilization, which has already engulfed more than one-half of the tribes on the continent, that somewhere in the western horizon the last of their race will soon be extinguished.

The first shocks to Indian civilization and advancement, which have been related in the fore going chapters, were the results of natural accidents, which none but God controls; and if those awful events could have been avoided, Columbus would have discovered a continent in the west as high in civilization, in agriculture and the arts, as the eastern continent was at that date.

Staggering under this death-blow, the *genius* of civilization lay for centuries and centuries in embers, until it again began to blaze out in Mexico and Peru, when the inhuman onslaughts and revolting cruelties of civilized men, stimulated by the thirst for gold, set honesty, morality, religion, and Heaven itself at defiance, in extinguishing the last lights that were lifting these poor nations from savage darkness and ignorance.

The last gleams of Indian civilization thus extinguished by deceptions and cruelties, at the recital of which the hearts of honest men and philanthropists sicken, the poor Indians, from one end of the continent to the other, have stood aghast at white man's cruelty; and, suspicious, have everywhere resisted his proffered civilization and religion, and yet the dupes of only one inducement - his rum and whiskey.

Crazed by and for these, from one side of the continent to the other, they have bartered away their game, their lands, and even their lives; for wherever rum and whiskey have gone, the small-pox has also travelled, and in every tribe one half or more have fallen victims to its mortality.

Columbus, perhaps, was the first white man who ever saw an American Indian, in October, 1492; landing on the island of San Salvador, one of the Bahamas, "he discovered Indians running to the shore, naked, and gazing at the ships."

In Hayti, where he met greater numbers, he says, in a letter to Louis de St. Angel, "True it is that after the Indians felt confidence, and lost their fears of us, they were so liberal with what they possessed, that it would not be believed by those who had not seen it. If anything was asked of them, they never said no, but gave it cheerfully, and showed as much anxiety as if they gave their very heart; and if the things given were of great or little value, they were content with whatever was given in return."

"Columbus was afterwards wrecked on the island of Hispaniola. The cacique (chief), *Gua-can-a-gan,* living within a league and a half of the wreck, shed tears of sympathy, and sent all his people in canoes to his aid; and the cacique rendered all the aid he could in person, both on sea and on land, consoling Columbus by saying that everything he possessed should be at his disposal. All the effects of the wrecked ship were deposited near the cacique's dwelling, and not the slightest article, though exposed to the whole population, was pilfered!"

And Columbus, in his letter to the King and Queen of Spain, says, "So tractable, so peaceable, are these people, that I swear to your majesties there is not in the world a better nation. They love their neighbours as themselves, and their discourse is even sweet and gentle, and accompanied with a smile; and though it is true that they are naked, yet their manners are decorous and praiseworthy."

Columbus, amongst these people, was loaded with presents the most costly that they possessed; and as he says himself, "this generous cacique, and a variety of other chiefs, placed *coronets* of pure gold on his head." And what was the sequel? This "generous cacique," and all the "variety of other chiefs," and their people, who had not even bows and arrows to defend themselves with (so peaceable they were), were driven from their dwellings into the mountains, and their villages burnt to the ground. The Caribbes were more warlike, and, armed with bows and arrows, made a stronger resistance; but they were at length defeated by one of the most disgraceful stratagems that ever appeared in the history of warfare. These Indians, who possessed large quantities of gold, got an idea that silver, first produced amongst them by the Spaniards, was of much greater value, exchanged gold at the rate of ten ounces for one. To turn this to the best account, a massive pair of steel manacles were highly polished for the purpose, to resemble silver (and, of course, of an immense value) were represented to *Ca-on-e-bo,* the chief, at the head of the Indian army, as a magnificent pair of bracelets of silver, sent to him by the King of Spain. Dazzled by so brilliant a present, and from the king, he submitted to mount a powerful steed and have them put on. They were locked to his wrists, and by a mailed troop of horse in readiness he was galloped through the Indian lines and to the coast, where he was put in additional irons, and sent a prisoner to Spain. And in the space of five years of deadly and the most cruel warfare, waged with guns and coats of mail and sabres against these harmless and inoffensive people, by the man whose honours were to be immortal, over 200,000 of these poor people were slain on their own ground, and more than 5000 were made prisoners and shipped to Spain, and sold as slaves, where they slew, themselves, or perished from diseases of the country.

Here began American history, and here was the beginning (not the end) of the Indians' second series of calamities.

This cruel and disgraceful warfare was all for gold, but the shining god proved to be farther west, and another fleet and another army were on its track, and another monster at its head. Fernando Cortes was this man, this educated demon, with a fleet and an army of mounted and mailed soldiers under his command, and the gold and jewels and blood of Mexico his idols.

History has well recorded the more than savage cruelties, and massacres, and robberies of this *civilized* expedition, in which the second growth of spontaneous civilization was crushed, and smothered, and strangled into a degraded and sickening amalgamation of conquered and subjugated, with selfish and fiendish conquerors.

An Indian (rich and beautiful) city was sacked and robbed of its gold - 100,000 of its inhabitants were slain - its king (Montezuma) was deceived, dethroned, and murdered - its palaces destroyed - its religion trodden under foot, and its sacred temples thrown down! and yet the thirst for gold, for plunder, and for massacre was not satisfied - there was another sun of Indian civilization above the horizon, and another mine of gold - it was Peru.

Pizarro (from the same *civilized* school) was the merciless wretch for this. Like Cortes in Mexico, with a fleet, and an army of mailed soldiers with fire-arms and sabres in hand, he cut and slaughtered his way through the defenceless ranks of the unoffending Peruvians, on their own ground, with the most disgraceful breach of proffered faith known to history, robbed the city of its gold - imprisoned and murdered its monarch, the Inca, and with the blades of his swords, taught to 150,000 peaceable and civilized Indians, as Cortes had taught in Mexico, their first lesson of the "blessings" of European civilization.

The "El Dorado" was yet an *idea* - still unsolved; the plundered heaps of gold were yet too small, and, the river of Indian blood must again be flooded! Civilization required another glorification, and De Soto was the ready cavalier for that. A knight Castilian was he, blood-snuffing, and mad for gold; and soon after the scenes of blood related, his little fleet anchored, and disembarked his cavalry legion on the sandy coast of Florida. His men were in coats of mail, and his horses also, which were of the noblest Castilian breed; and his cannons were drawn by horses covered with polished steel, and helmets plated with gold!

In helmet of gold himself, and sword in hand, he mounted his milk-white steed, and facing the west, where he dreamed of native cities, and wagon-loads of gold to be drawn back by his splendid *troupe* of Castilian chargers, and entered the swamps and everglades of Florida! Poor fool, that he could have known what was before him! He penetrated the impassable and interminable swamps and lagoons, and dragged his heavy cannons through them. And after wading the swamps, and through the blood of the poor savages, the cruelty arid butchery of which has no parallel in the pages of history, [1] he at last arrived on the bank of the Mississippi, in which his body found a grave, and his visioned cities and mines of gold were never reached.

After such examples of white man's injustice and cruelties, such illustrations of "glorious civilization," the news of which, of course, spread like the waves of a rising flood, over and through every tribe, from ocean to ocean, both in South and North America, *is it wonderful* that the American Indians should be suspicious of white man and his fair promises, his civilization, his faith, and his proffered religion? And *is it not* wonderful, under their traditions taught to their children, of such civilized barbarities and treacherous massacres, that these poor people should everywhere, in first interviews (as abundance of history informs us), receive white men with open arms, with hospitality and welcome, in their humble wigwams?

Reader, listen to a few of these, which are truths, and tell me *if it is not* a wonder. And after that I will name other civilized transactions; and then I will ask you, who is the *savage* - which the *brute*?

Columbus has already told us "that the caciques of Hispaniola embraced him in their arms, shed tears for his misfortunes, and placed upon his head coronets of gold." This is not *wonderful,* for it was natural; man has been everywhere made (not a brute, but) human, ready and disposed to meet his fellow-man in friendship and kindness, where there has been no cause given for a different reception.

Subsequent to the shocking invasions and cruelties recited above, colonization in North America commenced, and the beginning of this was the little colony of Puritans who sailed from England, and landed, with their wives and children, on the rock of Plymouth. "They were hungry and in distress, and the Indians received them with open arms, and fed them with maize and other food which they brought to them."

This was not *wonderful,* but *natural;* and *noble,* because these intelligent and discriminating people contemplated in this little domestic group of husbands, wives, and children, the elements of fellowship and peace, instead of the signals of war and plunder.

The entrance of this colony opened the door for others, and the stream of emigration that has continued ever since, peopling the whole Atlantic coast, and constantly moving on towards the west, and displacing and moving the Indian populations by treaty stipulations, or by force.

And we now come to what is *strictly* wonderful, and even astonishing - that, under all the invasions, the frauds, the deceptions and tricks, as well as force, that have been practised upon them, to push them from their lands, and towards the setting sun," these poor and abused people have exercised so little cruelty as they have; - that rum, and whisky, and small-pox, of the white man's importation amongst them, have been submitted to; and border warfare, until they are reduced, tribe after tribe, to mere remnants, and still pushed again and again to the west; and that even there, and under these irritating circumstances, white men travel unprotected, their lives secure, and their property transported with safety; - that "Lasalle and Father Hennepen," in 1678, with only thirty men, should have passed, in their voyages of discovery, through the whole of the great lakes, the Illinois and the Mississippi, during eight years of continual travels and explorations, amongst more than twenty tribes as yet ignorant of civilization; and Father Hennepen (as he relates), with only two men, ascending, amongst the numerous tribes (the first explorer there), to the Falls of St. Anthony; and under all the exposure and trying vicissitudes of those eight years, as they say, they were uniformly treated with hospitality and kindness by the Indians; that "Lewis and Clarke," with a small detachment of men, in 1805, should have ascended the whole length of the Missouri River, crossed the Rocky Mountains, and reached the Pacific Ocean, and returned, a distance of more than 8000 miles, in which they paid the first visits of white men to more than thirty of the wildest and most warlike tribes on the continent, without having to wield a weapon in self-defence! "And," (as I had it from General Clarke's lips, in his old age), "we visited more than 200,000 of those poor people, and they everywhere treated us with hospitality and kindness." And that hundreds of other travellers, and amongst them, *myself*, whose lives and whose property have been at their mercy, that they have been so merciful, and so friendly, and honourable, under the sense they have of white men's cruelties and wrongs, is truly a matter of *wonder!*

In the epitome of my wanderings, given in this little work, it has been seen that I have found my way into and through 120 different tribes, in North, South, and Central America, and the reader who has got thus far in the book, will easily imagine that my life and my property have been, much of the time, at their mercy; and will here learn that, not only have I found it unnecessary ever to raise my hand against one of them, but that they have everywhere treated me with hospitality and kind ness: and nowhere, to my knowledge, stolen a sixpence worth of my property, though in their countries there is universal poverty to stimulate to crime, and no law to punish for theft, and where travellers carry no trunks with locks and keys!

The above statements, if they be true, show us a people who are not only by nature human, but humane; and evince a degree of submission and forbearance on their part which would be a virtue and an honour for any race; and which, with their other claims, entitle them to a better fate than the unlucky one they are hastening to.

In the past pages we have seen these unhappy people in the midst of the cruel onslaughts for gold - by cataclysms *sunk* down; and by sabres *struck* down, in the progress of their own civilization; and we have contemplated them in "floods" from which tradition tells us, a few only were saved on the tops of the mountains - but we have yet to view them in another deluge more fatal, and from the drowning waves of which it is to be feared the mountaintops will save no one of them - the *Flood of Emigration!*

After cataclysms, the Indians' misfortune in South America, in Mexico, and Hispaniola, was in their gold; and that done, there is yet a chance of their living. Their misfortune in North America, that they owned the broadest and richest country on the globe, teeming with all the luxuries tempting to white man's cupidity - the temperature of its climate - the richness of its soil - its vast prairies speckled with buffaloes, and its rivers and mountains abounding in valuable furs, in latitudes most suitable for emigration, and that emigration led and pushed on by a popular government which could have but one motion, and that onward, to the Rocky Mountains and the Pacific Ocean.

Under such accumulated circumstances the Indians' fate was sealed their doom was fixed; and in that "flood," which has been for a half century spreading over their country, the last of them are now being engulfed; and as if *gold* must necessarily have its share in *their* destruction, its shining scales are being turned up in various parts of the Rocky Mountains, adding fury to the maddened throng who are now concentrating for its search in the very centre of the vast solitudes to which advancing civilization has been driving the poor Indians, both from the east and the west, as their last possible hold in existence.

Unlike the gold searchers in Mexico and Peru, who *struck* their *blows, got* their *gold* in *masses,* and were off, the gold seekers in the Rocky Mountains will hold on - *their* mines will last, and the poor Indians, between gold diggers, and squatters, and whisky sellers, who are all armed with repeating rifles and revolvers, will lengthen their days as long as they can, but there will be few of them.

For the last fifty years a lucrative traffic in whisky, paid for in beaver and other furs, and buffalo robes, has led to dissipation and poverty of the poor Indians, and introduced small-pox and other diseases, which have often swept off in a few months one half in many tribes, and two-thirds and even three-fourths, in others.

The disastrous and cruel consequences sure to flow from this traffic, with two or three thousand unprincipled men in the mountains and valleys of the Far West, under the direction of rich and powerful companies, has often been pointed out to the government; but in countries so far beyond the reach of laws, nothing has been done effectually to check it; and now the predicted consequences are seen in their full force.

The combined causes of border emigration moving on faster than the government can purchase the lands of the Indians - the unemployed hunters, and trappers, and whisky sellers, whose business is declining, and a headlong stampede of half-crazy adventurers flying to the gold fields of the Rocky Mountains, form a phalanx of the most desperate men, who take possession of the Indians' country - claim it, and hold it - pronounce the Indians all "brutes, who can hold no title" - build towns of log huts, and call them "cities" - publish newspapers, and announce "Indian murders! Indian murders of white men!" (whether perpetrated or not), call upon the government for regiments and armies of soldiers to protect them, and these soldiers in their country openly advocate "extermination" - offer rewards of twenty dollars for every Indian's scalp that can be taken (with the *civil* condition annexed), "provided that both ears are attached to them!"

Here, my young readers, we are upon facts, and I am ashamed for the character and honour of my country to acknowledge them as such; and I now put the question which I promised to ask, "Who is the *savage,* and which the *brute?*" My heart bleeds at this, but I cannot prevent it.

Twenty dollars offered by the corporation of Central City, in the middle of a state of the Union, for every Indian's scalp - for every deliberate murder! - What a *carte blanche!* what a thriving business the trappers and whisky-sellers can make of this! How much better than killing wolves at two dollars per head, or catching cunning beavers for three dollars! The poor, unsuspecting Indian of any distant tribe, whilst hunting for food to feed his wife and children, may be shot down, or decoyed from his wigwam, made drunk with a pint of whisky, and scalped, as the trapper's exigencies may demand; or taken out of his grave, where he has been recently buried, and his scalp, "with both ears," taken without the merit, and without the trouble, of a murder!

Why, the butcheries by Cortes and Pizarro and De Soto were not half so bad as this! *Can* it be that, in the present age of civilization and emancipation, scenes so abhorrent as these are to be countenanced or permitted by the government of my country, in the centre of one of her confederated states? It is said that an army of men sufficient to protect all the white inhabitants in the mountains and in the plains is on the move, and that *"extermination to the savage"* is to be the "watch-word." I do not believe it - I think better of my country than this.

What! the government that has just gained everlasting honour before the civilized world by giving *freedom* and rights of citizenship to two millions of Africans, now, at the point of the bayonet, to *disfranchise* and *enslave* a *free* and *independent* people - to *disinherit* her *"red children,"* whose lands she holds, and (to protect a set of murderous adventurers in the Rocky Mountains), to dispute their existence! I *cannot* believe this, and I *will* not, for I wish yet to lay my bones in my native land.

I have so far briefly enumerated the principal misfortunes of the poor Indians, but there is yet one other, not less unfortunate or less lamentable for them in its results they have no *newspapers,* no missiles to herald, post-haste, *their* griefs, their wrongs, to the ears of the world; but all deaths, when *they* are shot down by the rifles of their enemies, and all abuses of their wives and children, are muffled and silenced in the vast solitudes around them, whilst every blow struck by an Indian in retaliation, rings and echoes over every part of the continent as "wilful murder and massacre by the infernal savage!" Glorious institution, the "Press," but how much more glorious if it were not one sided!

I have long been aware of the approaching Indian crisis which now is evidently at hand, and in my notes written on the Upper Missouri, and published thirty years since, I predicted it in the following terms: - "The Sioux of 25,000, the Mandans of 2000, the Assineboins of 7000, the Minatarrees of 2500, the Chayennes of 6000, the Pawnees of 10,000, and numerous smaller tribes of the prairies which I have visited, and who are living exclusively on the flesh of the buffaloes (their only food, for in the vast plains where these cattle range, there are no other animals for food), making their tents of their hides, and robes and clothing for themselves and families, are soon to be left in a state of destitution, and, in fact, in absolute starvation, in which they will have to flee to the base of the Rocky Mountains to get animals for their subsistence.

"The cause of this approaching misfortune, which is soon to come upon them, is the nefarious business of rum and whisky selling, which is driven to that extent, by rich and rival companies, that in a very few years the vast herds of buffaloes that now graze on the prairies in the plains of the Platte and the Missouri will be destroyed. These are every year concentrating into a narrow compass, and being followed up by the various tribes on all sides, the last of them will suddenly disappear; the last animal will be skinned, and 200,000 Indians who now subsist on their flesh, and at least 500,000 wolves that live by picking the bones of the animals slain, will come together, and face to face will have to contend for existence.

"Though the government at Washington have passed laws prohibiting the passing of whisky into the Indian countries, they appoint Indian agents, who are silent members of the trading companies, and, having control over the whole Indian country, facilitate the entrance of as much whisky as the traders require.

"This whisky, which is distilled by these companies at St. Louis or other towns on the frontier, is conveyed into the Indian country in 'high wines' (alcohol), and for the Indians' use is diluted, each pint of alcohol making three pints of Indian whisky. At the mouth of the Yellow Stone, on the Upper Missouri, the principal factory on the Missouri, the price of this diluted whisky is eighteen dollars per gallon; and transported from that on horses to the Crows and Blackfeet, the price becomes thirty-two dollars per gallon! Such are the prices that these poor people pay for their dissipations.

"At this post, and the other trading establishments on the Missouri and Platte, the uniform price of buffalo robes, beautifully dressed by the Indian women, is a pint of Indian whisky; so that one pint of alcohol buys three buffalo robes, worth, in St. Louis, from five to eight dollars each! And here (discovered perhaps by accident, and probably never patented), it was ascertained that tobacco soaked in whisky made the whisky much more pungent and more intoxicating, and this important discovery, being brought into a working process here, results, greatly to the fur company's advantage, in the following simple and beautiful manner.

"In the fur company's retailing store, inside of their fort, they have two barrels of whisky standing on end, side by side, with taps near their bottoms, for drawing out the liquor. One of these barrels has a part of the heading taken out, and a keg of plug-tobacco being knocked to pieces, the tobacco is thrown into the barrel of whisky, and every morning, with a stick long enough to reach to the bottom, the tobacco and whisky are well stirred about.

"This precious barrel is marked No. 1, and the other No. 2. And when the poor Indians come in with their buffalo skins and throw them down, the clerk inquires which kind they desire, No. 1 or No. 2; if No. 1, two robes are taken instead of one! And as most important discoveries, lead to others, this has resulted in this way: when the whisky is out, and the tobacco dried and prepared for smoking, it has been ascertained that the Indians are quite willing to pay a double price for it, from the flavour it has acquired by lying in the whisky!

"The profit arising from this sort of commerce is easily calculated, and also the results that it must sooner or later lead to; and from forty to fifty thousand buffalo robes are taken down the Missouri to St. Louis every summer, (for which the animals are mostly killed in the winter, when their hair is the longest, and their flesh too poor to eat), in addition to the vast numbers killed for the subsistence of 200,000 Indians. From these statements something like an estimate can be made of the rapid decrease of these animals (which reproduce only at the rate of common cattle), and, as I have said, of their approaching extinction."

For the above prophecy and *"unjust attack upon the Fur Company,"* I have had some unfriendly denunciations by the press, and by those critics I have been reproachfully designated the *"Indian-loving Catlin."* What of this? What have I to answer? Have I any apology to make for loving the Indians? The Indians have always loved me, and why should I not love the Indians?

I love the people who have always made me welcome to the best they had.

I love a people who are honest without laws, who have no jails and no poor-houses.

I love a people who keep the commandments without ever having read them or heard them preached from the pulpit.

I love a people who never swear, who never take the name of God in vain.

I love a people who "love their neighbours as they love themselves."

I love a people who worship God without a Bible, for I believe that God loves them also.

I love the people whose religion is all the same, and who are free from religious animosities.

I love the people who never have raised a hand against me, or stolen my property, where there was no law to punish for either.

I love the people who never have fought a battle with white man, except on their own ground.

I love and don't fear mankind where God has made and left them, for there they are children.

I love a people who live and keep what is their own without locks and keys.

I love all people who do the best they can. And oh, how I love a people who don't live for the love of money!

It has been sneeringly said that I have "spoken too well of the Indians," (better to speak too well of them than not to speak well enough) - "that I have flattered them" - (better to *flatter* them than to caricature them; there have been enough to do this). If I have overdone their character, they have had in *me one friend,* at least; and I will not shrink from the sin and responsibility of it.

I was luckily born in time to see these people in their native dignity, and beauty, and independence, and to be a living witness to the cruelties with which they have been treated worse than *dogs;* and now to be treated worse than *wolves!* And in my former publications I have predicted just what now taking place - that in their thrown, and hunted down, and starved condition, the future "gallopers" across the plains and Rocky Mountains would see here and there the scattered, and starving, and begging, and haggard remnants of these once proud and handsome people - represent *them,* in their entailed misery and wretchedness, as *"the Sioux," "the Chayennes," "the Osages,"* &c, and *me,* of course, as a liar.

From the very first settlement on the Atlantic coast, there has been a continued series of Indian wars. In every war the whites have been victorious, and every war has ended in *"Surrender of Indian Territory."* Every battle which the whites have lost has been a *"massacre,"* and every battle by the Indians lost, a *"glorious victory!"* And yet, to their immortal honour, be it *history* with its *inferences,* (for it is truth), they never fought a battle with civilized men, excepting *on their own ground!* What are the inferences from this; and to whose eternal shame stands the balance in the books?

I have said that I was lucky enough to have been born at the right time to have *seen* these people in their native dignity and elegance; and, thanks to Him in whose hands the destinies of all men are, that my life has been spared to visit most of the tribes in every latitude of the American continent, and my hand enabled to delineate their personal looks and their modes, to be seen and to be criticised after the people and myself shall have passed away.

I have devoted fourteen years of my life, and all my earthly means, in visiting these scattered and remote people, and with my toils and privations, I have had my enjoyments. These have been curiously mixed, and generally by chance and by accident, which probably have beneficially relieved the one and the other from injurious anticipations and excitement.

My works are done, and as well as I could do them under the circumstances. I have had no government, society, or individual aid, but travelled and labored at my own expense. In my writings and my paintings I have quoted no one; but have painted and written of things that I saw and heard, and of nothing else. My works will probably be published in full (too late for *my* benefit), but for the benefit and instruction of others who come behind me.

The native grace, simplicity, and dignity of these natural people so much resemble the ancient marbles, that one is irresistibly led to believe that the Grecian sculptors had similar models to study from. And their costumes and weapons, the toga, the tunique, and manteau (of skins), the bow, the shield, the lance, so precisely similar to those of ancient times, convince us that a second (and last) strictly classic era is passing from the world.

In a political and ethnological point of view, also, from their evanescent position, these people and their modes, at this time, are surely subjects of peculiar interest, reduced, since the discovery of America, from seven or eight millions to an eighth part of that number at the present time; and that remainder, from the causes already mentioned, with no other prospect than rapid decimation and final extinction.

Of the irresistible, individual means that have been used, and of the various policies of the United States government, tending to (though not intended for) the destruction of these people, it has not been the intention of this little work to speak other than in brief and general terms; nor would it be justice towards the Indians, or to those who read, if I were to omit to say in this place that the causes which have so far led to their destruction are still dispensed amongst them from one end of the frontier to the other; and (what pains me most to say) that my ancient friends, the *Sioux,* the *Chayennes,* and other tribes of the plains, who treated me with uniform kindness and hospitality, and made me welcome in their villages thirty-three years ago, are now being swept from their beautiful plains into the Rocky Mountains by armies of men armed with cannon and revolvers!

These poor people, whose cruel fate posterity will lament, whose countries for more than half a century have been scourged (and in some places depopulated) by rum and whisky and smallpox, and who are now being driven into the mountains, will certainly perish there; but, in their death-struggle, will as certainly wreak a cruel and costly vengeance on the powers that are sending them there, as well as upon the settlers of the frontiers and the innocent travellers who venture to cross the vast and uninhabited solitudes of the great plains and the Rocky Mountains.

The remnants of numerous tribes driven from both sides into the desolate wilds and wastes of the Rocky Mountains, alike impressed with the undying sense of white man's cruelty to teach to their children, will there unite for sway and vengeance in regions which require but little in addition to their natural features to bid defiance to white man's existence.

Across those vast and frozen and uninhabitable tracts the United States are sending mailbags on the backs of ponies, and telegraphs by a single wire, and might have done so for the fifty years past and for the fifty years to come, without molestation from the Indians; but how long, in a state of war for *extermination,* can this be done?

Other wires are to be stretched amongst the rocks, and a railway is to be built, and is being built, and goods and valuable treasures and human life are to be wheeled by day and by night over and through those vast and desert solitudes, and what security will there be for either?

I have seen some estimates in the American papers that the "Pony Express" alone is going to require 10,000 men, at an expense of a million of dollars per annum, to protect it! If that be so (and I do believe it), what force and at what cost, will protect a single wire when the Indians are in a state of starvation and death, fighting for existence; their scalps advertised for at twenty dollars each, and the telegraphic wire (the very thing they want to point their arrows with) stretched through a thousand miles of rocks and snowdrifts? Or the nightly passing train, that a simple rock or block of wood upon the rail would enable an ambuscade of Indians, in five minutes, in the dead of night, to revenge the death of hundreds of their brothers, wives, and children, and enrich themselves with plunder, to be hidden in the unapproachable solitudes and caves of the mountains; or the same rocks and blocks of wood laid, and the hellish booty shared, by pale-faced (*moccasined*) bandits (there will be enough of them), to be avenged upon the Indians?

I have seen the country and I know the people, and I imagine the time near at hand when a *Pony Express, a telegraphic wire,* and a *railway* will *each* require 100,000 men to ensure them security; and then will be shouted by the acquisitive race, like thunder from the heavens, *"On, on, merciful civilization!* the treasures of the earth are thine, and death to the savage!" when the last of the race will be tracked by bloodhounds, and sent to the dust with "Sharp's rifles!"

www.ingramcontent.com/pod-product-compliance
Lightning Source LLC
LaVergne TN
LVHW011421080426
835512LV00005B/183